A More Civil War

CIVIL WAR AMERICA

Peter S. Carmichael, Caroline E. Janney, and Aaron Sheehan-Dean, *editors*

This landmark series interprets broadly the history and culture of the Civil War era through the long nineteenth century and beyond. Drawing on diverse approaches and methods, the series publishes historical works that explore all aspects of the war, biographies of leading commanders, and tactical and campaign studies, along with select editions of primary sources. Together, these books shed new light on an era that remains central to our understanding of American and world history.

D. H. DILBECK

A More Civil War
How the Union Waged a Just War

The University of North Carolina Press *Chapel Hill*

© 2016 The University of North Carolina Press

All rights reserved

Set in Arno by Westchester Publishing Services

Manufactured in the United States of America

The University of North Carolina Press has been a member of the
Green Press Initiative since 2003.

Library of Congress Cataloging-in-Publication Data

Names: Dilbeck, D. H., author.

Title: A more civil war : how the Union waged a just war / D. H. Dilbeck.

Other titles: Civil War America (Series)

Description: Chapel Hill : University of North Carolina Press, 2016. |
    Series: Civil War America | Includes bibliographical references and index.

Identifiers: LCCN 2015049991 | ISBN 9781469630519 (cloth : alk. paper) |
    ISBN 9781469630526 (ebook)

Subjects: LCSH: United States—History—Civil War, 1861–1865—Moral
    and ethical aspects. | United States—History—Civil War, 1861–1865. |
    War—Moral and ethical aspects—United States—History—19th century.

Classification: LCC E468.9 .D55 2016 | DDC 973.7—dc23
    LC record available at http://lccn.loc.gov/2015049991

Jacket Illustration: Reg't. Michigan Engineers & Mechanics destroying
R. R. track in Atlanta, ruins of the car shed to right hand (photo by
George N. Barnard, ca. 1864). Courtesy of the Library of Congress,
Prints and Photographs Division, LC-DIG-stereo-1S01415.

Portions of Chapter Three were previously published in " 'The Genesis
of this Little Tablet with My Name': Francis Lieber and his Reasons for
Drafting General Orders No. 100," Journal of the Civil War Era (June 2015):
231–53. Portions of Chapter Four were previously published in " 'The
Sternest Feature of War': The Moral Dilemma of Retaliation and
the Limits of Atrocity in the American Civil War," Fides et Historia
48:1 (Winter/Spring 2016): 32–60. Both are used with permission.

To Mackenzie and Pearl

Contents

Acknowledgments

What a pleasure it is to give thanks properly now to the family, friends, mentors, colleagues, and institutions that made this book possible.

While completing the archival research necessary for this project, I benefited immensely from expert assistance offered by the staffs of the Missouri History Museum, the Huntington Library, the U.S. Army Military History Institute, the Milton S. Eisenhower Library at The Johns Hopkins University, and the Manuscript Reading Room at the Library of Congress. I am particularly appreciative to have received a W. M. Keck Foundation Fellowship from the Huntington Library and a Ridgway Research Grant from the U.S. Army Military History Institute, which provided essential financial support for extended research trips

I am pleased this book found a home at the University of North Carolina Press, and I appreciate all that Mark Simpson-Vos did to shepherd me through the publication process. I owe an especially large debt to Aaron Sheehan-Dean and the second anonymous reviewer of my manuscript. Both treated my work like it was their own, and their thoughtful and thorough suggestions have made this an exceedingly better book.

I had the ridiculously good fortune of learning how to be a historian from the best in the country at the University of Virginia. Peter Onuf offered keen advice and persistent encouragement throughout my time at the University of Virginia, even after our amicable "divorce" and my drift into the Civil War era. Elizabeth Varon's captivating lectures on nineteenth-century southern history helped set in motion that drift. Gary Gallagher gladly accepted me as one of his students, despite his already sizeable cohort of advisees, and since then he has been gracious beyond measure with his support. He is a perceptive and generous critic as well as a model teacher and scholar. Peter, Elizabeth, and Gary are all fiercely committed to the success of their graduate students. I am honored to count myself as one of the many they have trained.

My parents, Hance and Julie Dilbeck, have persistently affirmed me in my calling as a teacher and historian. I consider it a rich blessing to have begun this vocation by first learning from them how to read in a parsonage in Marshall County, Oklahoma. They are my first and finest teachers, who showed me how to live like a tree planted by streams of water, which yields fruit in its season and whose leaf never withers. I am grateful for that instruction.

More than six years ago now, my wife, Mackenzie, made a great sacrifice in moving from our home in Oklahoma to Charlottesville, Virginia, a foreign place to us where we knew no one. More often than not, especially early on, we felt Jeff Tweedy was right: our love, our love, our love is all we have. For that, I am thankful. Mackenzie is a faithful partner in success and failure, joy and disappointment. This book is a testament to the strength I find in her love.

Our daughter, Pearl Caroline, arrived in April 2014 mere days before my graduation from the University of Virginia and our family's move back to Oklahoma. Her timing was impeccable! We had longed for her, and she has brought us joy unspeakable. This book is dedicated to Mackenzie and Pearl, in the fond hope that my daughter will inherit her mother's humor and heart.

A More Civil War

Introduction

Responsible to One Another and to God: The Union's Moral Vision of War

On New Year's Eve 1863, an anxious George W. Lennard sought blessed assurance of his eternal fate. Lennard began the American Civil War as a private in an Indiana regiment and was eventually commissioned lieutenant colonel of the Fifty-Seventh Indiana Volunteer Infantry. He survived some of the most gruesome fighting of the Western Theater, from Shiloh to Stones River to Missionary Ridge. As another year of war dawned, Lennard confessed in a letter home that he dreaded nothing more than the thought of what awaited him after death. He longed for "a clear and well defined hope that all would be well with me in the world to come." "You will say," he wrote his wife, "why dont you be a Christian? I say, how can a soldier be a Christian?" He continued: "Read all Christs teaching, and then tell me whether *one engaged in maiming and butchering men*—men made in the express image of God himself—*can be saved* under the Gospel. Clear my mind on this subject and you will do me a world of good." Lennard was still searching for answers when he was killed in May 1864 as he marched toward Atlanta.[1]

George Lennard doubted he could reconcile the gospel of the Prince of Peace with his duties as a soldier, which made him unusual in the Union army. But he was not alone in earnestly contemplating the morality of warfare. Can a soldier be a Christian? Can a self-proclaimed Christian society send more than two million men off to "maim and butcher" other men? Is killing and destruction acceptable in war if done in service of a sacred cause? Is it possible for a soldier to fight in a just war and himself remain just, or must he inevitably surrender his own righteousness before the brutal demands of war? Can a supposedly civilized people constrain the death and devastation unleashed by their armies? Is it really possible to wage war justly?

One year before George Lennard wrote his forlorn letter home, another man worked to resolve the moral quandaries that plagued Lennard's mind. Francis Lieber did so not by turning to the New Testament but to international law. Lieber was a scholar, not a soldier, a Berlin-born professor at Columbia College in New York City who taught history and political economy.

He was also an acknowledged expert on the laws of war, a component of international law that addressed legitimate justifications *for* and conduct *in* warfare. In the winter of 1862, Lieber convinced President Abraham Lincoln's administration to produce a code of conduct for Union soldiers distilled from the laws of war tradition. Lieber drafted the document and called it "Instructions for the Government of Armies of the United States in the Field." Issued to Federal armies in May 1863 as General Orders No. 100, it soon became known informally as the Lieber code. The code's 157 articles addressed a wide range of topics. Taken together, they sought to instruct men like George Lennard how to wage a just war.[2]

While Lieber's code authorized far-reaching destruction and stern measures to crush Confederate resistance, it also imposed constraints on Union armies. Both were vital components of a just war, Lieber believed. Clearly defining the limits of just warfare remained far more than a mere intellectual exercise for Lieber. His three sons fought in the Civil War. One lost an arm serving the Union at Fort Donelson, Tennessee, in February 1862. Another died fighting for the Confederacy on the Virginia Peninsula later that year. Lieber began work on his code six months after his son's death, motivated by an unshakeable conviction about morality in warfare: "Men who take up arms against one another in public war do not cease on this account to be moral beings, responsible to one another and to God." Lieber hoped to show Union soldiers how they might reconcile their obligations as a warring but still morally responsible people.[3]

Did Lieber succeed? Anyone inclined to answer yes quickly should pause and remember that as many as 750,000 soldiers died in the war.[4] The conflict's death toll can make it easy to scorn Civil War Americans for apparently allowing their self-righteous zeal to lead to near-limitless destruction. Yet the meditations of northerners like George Lennard and Francis Lieber suggest there might be a more complicated and compelling story to tell. I seek to tell that story by answering several questions about the loyal Union citizenry— chiefly about its political and military leaders and enlisted soldiers, but also about certain civilians on the home front such as northern ministers and newspaper editors. What did they think it meant to wage a just war? What were the most significant ideas and assumptions that informed their thinking? How did Federal officials refine these ideas into military policies, and when and where did these policies first appear? To what extent did Union military and political leaders, as well as regular soldiers, abide by these policies and agree with their underlying vision of just warfare?

In answering these questions, I explain why Union armies waged the kind of war they did, because Federals' ideas about just warfare shaped how they prosecuted the war. My goal is to better explain the strange paradox at the center of the Civil War: It occasioned both great destruction and remarkable restraint. Federals perpetuated once-unthinkable carnage yet also sincerely considered the humane limits to warfare. To understand why, it is necessary to look to the array of legal, religious, and political ideas that informed Union just-war thinking. These ideas both inspired immense violence and imposed restrictions on Union army actions. The Federals I write about who embraced this just-war thinking believed that enormous destruction in war could be just. Yet most of them also sought to abide by certain limits in their treatment of enemy soldiers and civilians. They thought destructiveness and restraint in war were not irreconcilable opposites but complementary and equally vital aspects of a truly just war.

Although historians have written a great deal about the nature of Civil War violence, what is still needed is a thorough consideration of the content of Union just-war thinking and the effect it had on how Federal armies waged war. At present, Civil War scholars have largely ignored these ideas or underappreciated their significance. One camp of historians tends to emphasize the war's particularly gruesome and remorseless violence. They even sometimes suggest that the scope and scale of the war's destruction was unprecedented, a grim harbinger of a modern era of total war.[5] Not surprisingly, these historians typically assume Federals and Confederates gave little to no serious thought to how they might wage war justly.[6] Another camp of historians has challenged this bleak account of the war's violence and demonstrated that its destruction was neither total nor unprecedented.[7] Yet even as they convincingly chronicled restraint in the Union military effort, these historians were less successful in fully explaining *why* this restraint existed.[8]

Despite their profoundly different depictions of the Civil War's violence and destruction, both camps of historians have devoted inadequate attention to just-war ideas and policies and their impact on Union army actions. As a result, neither perspective fully captures the nature of the violence committed by Union armies, both its inspirations and limitations. By taking seriously mid-nineteenth-century ideas about just conduct in war and the ongoing process of refining these ideas into military policies to govern Federal behavior, my goal is to provide a better framework for understanding the destruction unleashed by Union armies.

The Federals who populate this book possessed a distinct "moral vision of war," a set of ideas and assumptions that informed their thinking on the nature of a justly waged war. This moral vision was ambiguous enough to allow its adherents to disagree in practice on how exactly to wage war. Yet it is still possible to identify core claims that lent coherence to this moral vision. The most important idea was one Francis Lieber succinctly expressed in his code: "The more vigorously wars are pursued, the better it is for humanity. Sharp wars are brief." Lieber claimed that the most humane and just wars were usually the ones most vigorous in their prosecution, which he understood to mean a military effort that deployed all possible means (within certain restrictions) to achieve victory as swiftly as possible. While "sharp wars" might require an army to deliberately target enemy civilians and their property, they presumably also ended more quickly and therefore occasioned less *total* suffering, destruction, and evil. Not all loyal citizens embraced this moral logic. Many northerners criticized it strongly. But, especially as the Civil War progressed, the prevailing Federal opinion about the justness of the Union military effort agreed with Lieber that "the shorter [war] is the better; and the intenser it is carried on, the shorter it will be." Or, as an Indiana infantryman put it bluntly, "The only way to stop the war is to fight it out."[9]

In reality, waging a just war against the Confederacy was never that simple, because even as Union armies embraced a vigorous military effort, their war continued. Federals did not wage a sharp and short war but a sharp and protracted one, which always threatened to render absurd the claim that "intenser" wars were more humane. And if short wars were better for humanity, then why should Federals *not* temporarily resort to cruel and grotesque tactics if they ended the war more quickly? Maj. Henry Hitchcock, a staff officer for Gen. William Tecumseh Sherman, recalled one conversation he had with a Federal captain on precisely this question during the March to the Sea across Georgia in late 1864. "Had quite warm discussion with Dayton," Hitchcock wrote in his diary, "I advocating our self-restraint, 'laws of war' etc., etc., he contending we should do whatever and as bad as the rebs, even to *scalping*." The story of the Union's effort to wage a just war is no simple, orderly tale of moral triumph. It is instead a tension-ridden and morally complex story of the contest between two potentially, but not necessarily, compatible convictions: that vigorously prosecuted wars are humane wars and that Union armies must always adhere to certain restraints in how they wage war.[10]

The moral conviction, well stated in the Lieber code, that the "more vigorously wars are pursued, the better it is for humanity" hardly by itself shaped Union just-war thinking. In fact, Federals relied on a quite vast range of ideas—legal, religious, cultural, and political—when considering how to wage a just war.

The laws of war proved influential to the Union's military effort largely because of Henry W. Halleck and Francis Lieber, America's two leading authorities on the subject. Expertise in the laws of war demanded an extensive study that few nineteenth-century Americans undertook, professional army officers included.[11] But it so happened that during the Civil War Halleck and Lieber held positions of authority and influence that allowed them to lead the effort to conform the actions of Federal soldiers to the laws of war.

Halleck began the war as a commander in the Western Theater, but in late July 1862, Lincoln promoted him to general-in-chief of all Union armies, an office he held with decidedly mixed success for nearly two years before assuming the more strictly administrative role of chief of staff. In early 1861, Halleck published *International Law; or, Rules Regulating the Intercourse of States in Peace and War*, which solidified his reputation as a leading expert on international law. The erudite book contained a historical overview of international law, a philosophical discourse on natural law and positive law, and practical guidance on how to wage a just war. Two assumptions ran throughout Halleck's work. Not only did the laws of war compel belligerents to abide by certain restraints, but wars also sometimes produced "immeasurable blessings" and "unspeakable goods." Halleck explained: "Wars have frequently been, in the hands of providence, the means of disseminating civilization, if carried on by a civilized people." The laws of war instructed civilized people how to wage war in a civilized manner, and thereby reap some of war's "immeasurable blessings," Halleck believed.[12] Lieber similarly assumed that war, for all its horrors, sometimes produced "blessings" and "goods." As Lieber put it, "Blood is occasionally the rich dew of history."[13] Lieber and Halleck shared a commitment to distill the laws of war into guidelines that Union officers and soldiers could easily understand and follow. Both men saw in the laws of war robust justification for a vigorous military effort, yet not one entirely devoid of restraint.

The laws of war usually remained the domain of elite and learned men like Halleck and Lieber. Yet the wider literate public sometimes could acquire a working knowledge of key elements of the laws of war. For example, from October 1861 to February 1862, Lieber delivered a series of public lectures at Columbia College on the "Laws and Usages of War," attended by as many as one hundred people and later published in New York newspapers in an abbreviated form. Similarly, in late 1861, the *Daily Missouri Republican*, a city's leading Democratic paper, ran a four-part editorial on the "Laws of Warfare." These four lengthy editorials surveyed the laws of war in a plain but not rudimentary style. "The great principles of morals apply to nations as well as to men, and the violation of national duties produces national injury, and may result in national ruin," the newspaper declared. Not surprisingly, given Missouri's problems with guerrilla warfare, the editorials focused extensively on how the laws of war distinguished legitimate combatants and noncombatants from illegitimate marauders, guerrillas, and murderers—and also sketched out the different punishments and protections each category of persons deserved. The *Daily Missouri Republican* attempted to educate civilians and convince them "men in arms and in rebellion, must submit to the laws of war."[14]

It was possible, then, for loyal citizens to acquire a basic understanding of the laws of war, perhaps by reading newspaper editorials or even Lieber's code, which was widely reprinted in the North. Yet the laws of war remained influential to the Union war effort not because most soldiers and civilians understood this technical body of legal thought in intimate detail. Instead, the laws of war proved significant because of the influence it had on *official* Union military policies, particularly General Orders No. 100, an influence indebted above all to the efforts of Henry Halleck and Francis Lieber.

In addition to the laws of war, a richly varied set of religious ideas—less technical than ideas drawn from international law but certainly more widely held—also shaped Union just-war thinking. Federals who contemplated how to prosecute a just war often asked themselves, "How should a *Christian* nation wage war?" Some northern ministers turned to Christianity to sanctify seemingly limitless violence in service of the Union war effort. Yet, to a greater extent than historians have recognized, many ministers insisted in their wartime sermons that Federals must wage war in a humane spirit and without vengeful hatred for Confederates. "Let us leave indiscriminate slaughter, piracy, and desperate measures to desperate men," proclaimed Henry Bellows, Unitarian divine and president of the United States Sanitary Commission. "We can afford to be humane . . . and we are bound to be so by the standard of our Christian civilization." This was no call to lay down arms and embrace pacifism. "We cannot spare them our blows; for we have the holy cause of universal justice," Bellows explained. Yet, he hoped this humane spirit would prompt Federals to "rid the contest of vindictiveness and personal hatred and malice." One minister likewise called upon his parishioners in the late summer of 1862 to reject "any spirit of malignant vindictiveness" in its war against the Confederacy. Another clergyman proclaimed, "I would not have now, never have wished to have, any element of vindictiveness in our treatment of [Confederates]."[15] But northern ministers ultimately offered somewhat imprecise guidance for waging war justly. It was not plainly evident how exactly to fight humanely and without vindictiveness, virtues that did not easily translate into military policies. Even so, Federals still turned often to religious ideas to help them define the boundaries of just action in war.

For many loyal citizens, to ask how a *Christian* people should wage war was more or less the same as to ask how a *civilized* people should wage war. Federals frequently used "Christian" and "civilized" interchangeably when describing their war effort. As one Ohio civilian opposed to retaliation in kind against captured Confederates said, "How much nobler it will be to take a Christianized or civilized position in reference to the wrongs the rebels are inflicting upon our gallant soldiers." Behind this talk of civilized warfare were powerful assumptions about the superiority of northern society compared to the Confederacy. If Federals did not always precisely define civilized warfare, they often suggested it was simply the opposite of how Confederates prosecuted the war. Frederick Douglass thought that Confederate armies had become "more savage, more fierce and brutal in their modes of warfare, than any recognized barbarians making no pretentions to civilization." The *New York Herald* affirmed the same idea in even more explicitly racial tones. Confederates did not wage war like civilized (that is, white) people; instead, the "Chinese and the Sepoys have become the chosen models of Southern men."[16]

By avoiding Confederates' barbaric tactics, many loyal citizens believed their armies would preserve America's lofty moral standing in the world. Indiana Republican senator Henry Lane, for one, feared that if Union armies imitated Confederate behavior, they would "with impunity trample upon all their obligations to God as Christians and all their obligations to the world to abide by the laws of civilized warfare."[17] If Federal armies resorted to a style of warfare that utterly contradicted the enlightened, civilized values that defined the Union, then, even if victorious over the Confederacy, the loyal citizenry would still in a sense lose their Union by tarnishing its exceptional moral character. Today, words like "civilized" undoubtedly carry controversial connotations. But I use the term "civilized warfare" through-out this book precisely because the loyal citizenry used it so frequently (even when disagreeing on its meaning) to describe the nature and importance of just conduct in war.

Distinctly political concerns also influenced the Union citizenry's just-war thinking, especially on how and why to restrain devastation. Many Federals desired to punish or target white southerners in rough accordance with their disloyalty. The historian Mark Grimsley persuasively argues that Union armies unleashed a "directed severity" against southern civilians, act-ing on the belief that patently disloyal civilians should suffer more than loyal or neutral ones. Many Federals also assumed that because a domineering Slave Power aristocracy duped or coerced most white southerners into sup-porting the Confederacy, a just war effort must hone its devastation upon the elite slaveholders. This assumption revealed itself dramatically when, in 1865, William Tecumseh Sherman's army marched through South Carolina, especially Columbia, the supposed home of the most meddlesome and culpable members of the slaveocracy. One Iowa private, as he arrived in Co-lumbia, reveled in finally making suffer "this hotbed of treason and the foul nest where secession was first hatched." Another Ohio infantryman in Sher-man's army rejoiced that the oligarchic lords of the "Mother State of Seces-sion" were now "severely yet justly reaping" the chaos and calamity they sowed with secession.[18] Union armies needed, above all, not to devastate or punish white southerners but disenthrall them from the domineering con-trol of the aristocratic slaveholding elite.

Another equally important political consideration was the goal of ensur-ing a magnanimous, lasting reunion after Federal military victory. One Pennsylvania infantry captain who witnessed firsthand the devastation of the Shenandoah Valley in 1864 confided to his wife his concern that there was "no telling when & where all this is going to end. There is such a sea of bitterness & hatred between the two parties in this war that it occurs to me the prospect of peace is yet far distant." In fact, many northerners assumed that how Union armies conducted the war had the power to make lasting reunion either possible or illusory. Restraint toward Confederate civilians and their property might prove essential to achieving President Abraham Lincoln's dream: a just and lasting peace within a restored Union. As Sena-tor Thomas A. Hendricks put it, Union armies ought to abide by rules "for the regulation of belligerents" not merely to avoid "inhumanity, barbarism, and cruelty," but also "so that when the war is over there may be mutual respect and confidence, that the ancient relations of commerce and trade may return unimpaired ... [and] make us once more one Government and one people with one destiny."[19] The Pennsylvania infantry captain in the Valley in 1864 knew how exceedingly difficult it would be to achieve Hendricks's goal. Yet Federals' hopes for permanent, peaceful reunion had far-reaching implications for how they approached waging a just war

My main goal in this book is to explain how Union officials refined wide-ranging legal, religious, cultural, and political ideas into coherent rules to govern their army's behavior. When translated into particular policies and measures, these just-war ideas amounted to a military effort I refer to as "hard yet humane." Union armies eventually waged a "hard war" that abided by Lieber's call for "intenser" fighting and did not shield enemy civilians from hardship and devastation. The conviction that vigorous wars were just wars infused the Union military effort with a stern determination to defeat the Confederacy as swiftly as possible, however immense the temporary carnage and hardship. Yet, at the same time, Federals devoted equally earnest attention to defining the boundaries of just conduct in war. They endeavored to wage "a more civil war" by adhering to the restraints imposed by the laws of war or other just-war ideas.[20] The same moral vision of war that justified great destruction also insisted on certain limits to the violence Union armies unleashed.

The first two chapters of this book look to the Mississippi River Valley in the initial eighteen months of the war to trace the origins of the Union's "hard yet humane" just-war policies. Some historians have argued that when Federal armies in this region faced guerrillas and hostile Confederate civilians they responded by resolutely embracing the hard hand of war—which is true, but only half the story.[21] These same challenges also simultaneously inspired many Union officials to work to establish and abide by certain constraints. In guerrilla-ravaged Missouri and Union-occupied New Orleans and Memphis, a distinct understanding of just warfare began to take hold among Federals, one that consciously sought to reconcile hard war measures and humane restraints. Because the first two chapters trace the origins of Federal "hard yet humane" just-war policies, my focus here remains chiefly on the upper echelon of the Union military command in the Mississippi River Valley. Ultimately, Union generals such as Henry W. Halleck, Benjamin F. Butler, and William T. Sherman—far more than junior officers or enlisted soldiers—were responsible for creating the earliest military rules for waging war in a hard yet humane manner. Union generals in the region crafted these policies without much consideration of the *opinions* of common soldiers about the nature of just warfare. However, these same generals certainly contemplated the *experiences* of the soldiers under their command, the realities soldiers faced while battling guerrillas or interacting with civilians, as they drafted their just-war policies.

Chapter 3 explains how Francis Lieber refined this moral vision of hard yet humane war into a coherent set of rules applicable to the entire Union army. The 157 articles of General Orders No. 100, the Lieber code, sought to instruct Federals on how to reconcile in practice the hard hand of war with humane restraints. It also attempted to vindicate vigorously waged wars as truly moral wars. Admittedly, it is difficult to assess how thoroughly Lieber's code actually shaped the behavior of Union soldiers. The process at work here is far more complex than a simple cause and effect, as if soldiers always obeyed whatever the code commanded. There are innumerable examples of Union soldiers disregarding the constraints set forth in the code; moral principles and military policies never perfectly aligned with soldiers' practices. It is also often impossible to determine if soldiers *intentionally* acted in accordance with the code, if they were consciously aware of the demands of the code's articles and deliberately tried to live up to them. Even so, there remained a striking similarity between the content of Lieber's code and the actions of Union soldiers. The reason for this similarity is that many Federal officers and soldiers possessed the same moral vision of war that defined Lieber's code, the same convictions about the justness of a hard yet humane war.

Two concluding chapters reveal how Federals adhered to the moral vision of hard yet humane warfare in the conflict's final year. I look first to the Union's use of formal retaliation against Confederate soldiers, and argue that Federal officials involved in major retaliation-related episodes largely abided by the Lieber code's cautious attitude toward retaliation. Then I consider the Union army's treatment of Confederate civilians and their property in two notorious campaigns: Philip H. Sheridan's 1864 Shenandoah Valley Campaign and William Tecumseh Sherman's March to the Sea and through South Carolina. These campaigns witnessed great destruction (often utterly unwarranted) and also persistent restraint. Federals' moral vision of hard yet humane warfare inspired both, for many Union soldiers believed both were necessary in a justly waged war. Taken together, these five chapters do not trace a drastic change during the war in prevailing Union just-war thinking. Instead, I show how Union officials and policymakers refined common moral convictions about the nature of just warfare into detailed military policies that many Union soldiers then endeavored to implement.

The story I tell here is of Federals embroiled in the moral dilemmas of waging a war that became the most destructive in their nation's history. I have tried along the way to avoid quick caricature or condemnation of Civil War Americans. If Francis Lieber was right, a day of terrible reckoning awaited those among them who failed to take seriously their moral obligations; they remained accountable to God for their actions in war. I seek neither to romanticize Federal armies as morally superior nor sanitize the war's carnage. After all, even as Union armies endeavored to wage war justly, they still committed themselves to a war vigorous in its prosecution, and therefore also great in its destruction. This is the essential and sobering point at the heart of this story: Most Federals believed just wars *were by necessity* wars in which armies did nearly whatever was necessary to end war as quickly as possible. It was precisely for this reason that Lieber proclaimed not long after the war began, "The gigantic wars of modern times are less destructive than were the protracted former ones."[22] Civil War Americans such as Lieber lived at the cusp of a modern world in which war endured. They responded by embracing a particular vision of just warfare that they believed would limit the total suffering and destruction their war unleashed. Federals hoped that in waging hard yet humane war they would best fulfill their obligations to God and humanity as moral beings engaged in war.

CHAPTER ONE

A War of Barbarism or of Comparative Humanity
Combatting Guerrillas

In the opening months of the Civil War in Missouri, as the Union army embraced hard war measures to subdue rebel guerrillas and civilians, it also established rules intended to limit the war's killing and destruction. The war in Missouri posed innumerable moral challenges. Guerrillas plundered civilians and destroyed railroad and telegraph lines. Zealous Jayhawkers carried forth the crusading spirit of John Brown and wreaked havoc in western Missouri. Union soldiers punished secessionists by raiding or destroying their property. Brash Confederate sympathizers exacerbated tensions among the divided citizenry and often eagerly aided guerrillas. Maintaining peace and order by any means would be no easy task. To do so according to the laws of war might prove impossible.

In early November 1861, Maj. Gen. Henry W. Halleck assumed command of the Department of the Missouri and appeared equal to the task. Halleck, the bookish West Point graduate, army engineer, and authority on international law, recognized that the dire situation in Missouri presented acute challenges to waging war justly. Did guerrillas deserve any rights usually afforded to regular soldiers, or were they lawless marauders and murderers who deserved swift death? Should Union forces unleash the hard hand of war against noncombatants who supported guerrillas? When should Union soldiers confiscate or destroy civilian property? Should civilians in an area known to harbor guerrillas be held responsible for their killing and destruction? Did the all-important end of restoring order in Missouri justify any means?

The Union army in Missouri responded to these questions with stern measures that signaled the start of a more brutal and uncompromising style of warfare, but that is only half the story. The military situation in Missouri also inspired some of the earliest official rules meant to govern and restrain Federal soldiers' actions. From the spring of 1861 through the summer of 1862, the guerrilla war in the state prompted Halleck and other Federals to work to reconcile hard war measures with the constraints imposed by the laws of war and their notions of how a civilized people should wage war.

This was a messy task, imperfectly completed, and complicated by the fact that not all Federal soldiers strictly adhered to official just-war policies issued by their commanders. Even so, the first eighteen months of the Civil War in Missouri proved consequential to the Union war effort not because it helped inaugurate a style of near-total warfare that encompassed soldiers and civilians alike.[1] Historians have neglected to recognize that early encounters with guerrilla warfare in Missouri instead prompted many Union officers and soldiers in the state to embrace a moral vision of just warfare that advocated both hard war measures and humane restraints.[2]

This intentionally hard yet humane military effort emerged across roughly four stages from May 1861 to August 1862 in response to frustrating realities Union soldiers faced on the battlefield. In late spring and summer of 1861, Federals first confronted the guerrilla problem mostly without clear guidelines from the highest levels of Union command. However, a few key ideas took hold about how to deal justly and effectively with guerrillas—above all, that civilians could be held responsible for ensuring guerrilla-free peace and order where they lived.

Throughout the late fall and winter of 1861, Henry Halleck launched a sustained effort to codify rules to govern Union troop behavior in everything from the seizure or destruction of property to the treatment of guerrillas and Confederate-sympathizing civilians. Although Halleck undoubtedly led this effort to refine Union thinking about just conduct in war, loyal citizens in Missouri, especially ministers and newspaper editors, also voiced their opinions.

By the spring and summer of 1862, Union forces then went about implementing, revising, and reimplementing policies specifically for subduing guerrillas. Brig. Gen. John M. Schofield made a particularly bold and ultimately unsuccessful effort to hold civilians responsible for ending guerrilla activity by calling up all able-bodied men to serve in the newly formed Enrolled Missouri Militia. These efforts failed to end guerrilla activity in Missouri, but they did embody a vision of just conduct as equally hard and humane.

This initial antiguerrilla effort culminated in late August 1862, as Halleck, then general in chief of Union armies, looked to Francis Lieber for expert legal advice on how best to conquer guerrillas in the sternest possible terms allowed by the laws of war. Lieber's solutions to the problems in Missouri shaped the spirit and content of later Union just-war policies, especially his own General Orders No. 100, issued to Union armies in the spring of 1863.

In confronting guerrillas in Missouri, Federals worked to reconcile two styles of warfare: one that sought stern, vigorous punishment of rebel guerrillas and their sympathizers, and one that adhered to restraints imposed by the laws of war and common notions of civility in warfare.

The Guerrilla War Begins: May to August 1861

Almost as soon as the Civil War began, guerrillas upended normal life in Missouri. When Henry Ankeny arrived in the state with his Iowa infantry regiment and surveyed the turmoil firsthand, he concluded, "this is the most uninviting country I ever saw." James Overton Broadhead, a prominent lawyer in St. Louis, warned Secretary of War Edwin M. Stanton in early June 1861 that Confederate sympathizers not part of regular armies were "drilling, arming, manufacturing arms and preparing munitions of war, and where they have the power still threatening Union men and driving them from their homes." Guerrillas destroyed railroad and telegraph lines. They harassed civilians and destroyed private property, often for mere plunder, often to intimidate Unionists.[3] From the very start of the war, the guerrilla fighting raised three particularly difficult just-war questions.

First, how exactly should Union troops subdue and punish guerrillas? Ad hoc arrangements worked out by Union officers prevailed in the war's early months. For example, Federals responded to an attack on the North Missouri Railroad outside St. Louis by hanging one man immediately, shooting another who tried to flee, imprisoning the remaining guerrillas, and seizing nearly thirty horses. Union soldiers relied on a variety of tactics fitted to unique circumstances, yet the *Daily Missouri Democrat*, St. Louis's leading Republican-leaning newspaper, insisted that Union punishment of guerrillas "must be swift, certain, and dreadful."[4] Ulysses S. Grant, recently appointed brigadier general in the United States Volunteers, similarly wrote to his wife from Mexico, Missouri, that guerrillas should face stern retribution from the Union army. "They are great fools in this section of country and will never rest until they bring upon themselvs [*sic*]all the horrors of war in its worst form. The people are inclined to carry on a guerilla Warfare that must eventuate in retaliation." Yet Grant grimly acknowledged that once begun, a harsh and uncompromising war against guerrillas "will be hard to control."[5]

Second, should local civilians be held responsible for nearby guerrilla destruction? When Brig. Gen. William S. Harney assumed command of the

Department of the West in mid-May 1861, he assured civilians he would not "harass or oppress the good and law-abiding people of Missouri" and would do all he could "to protect their persons and property from violations of every kind."[6] At the same time, a Missouri regimental newspaper, *The U.S. American Volunteer*, claimed that Union troops were stationed in Missouri "to keep the peace, not to break it," which meant they would protect loyal Missourians from anyone guilty of "treasonable purposes."[7] Eventually, this commitment to protecting Missouri Unionists and their property prompted more severe measures against disloyal citizens aiding guerrillas. But Federals still faced the difficult challenge of discerning who were the "good and law-abiding people of Missouri" and who were not. A person's true loyalty or their involvement with guerrillas was not always readily apparent. Col. Lorenzo Thomas warned Harney in late May that many of the state's political leaders professed loyalty to the Union but plotted with Confederates: "They have already falsified their professions too often and are too far committed to secession to be entitled to your confidence." Galusha Anderson, pastor of Second Baptist Church in St. Louis, recalled the trepidation he felt in preaching each week as the war began, for although he assumed his congregation contained staunch Union and Confederate sympathizers, he did not know the precise loyalties of most members.[8] Uncertainties about a person's true loyalty only made it all the more difficult for Union armies to deal justly with civilians.

Third, what could Union officers do to prevent and punish unwarranted abuses committed by their own soldiers while fighting guerrillas? Quite often this question specifically concerned the legitimate treatment of civilian property. What exactly could soldiers seize or destroy? When and for what reasons? In mid-May 1861, a Union captain arrested over fifty Confederate sympathizers in Potosi who had recently harassed local loyal citizens. The captain decided not to destroy a vast quantity of property initially seized during the arrests, except for two smelting furnaces used to furnish lead to Confederate forces.[9] But not all Federals always showed the same discretion. L. W. Burris of Liberty worried that Union soldiers turned local civilians against the Union cause by "the searing of private homes, drawers and trunks, where there is no need for suspicion."[10] When Ulysses S. Grant arrived at Mexico, he discovered that some men in regiments now under his command had a history of ransacking homes without justification and helping themselves to whatever food and drink they could find. Grant promptly prohibited his soldiers from entering homes uninvited and seizing property without his authorization.[11] In late July 1861, Brig. Gen. Nathaniel Lyon issued one of the earliest comprehensive policies for the seizure of property in the state. Lyon promised to protect "all law-abiding citizens," and therefore ordered that Federals only seize the property of persons "exciting others to acts of rebellion, and are themselves in arms against the General Government." Lyon also reminded his troops that they should only seize property to prevent pro-Confederates from committing "mischief," and should not seek "the injury of families or the wanton destruction of property."[12]

Union soldiers and their commanders inevitably confronted these three questions as they waged war against guerrillas. But Lyon's early orders were hardly the final official word on how Federals ought to combat guerrillas and their supporters. In the opening months of the Civil War, other Union officers also constructed rules of conduct for the guerrilla fighting that embodied the moral vision of a hard yet humane war. Implementing these rules sparked controversy and conflict. The earliest major controversy arose in northeast Missouri and involved Brig. Gen. John Pope, a brash Kentuckian prone to hubris.[13] On 31 July, Pope issued General Orders No. 3, the most vigorous effort to date by a Federal officer to hold civilians responsible for nearby guerrilla activity. By late August, Pope found himself embroiled in a bitter fight over the responsibility of civilians in Marion County for a recent guerrilla attack on a train carrying Union troops. The controversy revealed the difficulty of subduing guerrillas and pacifying their civilian supporters in a way that deftly balanced measures both hard and humane.

The guerrilla conflict in northeast Missouri was as violent, perilous, and irrepressible as anywhere in the state. The *Daily Missouri Democrat* reported in early August 1861 about the "tyranny . . . of the most atrocious character" of secessionists in that portion of Missouri. Reports surfaced of Union men murdered "in an unprovoked and heartless manner . . . for no crime but that they half kept their allegiance to a good government and advised their neighbors to do the same." Guerrillas targeted railroads and harassed loyal citizens. Attorney James Overton Broadhead warned a fellow Unionist that guerrillas were "overrunning the country and forcing all union men to take an oath not to take up arms against the state of Mo nor the confederate state. The Union sentiment is fast being crushed out." Gert Goebel, a German immigrant, later wrote that the dire threat to loyal citizens that guerrillas posed in the region demanded a response: "continued clemency toward bands of murderers, who shrank from no crime as long as they were not punished, would have been an unjustifiable cruelty toward the unprotected Union people."[14]

When Pope assumed command of the District of North and Central Missouri in July 1861 he immediately threatened quick retribution against anyone who committed "depredation upon the public or private property or who molest unoffending and peaceful citizens." Pope desired to restore safety and security in the region, especially for Unionists, and he thought this required preventing the further destruction of railroads. By late July, Pope believed the best way to do so was to hold civilians responsible for nearby guerrilla destruction. He publicly pledged that every time guerrillas destroyed part of the often-attacked North Missouri Railroad, he would hold citizens living within a five-mile radius of the destruction financially responsible (unless they had actively resisted the guerrillas). If local citizens did not immediately inform Union commanders of the whereabouts of the guilty guerrillas, Federals would seize money and property equivalent to the costs of the destruction. Pope admitted in a letter to Maj. Gen. John C. Frémont that his measures "may seem at first sight to be harsh," but he insisted they were justified—even mild—given the true loyalties and subversive activities of many citizens in northeast Missouri. Supposedly loyal citizens made no effort to "resist these lawless acts of outrage," Pope argued, which he believed amounted to open aid to the enemy. Pope concluded that the lifeblood of guerrilla activity was the aid and support it received from local civilians. But if supporting guerrillas resulted in severe financial duress, Pope wagered most civilians would help stop the destruction of railroads.[15]

On 31 July, Pope followed up this warning by issuing General Orders No. 3, his most extensive statement to date on how the Union forces under his command would deal with guerrillas and their supporters. Pope's orders crystallized two key ideas that eventually guided Federal antiguerrilla efforts throughout all of Missouri. The first idea was that Federals could hold civilians responsible for guerrilla lawlessness and destruction. Pope said the people of northeast Missouri had an obligation to maintain "the peace and quietude of their own section." To ensure that civilians fulfilled this obligation, Pope sought to establish in every county seat and major town a "committee of public safety" comprised of no more than five people responsible for maintaining peace and order. They had the power "to call out all citizens of the county to assemble at such times and places and in such numbers as may be necessary to secure these objects." Pope warned that if civilians did not maintain peace themselves, he would send out Union troops to do so, and charge the county for the expenses incurred. Well aware that many northeast Missouri residents loathed the permanent presence of "occupying" Union troops, Pope insisted that if citizens proved able to ensure peace in their counties, "there will no longer be a necessity for the presence of armed forces." Pope did not clarify important details. What exactly constituted maintaining "peace and quietude"? Could a county avoid financial penalties if its committee of public safety made a genuine yet unsuccessful effort to maintain peace? Were there limits to the penalties that could be levied against a county? Still, the orders did make one thing abundantly clear: Pope acted in the conviction that "[to] preserve the peace is the duty of all good citizens."[16]

The second key idea in Pope's orders was that Federals should resort only to well-defined and limited punishments of civilians who supported guerrillas. Here Pope granted that a degree of humane restraint must accompany the hard war measures he advocated. Pope suggested that he might have responded to the widespread disarray and destruction by sending out "in all parts of this region small bodies of troops, to hunt out the parties in arms against the peace, and follow them to their homes or places of retreat." But this heavy-handed show of force would have resulted only in unnecessary violence, Pope reasoned. He thought his chosen course of action would restore peace and safety "with the least bloodshed, the least distress to quiet persons, and the least exasperation of feeling among the people." Less than one month prior to Pope's orders, the *Military News of the Missouri Volunteers*, published by the Fifth Missouri Infantry, had similarly insisted that the Union army must deploy its destructive power in a discriminate and limited manner: "Though accompanied with arms and implements of war, though moving in martial order, these arms, this order are only prepared for use against the lawless, violent and treacherous disturbers of public peace." General Orders No. 3 might seem harsh or imperfect but Pope believed it still reconciled vastly different goals: winning the guerrilla war while respecting as best as possible the person and property of Missouri citizens and sparing the "effusion of blood."[17]

But not all loyal citizens in Missouri deemed Pope's orders wise and prudent. J. T. K. Hayward, a St. Louis resident, acknowledged in a letter to Pope that large portions of northeast Missouri favored secession and aided local guerrillas. But Hayward also claimed that Union troops committed some of the worst depredations in the region. More importantly, he feared Pope's policy of holding civilians responsible for guerrilla destruction of railroads undermined Pope's chief strategic goals: "Retain all your present friends if possible, and strengthen their hands, while weaken the enemy, and give them the least possible just occasion to complain." Hayward concluded General Orders No. 3 had not subdued guerrillas but did harm and anger innocent loyal civilians: "The principle of holding peaceable, quiet men responsible in a military contribution for damages done by lawless and violent men is one which can never meet with favor in the popular mind."[18] Hayward criticized Pope's policy for weakening Union sentiment and unjustly punishing genuinely loyal citizens who had the misfortune of living in an area largely supportive of guerrillas.

Opposition to Pope's measures intensified as he embarked on an uncompromising effort to implement them in Marion County in late August 1861. Guerrillas fired on a train carrying Union troops as it left Palmyra, the county seat of Marion, killing one soldier and wounding another. Federals killed five guerrillas as they scattered into the countryside after the attack. A furious Pope warned he would "inflict such punishment as will be remembered." He gave Palmyra officials six days to hand over those responsible for the attack. If they failed to do so, Pope threatened to send a whole brigade into the area and levy a ten-thousand-dollar fine on Marion County and five-thousand-dollar fine on the city of Palmyra. "Some severe example is needed or we shall be harassed constantly by these robbers and assassins," Pope explained.[19] He saw in this latest incident an opportunity to prove that his preferred policy for waging the guerrilla war in Missouri was effective, feasible, and just.

Citizens of Marion County immediately protested Pope's punishment, and some appealed directly to Maj. Gen. John C. Frémont, commander of the Department of the West, to have it rescinded. They denounced the measure as illegal and counterproductive. "It is without warrant of law," they protested, and only alienated Marion County residents from the Union: "It is irritating to the people and deeply injurious to the union cause." By punishing equally the innocent and the guilty, the loyal and disloyal, the penalties have "already driven thousands from our ranks." If Pope imposed the levy, the vast majority of people living in the region would engage in "open rebellion," the citizens predicted.[20] Pope argued his policy restored peace, security, and loyalty to the Union; his opponents protested that his measures did exactly the opposite, aggravating civilians and driving them away from the Union cause.

Pope wrote Frémont to respond directly to the appeal from Marion County citizens. He reiterated earlier arguments that his policies dealt fairly and humanely with guerrillas and their supporters. Pope demanded a great deal from the civilians of northeast Missouri, he said, because the present war would end only "by making all engaged in it suffer for every act of hostility committed." The proper limit to this suffering was an open question, one that Union officers in Missouri would revisit repeatedly. But at the moment, Pope expressed little discomfort over the prospect of genuinely loyal citizens unduly punished by his measures—in part because he believed the overwhelming majority in the Palmyra area sympathized with the guerrillas, and in part, as he put it in General Orders No. 3, because he believed every citizen had a duty to actively preserve peace. Pope further warned Frémont that his orders would only effectively subdue guerrilla activity if consistently enforced: "One failure to enforce rigidly penalty will destroy all belief it will ever be enforced at all."[21]

The editors of St. Louis's *Daily Missouri Democrat* agreed with Pope that Federals would win the war in Missouri not through leniency but through "the stern arm of justice." In a late August editorial, the newspaper mocked earlier hopes "that forbearance and leniency might calm excitement, and bring the guilty to reason." This policy only encouraged guerrillas, disheartened Unionists, and produced "serious mischief to the Republic." The editorial heartily endorsed the spirit of Pope's measures. It insisted that anything less than the stern arm of justice led to destruction, harassment, lawlessness, and bloodshed. But swift and decisive retribution would humanely restore security and order.[22] A Union soldier in a Missouri infantry regiment, having seen the chaos unleashed by guerrillas, similarly endorsed the logic of a hard yet humane war in late July 1861: "A little severity just now would save hundreds of useful lives hereafter."[23]

Eventually, the public outcry against Pope's orders prevailed. Governor Henry Gamble and Francis Preston Blair Jr. soon pressured Pope to rescind the financial penalties imposed on Marion County, which he did on 30 August. Although Pope still believed in the wisdom of his policy, he deferred to "the earnest wishes of the executive civil authority of the State." Even so, Pope warned the citizens of northeast Missouri that any "abuse of this leniency" would result in retribution of unprecedented fury.[24] The controversy provoked by Pope's orders amounted ultimately to disagreements about the limits of a just war against guerrillas and their supporters. The conflict played out against the unsettling reality that as the summer ended the guerrilla war in Missouri continued unabated.[25] Policies such as Pope's were clearly controversial, but it remained to be seen if they were also effective.

At the same time Pope faced great opposition in northern Missouri, John C. Frémont also became embroiled in a controversy over legitimate conduct in war. It began on 30 August when Frémont sought to act boldly to end "the total insecurity of life" lately caused by guerrillas in the state. The "severest measures" were necessary, Frémont said, so he declared martial law throughout Missouri. (On the same day he declared martial law, Frémont also issued General Orders No. 6, a stern reminder to Federal soldiers that they must still uphold "good order and rigorous discipline," which meant especially not committing "unauthorized searches, seizures, and destruction.") According to Frémont's proclamation, guerrillas caught in arms behind Union lines would be tried by court martial and executed if found guilty. Frémont also warned that Federals would confiscate the property of any person "who shall take up arms against the United States," including slaves, who would then be "declared freemen." This final threat directly contradicted the so-called First Confiscation Act, passed by Congress earlier in the month, which authorized the confiscation only of property (including slaves) used directly to aid the Confederate war effort. In threatening to target slavery, Frémont jeopardized President Abraham Lincoln's daunting effort to unite the northern citizenry in a war to save the Union and ensure the continued loyalty of the Border States.[26] Ethan Allen Hitchcock, retired general and eventual member of the committee that drafted the Lieber code, believed Frémont was "an instrument in the hands of abolitionists . . . used by that sect in the effort to force the Government into an abolition war." Frémont did act in part to secure acclaim from abolitionists. Still, that did not stop New York lawyer George Templeton Strong from praising the bold action as exactly what the Union military effort needed: "War in earnest, at last."[27]

It was war in earnest on terms Lincoln could not tolerate. He ordered Frémont not to execute any guerrillas without his approval, for he feared a vicious cycle of retaliation would erupt: "The Confederates would very certainly shoot our best men in their hands, in retaliation; and so, man for man, indefinitely." Lincoln also worried Frémont's strike against slavery would "alarm our Southern Union friends." He requested that Frémont revise this portion of his order to align it the First Confiscation Act. Frémont stubbornly refused Lincoln's private request so the President "cheerfully" ordered him publicly to make the revision. As he explained to Illinois senator Orville Hickman Browning, Lincoln believed Frémont's proclamation was "*purely political*, and not within the range of *military* law, or necessity." While a general might temporarily seize private property, the general could not permanently revoke a person's ownership in that property; commanders like Frémont might find it necessary "to seize the farm of a private owner," yet that did not empower them "to say the farm shall no longer belong to the owner, or his heirs forever," especially once it was no longer "needed for military purposes." The same logic applied to slave property, Lincoln reasoned: "If the General needs them, he can seize them, and use them; but when the need is past, it is not for him to fix their permanent future condition." Lincoln feared Frémont's proclamation would signal "the surrender of the government"—not only because it defied the existing "Constitution and laws" which governed the nation but also because it alienated Border State Unionists.[28]

The Frémont episode revealed that what to do with slavery was one of the more controversial just-war questions that Federals faced. Should Union armies strike a deathblow against slavery to subdue guerrillas? Did an army commander, Congress, or the President as commander in chief have legitimate legal authority to declare enemy slaves free? Could a just war also be a war against slavery? *Must* it be a war against slavery? These questions hardly applied only to the war effort in Missouri. Their moral and political dimensions weighed heavily on the Lincoln administration and Union army commanders in the months ahead.

By the fall of 1861, Union armies had not subdued Missouri guerrillas, and they only had begun to resolve the many-sided problem of a justly waged war. While some Federals dismissed Pope's heavy-handed style, others came to agree with him that the only way to end the guerrilla war in Missouri was to hold civilians responsible for ensuring peace and security. This was precisely the sort of principle whose devil is in its details. What exactly were the limits to this civilian responsibility or the punishments meted out on persons who failed to fulfill it? Reconciling hard war measures and humane restraints would be a messy, imperfect, experimental business. This task awaited Henry Halleck as he assumed command of the Department of the Missouri in November 1861.

Henry Halleck and His Initial Hard Yet Humane
Military Policies: September to December 1861

By early January 1862, Halleck had issued a well-defined set of rules governing just conduct in war—ranging widely from the proper seizure of property, to the treatment of civilians, to the assessment of financial penalties against Confederates in St. Louis, to the punishment of guerrillas caught destroying railroads, to the enforcement of martial law and the trial of civilians by military commissions, to the punishment of Union troops guilty of plunder. In the months prior, across the fall and winter of 1861, the Union army appeared increasingly to act in the stern spirit of Pope's General Orders No. 3. The intractable guerrilla problem convinced many Federals in the state that vigorous measures like Pope's orders were necessary. Yet even as the Union army in Missouri traded conciliation for the hard hand of war, many Federals worked also to reconcile in theory and practice their harsh anti-guerrilla tactics with a degree of restraint.

Although officers like Halleck codified and implemented rules of conduct, the underlying just-war questions also interested Missouri civilians. Many of them called for a war of quick and decisive fury, yet not utterly devoid of limits. In late August 1861, St. Louis's most prominent minister, William Greenleaf Eliot, proclaimed from the pulpit that Missouri Unionists had the power to make the present conflict "a war of barbarism, or of comparative humanity and civilization." Eliot, a Unitarian from Massachusetts, had lived in St. Louis since 1834 and was instrumental in founding Washington University. "I am a lover of peace," Eliot confessed that August morning. "War is not a Christian work, and the time will come for its abolition." But the time had not come yet. The Christian during wartime had to reconcile two duties: to defend one's country in battle and to foster peace, righteousness, and social progress. The two duties were not necessarily compatible. Missourians must reject a war of barbarism for one of *comparative* humanity and thereby "keep Christian principles alive."[29]

Eliot was a man of the cloth, not a man of the sword; he did not command men in arms but instead preached the gospel. Therefore, he offered no specific guidance on how Union troops might act in battle to keep Christian principles alive. Union armies had an obligation to wage war by the sternest measures necessary for victory, Eliot said; if they did not, "society would be completely in the hands of the wicked." However, Eliot also pleaded with loyal soldiers and civilians to remember their goal remained not vengeful devastation but a "fair and just settlement," the Union peacefully restored. "It is one thing to be decided, energetic, resolute, quite another to be vindictive, overbearing, blood-thirsty," Eliot concluded. The former defined a justly waged war; the latter, utter barbarism. Soldiers who heeded advice such as Eliot's, one Missouri volunteer believed, and nobly sacrificed themselves for the Union, died "like a Christian." As *Camp Sweeney Spy*, a Union regimental newspaper in Missouri, insisted, Federal armies must continue to fight "not for revenge but to rescue from infamy our beloved land."[30]

But Barton Bates, for one, believed instead that what mattered most was ensuring that secessionists "feel themselves conquered." Bates wrote a fiery letter to his father, Attorney General Edward Bates, in early September 1861 about Missouri's truly "miserable state." Bates begrudgingly accepted that Federals ought to treat Confederate soldiers as legitimate combatants and not mere lawless bandits. But for irregular guerrillas or marauders, Bates thought the only legitimate course of action was to "shoot them promptly." Bates loathed the "lenient" treatment shown so far to guerrillas. "They need a severe lesson," Bates concluded. "They should be summarily shot by thousands. They have well earned the fate, and the example made of them may be of great value elsewhere in deterring rebels, within the lines of the army, from following their example."[31] Even though such summary executions by the thousands never occurred, Bates expressed in harsh terms the increasingly prevalent view that only stern retribution deterred guerrilla activity. His letter captured the visceral anger Unionists felt toward guerrillas and their sympathizers. Perhaps Federals could master and subdue this anger—and prevent it from spiraling into unchecked vengeance—but the anger rarely disappeared entirely, even from the hearts of those committed to restraining war's worst excesses.

Many Unionists in Missouri sympathized with the frustration and hatred underlying Bates' irate outburst. Yet the editors of the *Daily Missouri Republican* proved that sober reflection about just conduct in war could prevail. "Some pretty good people talk as if every sort of barbarity and horror, multiplied *ad infinitum*, were a necessary part of this war," the *Daily Missouri Republican* noted, which it labeled "a most *atrocious* view of [war]." An Iowa infantry private likewise found little thrill in the barbarities of war, even the act of killing: "I did not volunteer to kill many if it could be avoided and I would like very much if this matter or trouble could be settled (if it could be settled right) without having to shoot at or kill a single man." As the editors of the *Daily Missouri Republican* put it, to pursue a war without restraint or discretion only guaranteed the war would "leave our people neither liberty nor life worth having." The newspaper affirmed in an October 1861 editorial that participants in the war in Missouri must abide by the laws of war. The newspaper emphasized that officers should pay particular care to protect noncombatants "from the violence of the lawless part of their soldiery; for in every command there will be more or fewer lawless men." The paper called for the clearest possible guidelines for the confiscation of property; only by acting in accordance with such guidelines would soldiers avoid the same "lawless and irregular violence" that guerrillas committed.[32] Despite its desire to see lawless guerrillas punished, the *Daily Missouri Republican* still believed the Union military leadership in Missouri should issue clear guidelines for waging war with civility and restraint.

Henry Halleck and other officers went about this task in earnest in the late fall and winter of 1861. They did so because of both continued guerrilla activity and persistent abuses by Union troops. It is easy to imagine all Federal soldiers in Missouri as prone to plunder and mayhem, forever beyond the control of refined officers who sought to conform troop behavior to enlightened standards of civilized warfare. In reality, the situation was never that simple. One soldier, after witnessing firsthand guerrilla destruction in Missouri, confessed to his fiancée, "I feel strongly tempted to stay here and turn Jayhawker. It is the best business just now—it has only one objection to me, and that is it looks too much like stealing." In late December 1861, a Union soldier from Illinois wrote home to his family about confiscating horses and cattle to aid the Federal military effort, which did not bother him. However, the soldier continued, "Burning houses I did not participate in. It may be necessary, but it is not my style of warfare." Even as some soldiers persistently acted with a degree of restraint, or condemned excessive destruction, others could disregard such restraint.[33] In late October, John C. Frémont, still commander of the Department of the West, found it necessary to remind his soldiers that the plunder or unauthorized destruction of private property was strictly forbidden and punishable by "terrible penalty." Anything deemed necessary for the survival of Union troops could be seized only after Frémont approved. Even then, he explained, the seizure had to occur under the close watch of officers, who were to give owners receipts for their eventual reimbursement. Union armies in Missouri needed not only "to prosecute the war with the utmost vigor against all who are in arms against the Government," Frémont said, but also "to inspire confidence in the loyal inhabitants of this State, and to assure others of protection and immunity if they return to their allegiance."[34]

After assuming command of the Department of the Missouri, Henry Halleck issued guidelines in late November for property seizure and destruction that mirrored rules issued by Frémont one month earlier. He directed Union troops to seize property only when absolutely necessary and ordered officers to document the seizure and provide receipts to property owners. Halleck did issue a threat Frémont had not: Troops who committed an unauthorized act of seizure or destruction would be punished with the "extreme penalty imposed by laws of war, which is death." Because unwarranted depredations by Federal troops intensified the "discredit cast upon our patriotic army," executing guilty soldiers helped keep Missouri civilians loyal.[35] The *Daily Missouri Republican* applauded Halleck's efforts. Holding soldiers to well-defined rules would "do a great deal toward pacifying large portions of our State, where many people feel that their liberty and property are unjustly dealt with by men having no responsibility."[36] Not all Union soldiers succumbed to plunder and near-indiscriminate destruction, but enough did to compel commanding officers to reissue rules meant to govern the just treatment of private property.

But Halleck had much more than the treatment of civilian property on his mind. As December 1861 unfolded, he orchestrated the most extensive effort to date by a commander in Missouri to ensure that Union troops in the guerrilla-ravaged state prosecuted the war in a hard yet humane manner. Halleck drew upon his expertise in international law to draft General Orders No. 13, issued 4 December 1861, a summary of the laws of war and its relevance to the situation in Missouri. The orders firmly established a stark vision of how Union troops should wage war in Missouri—fierce and decisive in their punishment of guerrillas and civilian sympathizers yet constrained by rules of humane conduct.

"Peace and war cannot exist together," Halleck's orders began. Therefore, Union armies must promptly abandon the "mild and indulgent course heretofore pursued" against irregular guerrillas and their civilian supporters. "They have forfeited their civil rights as citizens by making war against the Government, and upon their own heads must fall the consequences," which meant they would receive no protections afforded to regular prisoners of war or noncombatants. Anyone found guilty of "murder, robbery, theft, pillaging, and marauding" would be "shot or otherwise less severely punished," a warning issued both to guerrillas and Union troops. Halleck condemned "cruel and barbarous acts" committed by Federals in response to guerrilla attacks and he rejected an eye-for-an-eye response to murder or robbery. But he still thought certain reprisals did fall "within prescribed limits" according to the laws of war. Halleck believed one recent offense in particular demanded a response: "The rebel forces in the southwestern counties of this State have robbed and plundered the peaceful non-combatant inhabitants, taking from them their clothing and means of subsistence. Men, women, and children have alike been stripped and plundered. Thousands of such persons are finding their way to this city barefooted, half clad, and in a destitute and starving condition. Humanity and justice require that these sufferings should be relieved and that the outrages committed upon them should be retaliated upon the enemy." Halleck, in St. Louis, found it impractical to track down the guilty parties in southwest Missouri. But some wealthy St. Louis residents had rendered "aid, assistance, and encouragement" to the original offenders. Although "less bold" than guerrillas in southwest Missouri, these secessionists in St. Louis were "not less guilty." Halleck planned to have refugees fed, clothed, and housed at the expense of "avowed secessionists."[37] *Harper's Weekly* praised Halleck's plan because it "struck consternation into the hearts of the secessionists, and at the same time provides an effective remedy."[38]

"These orders may by some be regarded as severe," Halleck concluded, "but they are certainly justified by the laws of war, and it is believed they are not only right, but necessary," both to restore peace and order in Missouri and protect "the lives and property of loyal citizens." But Halleck also believed he alone among Union officers could legitimately issue such orders. When a colonel in command at Cape Girardeau similarly tried to collect an assessment to support refugees in his district, Halleck revoked the order, wary of the injustices that might result if each of his subordinates devised and implemented their own assessment measures. Halleck did not order the prompt execution of regular Confederate soldiers. Nor did he authorize reprisal against noncombatants who did not aid irregular guerillas. But the laws of war afforded little mercy to irregular guerrillas and their active supporters, Halleck believed.[39]

What the laws of war stipulated about guerrillas and noncombatants not only interested military commanders such as Halleck. From late December to mid-January, the *Daily Missouri Republican* ran a lengthy four-part series on the "Laws of Warfare." The series offered an introduction to the restraints imposed by the laws of war. Why should a newspaper concern its readers with the details of the laws of war? According to the *Daily Missouri Republican*, because the moral health and credibility of the Union was at stake: "The great principles of morals apply to nations as well as to men, and the violation of national duties produces national injury, and may result in national ruin." If Union armies did not abide by the laws of war, the United States would no longer belong to "the civilized world." Moral anarchy might soon follow.[40]

Only nations could fight legitimate wars, not individuals. Therefore, only duly constituted "combatants entitled to fight, whom the State calls upon and commissions for that purpose," could take up arms in war. From this premise, the *Daily Missouri Republican* justified stern, swift punishment of irregular guerrillas. The newspaper also concluded that Union armies must respect the sacred distinction between soldiers and noncombatants and allow civilians to peaceably "follow their regular civil occupations." However, noncombatants could not freely furnish "supplies or assistances to their armies." Most importantly, Union troops ought to remember, even when dealing with civilians sympathetic to the Confederacy, that "war is a disease which is to be cured as soon as possible." The restoration of peace, order, and loyalty was always the paramount goal, one achieved by waging war free of unchecked personal passions and hatred. Since the Civil War was "not between individual citizens, but between the State and an organized faction striving to overthrow the Government," the newspaper hoped it might remain a war "for principle, and not for malice or revenge." Vengeance in war led to unwarranted killing and destruction. The closer Union armies adhered to the laws of war, the more they would avoid such behavior, which would make it easier after Union victory to restore peace and order. Disloyal persons were "enemies only for the time being," and a justly waged war offered the surest path to a lasting peace.[41]

As the *Daily Missouri Republican* published its editorials, Halleck continued to refine his vision of a military effort in which irregular guerrillas and civilians faced stern punishments according to the laws of war. He soon found that two issues afforded him such an opportunity—the assessment of financial penalties against Confederate-sympathizing St. Louis civilians and the punishment of guerrillas who destroyed railroads.

As refugees from guerrilla-ravaged parts of Missouri arrived in St. Louis, Halleck decided to hold secessionists in the city responsible for meeting the material needs of the refugees. While the majority of St. Louis residents were Unionists, many sympathized with the Confederacy. The refugees who arrived in the city seemed to have suffered the worst of the guerrilla war. They looked "poor and wretched beyond description," one resident of St. Louis remembered, "in rags, often hatless and shoeless, sallow, lean, half-starved, unkempt."[42] As the number of refugees swelled, providing for their basic needs became a more serious problem.

Halleck resolved to compel charitable support from three types of persons "known to be hostile to the Union": Confederate soldiers who owned property in St. Louis, those who furnished "pecuniary or other aid" to the rebels, and those who encouraged "verbally, in writing, or by publication" to rebel guerrillas or armies. On 12 December, Halleck empowered a three-person board of assessors to determine the contribution required of each secessionist. Those who did not comply faced a $10,000 levy. Persons wrongly labeled disloyal had one week to appeal to the provost marshal general and provide compelling evidence "to vindicate his character." Anyone who resisted the assessment faced immediate arrest, imprisonment, and trial by military commission.[43]

How could Halleck justify holding certain citizens of Missouri responsible for crimes they did not commit by compelling them to provide for displaced Missourians? One Wisconsin artillery officer in St. Louis rejoiced that the city's secessionists "were taxed so roundly to benefit refugees, who were compelled to flee from their all," a penalty he thought fully justified. But Franc B. Wilkie, a Unionist reporter traveling with an Iowa infantry regiment in Missouri, feared the measure was "a grave infraction of the organic law of our national liberties, thus placing in the hands of our enemies another powerful weapon with which to assail us." Halleck ultimately believed "there can be no middle course of individual neutrality" in the war. Residents of Missouri were either loyal or disloyal, and policies like the one punishing St. Louis secessionists uncovered a person's true loyalty. "We must know who are friends and who are enemies; the line will be distinctly drawn," Halleck wrote. A fellow Unionist in St. Louis also recognized Halleck's efforts as "trumpet-calls to every man to take his stand openly and show his colors," so that Union forces might "ascertain who were the enemies . . . [and] justly deal with them." Halleck acted as though neutrality did not exist in the present war in Missouri: "All citizens who are not rebels must loyally support the Government. If they aid rebels, they are traitors; if they refuse aid to the cause of the Union, they are disloyal." Confederate-sympathizers in St. Louis perhaps never took up arms against Unionists, yet by their "disloyalty [they] give countenance to those who are openly enemies."

Therefore, Halleck believed he could hold them financially responsible to provide for refugees.[44]

No order "created more excitement," a Unionist from St. Louis later remembered. It first "amazed" secessionists, then "vengeful resentment and bitterness took possession." Secessionists could pay outright the financial penalty assessed or supply the equivalent monetary amount in clothing, provisions, and housing. Either way, if Federal officials did not receive the assessment within five days, they levied an additional 25 percent penalty. Ultimately, the implementation of these orders stalled throughout December and early January. Halleck assured Francis P. Blair Jr. that the "growl of secessionists" had not led him to relax the orders. Instead, the official list of secessionist civilians "was not fairly made." Halleck gathered together a new board to revise and complete the list of disloyal persons but they "did not have the nerve to stand up to it." They wanted their identities kept secret. Halleck refused: "I want no secret boards. Hence the delay."[45]

As Halleck struggled to execute his measures against St. Louis secessionists, he also launched a new effort to end the destruction of railroads by guerrillas in northern Missouri. On 22 December, Halleck declared that guerrillas "under the guise of peaceful citizens" who destroyed railroad and telegraph lines were "guilty of the highest crime known to the code of war and the punishment is death." Guerrillas caught in the act would be shot immediately. Union officers had generally already followed this course of action. "In cases of outrageous marauding," Ulysses S. Grant wrote Col. L. F. Ross in early December, "I would fully justify shooting the perpetrators down if caught in the act—I mean our own men as well as the enemy." More provocatively, Halleck empowered officers in areas where guerrillas destroyed railroads and telegraph lines to impress into service the slaves of Confederate sympathizers to repair the damages. Like Pope, Halleck sought to hold local civilians responsible for guerrilla activity. While Halleck did not repeat Pope's most controversial measure—holding loyal and disloyal citizens equally responsible—he issued a threat, short on details, to that effect: "Hereafter the towns and counties in which such destruction of public property takes place will be made to pay the expenses of all repairs," unless they made a good faith effort to prevent the attack. "I have no doubt there will be a newspaper howl against me as a blood-thirsty monster," Halleck wrote to Thomas Ewing of Ohio, yet that did not diminish his conviction "that nothing but the severest punishment can prevent the burning of railroad bridges and the great destruction of human life." Halleck fumed over how a culprit could set ablaze a bridge or building and then return to "quietly plowing or working in his field." Only a "strong hand" could put down these rebels, Halleck resolved. "It must be done; there is no other remedy."[46]

Yet Halleck believed even these severe punishments had to proceed in a legitimate and limited manner. He loathed the infamous actions of troops commanded by Jayhawkers James Henry Lane and Charles Jennison. Halleck complained to Gen. George B. McClellan that the Jayhawkers had "done more for the enemy in this State than could have been accomplished by 20,000 of his own army." Halleck considered this sort of "rascality and robbing" deeply counterproductive to shoring up loyalty to the Union and subduing guerrillas. A severe show of force could end the marauding and destruction, yet Halleck insisted it must proceed in accordance with the laws of war.[47]

In late December, Halleck declared martial law in St. Louis and "in and about all railroads in this State" in a renewed effort to subdue rebel sympathizers and guerrillas. Halleck's martial law declaration made possible subsequent trials of civilians by military commission. The historian Mark E. Neely, in the most thorough study of these military commissions in Missouri, revealed that they were hardly sham trials destined for guilty verdicts. In fact, they might have restrained Union forces in areas under martial law, for they imposed "systematic record-keeping and an atmosphere of legality on the army's dealings with a hostile populace." Neely did not doubt that Civil War Missouri was often a "nightmare" for civil liberties. However, he concluded the "justice meted out by military commissions was of a rough sort, but justice was usually their goal. They did not victimize innocent and guilty alike in kangaroo courts or in show trials of predetermined outcome." Perhaps most tellingly, of the fifty-four trials recorded in the *Official Records* held prior to June 1862 (excluding the thirteen defendants who pleaded guilty), six persons, almost 15 percent, were acquitted; sixteen more eventually had their sentences mitigated upon review. The justice dispensed by these military commissions, in Neely's words, "could be tempered with mercy."[48]

By January 1862, Unionists in Missouri had gone a long way toward reconciling the "strong hand" of war, as Halleck put it, with the restraints imposed by the laws of war and common notion of just and civilized warfare. Conditions in Missouri inspired this effort to reconcile hard and humane war. Halleck and others realized that the success of the Union war effort in the state demanded policies both severe enough to end guerrilla activity yet also plainly legitimate according to the laws of war so as not to alienate loyal citizens.

The Guerrilla War Continues—John M. Schofield and the Enrolled Missouri Militia: January to August 1862

As winter gave way to spring and summer in 1862, the Union army still struggled to subdue guerrillas. Sterner measures had not rid Missouri of guerrilla activity. The quest to combat guerrillas in a just *and* effective manner continued. Throughout the spring and early summer of 1862, Union commanding officers revised and reissued orders concerning the treatment of guerrillas and their supporters. At the same time, they also hardened in their resolve to hold civilians responsible for ensuring peace and order. In late July 1862, John M. Schofield, as brigadier general of the Missouri militia, took this principle to an unprecedented, controversial, and ultimately ill-fated extreme. He sought to compel all able-bodied men to serve in a new militia force and help defeat irregular guerrillas. The war to pacify guerrillas and their civilian supporters did not end in decisive Union victory by the summer of 1862. Yet precisely because guerrilla activity still raged, Federals had the opportunity and obligation to refine their vision of how best to effectively wage a hard and humane war

William T. Sherman was a depressed, humiliated man when he returned to St. Louis in early December 1861. When Halleck placed Sherman in charge of Benton Barracks later that month, Sherman had not fully recovered from an earlier emotional breakdown. But he still saw clearly, albeit perhaps with an added touch of despair, the challenges facing Union forces in guerrilla-infested Missouri. "It is far worse in Missouri now than last spring," Sherman wrote to his brother John in early January 1862. Guerrillas continued to destroy railroads and telegraph lines and wreak havoc on Unionists. Even among seemingly peaceful civilians, "secession feeling . . . shows itself in Such a way that you Know it exists and yet you cannot touch it." Sherman seriously doubted if there was really any feasible solution to the problem. It seemed as if nothing short of "moving bodily the Inhabitants of Iowa, & Wisconsin down on the Farms of Missouri, and removing the present population, for imprisonment," would end the guerrilla activity.[49]

Sherman, at this moment of personal trial, accepted with uncharacteristic resignation that Union armies might never win the guerrilla war. Other Unionists in Missouri felt only deep anger at the continued violence and destruction. "Their object is plunder and the gratification of evil passions," William Greenleaf Eliot proclaimed of the guerrillas, "and having no property to lose, and no social interest at stake, they rejoice in the continuance of civil strife." In doing so, the rebels plainly showed "their true character, for what they are, plunderers and workers of mischief, and are in a position to be treated as such." The Democratic-leaning *Daily Missouri Republican* denounced the guerrillas as Missouri's worst "enemies to the peace and welfare of our State, and to freedom from molestation and duress on the part of its quiet citizens." Bernard Farrar, provost marshal general in Missouri, candidly advised a Union army major that the guerrilla problem had become "a question of power not one of law." The guerrillas ignored the laws of war; they "first discarded the law and have appealed to force." Union troops could only respond in kind, Farrar believed, by denying guerrillas the rights normally afforded regular soldiers or noncombatants and letting them suffer instead the terrible consequences of their actions. Halleck agreed wholeheartedly. In mid-March 1862, in response to persistent "depredations of insurgent and guerrilla bands," he again threatened to resort to "such measures as may be necessary to restore the authority of the Government and to punish all violations of the laws of war."[50]

Union forces continued to skirmish with guerrillas in the spring of 1862. These skirmishes posed chaotic, unpredictable challenges to Union officers committed to crushing guerrilla activity in a just manner. Union troops in Johnson County, Missouri, set out to arrest several guerrillas hiding out in a nearby home. When they arrived, the woman living in the house assured them she harbored no guerrillas. As she opened the door to let in the soldiers, four rebels sprang out and fired on the troops. One Union soldier was killed, but so too were all of the guerrillas. Afterward, the Federals burned down the home. Union troops near Santa Fe, Missouri, encountered a similar situation when they tried to apprehend a band of guerrillas led by the infamous William Quantrill holed up in a nearby house. The guerrillas fired at the Federals as they approached the front door. An officer called for the guerrillas to surrender, or at least release the women and children still inside. Once the guerrillas did so, Union soldiers set the house on fire. Most of the guerrillas, including Quantrill, fled the house successfully. Others were shot as they tried to flee. A few died in the fire. In both instances, Union troops approached the houses intending to arrest the guerrillas and only after being met with gunfire responded in kind. Their destruction of property known to harbor guerrillas was hardly uncommon. For example, Federals in

Montevallo burned down a hotel and nearby buildings—reportedly "of little or no value"—that guerrillas had used for defenses.[51] In each of these instances, Union soldiers resorted to severe measures to defeat guerrillas, but did not disregard all discretion and restraint. Federals shot dead the guerrillas and destroyed the civilian property that harbored them, yet the civilian owners and occupants of the property avoided the guerillas' grim fate.

In fact, in each instance, soldiers acted largely in accordance with the policies for dealing with guerrillas and their civilian abettors that Union commanders had handed down over the previous months. Even so, some junior officers such as Captain J. D. Thompson of the First Iowa Cavalry could still lament, in the spring of 1862, the "wanton destruction" often committed by Federals. But Thompson "positively refused to permit his men to engage in [such] nefarious business," he wrote, which served only to foster greater disorder and disloyalty. Henry Halleck was also under no illusions about the behavior of some Union troops, especially in the western part of Missouri. Stories continued to surface, Halleck admitted to Secretary of State Edwin Stanton, of outrages committed by Federals. Some soldiers "behaved very badly, plundering to an enormous extent." Halleck did all within his power "to prevent this and punish the guilty," but the abuses continued.[52] Commanding officers such as Halleck were usually clear-eyed about the depredations committed by Union troops. Perhaps they found some reassurance in the reports of soldiers dealing with the guerrilla problem in accordance with the laws of war. At the very least, they remained determined to continue to issue and seek to enforce rules of just conduct that deftly balanced vigorous antiguerrilla measures and legitimate restraints.

John M. Schofield, for one, in late May publicly pledged "magnanimous" treatment for those "who are tired of the rebellion and desire to become loyal citizens and to aid in the restoration of peace and prosperity." Union soldiers had an obligation "not only to abstain from molestation, but to protect from injury all loyal and peaceable citizens," Schofield said. Several weeks earlier, Schofield similarly advised Capt. Charles H. Warrens to avoid reckless treatment of the property of Confederate sympathizers because many "may be reclaimed by justice mingled with kindness." Just conduct might prompt some Missourians to renew their loyalty to the Union. John Dunlap Stevenson, colonel of the Seventh Missouri Infantry, likewise affirmed that his ultimate goal remained "to deal justly with all, and hope to induce all in the future to be loyal to the Government." But Schofield, in his May proclamation, also promised to hunt down unrepentant guerrillas with "utmost energy and vigilance," shooting on the spot anyone apprehended in arms. Any civilian who failed to aid Federals in capturing guerrillas would face punishment as "abettors of the criminals." S. S. Marrett, serving in the Third Illinois Cavalry Regiment, had by the late spring of 1862 seen first-hand the suffering faced by Confederate sympathizers and guerrilla support-ers in Missouri. "It is a hard case but the people have brought the trouble on," Marrett concluded, "and they must take the responsibility of bearing the expenses."[53] This uneasy balance between, in Schofield's words, "mag-nanimous treatment" and "utmost energy and vigilance" had characterized the Union war effort against guerrillas at least since midsummer 1861. One year later, it had a decidedly mixed record in actually quelling guerrilla activity.

By late July 1862, Schofield would embark on one of the most ambitious efforts to date to compel Missouri civilians to take responsibility for the res-toration of guerrilla-free peace and order in their state. On 22 July, Schofield ordered all able-bodied men to enlist in the militia "for the purpose of exter-minating the guerrillas that infest our State." Schofield labeled this force the Enrolled Missouri Militia to distinguish it from the preexisting, federally supported Missouri State Militia. The new militia primarily would help de-fend places like north central and southwest Missouri where guerrilla bands proved particularly intransigent. "Not a day passes without sharp fighting somewhere," Schofield reported to Secretary of War Edwin Stanton. Scho-field anticipated his orders might "create a stampede of secesh," as he put it to Col. Lewis Merrill, but he feared local guerrillas would soon grow even more determined "to wage a war of destruction and extermination upon the loyal people." The Enrolled Missouri Militia could meet these potential threats with "prompt and vigorous" action, while also freeing up other forces to fo-cus instead on preventing Confederate raids along the Arkansas border. All told, eighty-nine new militia regiments were formed in response to Scho-field's orders.[54]

Schofield's orders drew a stark line between loyalty and disloyalty, and left no real middle ground. Men were either committed to the Union and willing to take up arms to protect it from guerrillas, or they refused to enlist and proved their utter disloyalty. Missourians who privately harbored seces-sionist sentiments but did not actively aid guerrillas could no longer remain "neutral." Schofield's orders forced every man to declare himself publicly for or against the Union. Schofield hoped to compel Missouri's male citizens to take responsibility for ending guerrilla activity—not by levying indiscriminate financial penalties, like Pope, but by calling upon them to serve in the new militia.

Fearing that "enemies of law and order" misrepresented his orders, five days later Schofield tried to allay citizens' concerns by promising nothing ulterior in his motives. His goal remained "solely to organize law-abiding people of the State capable of bearing arms in such complete and thorough manner as to enable them at once and forever to put down robbery, plunder, and guerrilla warfare." These assurances did little to lessen the uproar over his orders. Col. John McNeil reported from Palmyra, Missouri, of the "general uprising of the rebels all over this part of the State," sparked by the militia orders. James Totten, commander of the Central District of Missouri, worried that because of Schofield's orders Confederate sympathizers were "now thoroughly awake and actively concentrating" for some future "determined and desperate effort for the mastery in Missouri." Totten also reported to Schofield that the "loyal people have rallied, however, and are waiting for authority and permission to wipe out rebellion." Many of these Unionists had suffered at the hands of guerrillas, Totten noted. Having been called upon to "exterminate guerrillas," they "justly demand the privilege of doing it."[55]

St. Louis' *Daily Missouri Republican* endorsed Schofield's militia measure as limited in its intention and necessary to winning the war against the "thieves and assassins" guilty of guerrilla activity. "There is no hidden design in this Order," the paper assured its readers. "It expresses distinctly what it proposes to accomplish, and that is, to *exterminate the guerrillas in the State*. It means this, and it means no more." The paper appealed to all men to comply with the order and thereby "strike terror into the hearts of [guerrillas], and drive them from the State." Schofield sought only to empower local communities to fulfill their responsibility to restore peace and order, the newspaper insisted. It concluded that if the only way for Union forces to end the guerrilla war was to enlist the support of Missouri citizens, perhaps the most prudent and just course of action was Schofield's effort to establish the Enrolled Missouri Militia.[56]

Schofield, for reasons beyond his control, almost immediately began to backtrack on the terms of his original order. On 24 July, he exempted foreign nationals living in Missouri. Two days later, Secretary Stanton intervened to force Schofield to exempt telegraph operators. By 28 July, under pressure from Governor Gamble, Schofield agreed to allow men to avoid militia service altogether by paying a penalty of ten dollars and a small tax on their

property. This exemption did little to pacify critics, and Schofield eventually revoked it. He decided instead to exempt secessionists entirely from
service in the Enrolled Missouri Militia. These men still had to enroll at the
nearest military post and surrender their arms. But Schofield agreed to tolerate their disloyalty so long as they "continue quietly attending to their or-
dinary and legitimate business and in no way give aid or comfort to the
enemy."[57] Confederate sympathizers succeeded in securing for themselves a
place between loyal service to the Union and complicity in guerrilla activity.

Schofield and John Pope ultimately encountered a similar problem. Both
men sought to compel civilians, regardless of their loyalty, to take part in
ending guerrilla activity—one through financial penalties, the other through
militia service. Both men faced criticisms that their orders unfairly paid no
regard to a person's loyalty. Pope's penalties affected Unionists; Schofield's
militia would have included secessionists. Both controversies revealed the
difficult dilemma of how to involve civilians in the war against guerrillas in a
just and effective manner. Any answer surely would offend some people,
yet, in the minds of Union leaders, certain answers were more legitimate
than others. The underlying question itself was an early variation on one of
the Union army's greatest challenges to waging war justly: How thoroughly
should Union troops expose noncombatants to war's sacrifices and horrors?
The guerrilla war in Missouri raised these questions and compelled serious
reflection about the nature of moral warfare.

Federals had not won the guerrilla war by late summer 1862, but they had
begun to refine a style of war uncompromising in its punishment of guerrillas and their abettors yet not without restraints imposed by the laws of war.
How well these restraints would hold as the guerrilla depredations persisted
remained unknown. *Frank Leslie's Illustrated Newspaper* denounced guerrillas who "openly ignored the code of honorable warfare and resorted to all
the odious devilries of the Chinese and other nations . . . poisoning wells,
hanging prisoners without distinction to age or sex, or assassinating unwary
men." These actions, the periodical promised, would result only in a terrible
"day of reckoning." Col. Fitz Henry Warren predicted the situation in Missouri would inevitably devolve into "a war of extermination." "We are to be
driven out and annihilated or they are," Warren continued, for nothing else
could result from the "inveterate, malignant hatred" Unionists and guerrillas felt for one another.[58]

Henry Halleck monitored the situation in Missouri even after he became
general in chief of Union armies. In late August 1862, as "inveterate, malignant

hatred" threatened to consume Missouri, Halleck turned to Francis Lieber for advice on what to do about the guerrilla problem. Once again, out of chaos, destruction, and bitterness came a redoubled effort to clarify what it meant to wage a just war.

Francis Lieber and *Guerrilla Parties Considered*, August 1862

First Lieutenant Hamilton Lieber, son of Francis Lieber, fought for the Union with the Ninth Illinois Infantry at Fort Donelson in mid-February 1862. A bullet struck the twenty-seven-year-old officer in the left arm, yet he continued to fight until another shattered his left elbow. Doctors later amputated Hamilton's arm. Francis left New York City in a panicked search for his son, unsure of his exact location. After failing to find him in Cincinnati, Francis spent ten days in St. Louis and eventually located Hamilton recovering in a Union hospital. While searching in St. Louis, Francis reacquainted himself with Halleck, then still in command of the Department of the Missouri. The two had dined together on several occasions many years ago. Halleck, in fact, had advised Lieber where he might find his son. Soon after, Lieber and Halleck, united by their expertise in the laws of war, began a lengthy and consequential wartime correspondence.[59]

Lieber's ties to Halleck only strengthened after Halleck became general in chief. Although events in Missouri were no longer Halleck's primary concern, he knew the unresolved guerrilla conflict demanded serious expert attention. He gladly welcomed Lieber's suggestion that he formally issue to Union officers the 6,000-plus-word essay on guerrilla warfare Lieber had recently finished, *Guerrilla Parties Considered with References to the Laws and Usages of War*. It marked a culmination of the Union army's early effort to respond to guerrilla activity not by pursuing a war of indiscriminate bloodshed but by codifying and implementing clear guidelines for just conduct in war.

Lieber recognized that all guerrillas were not equal. By carefully distinguishing ten different types of irregular combatants, Lieber offered a more complex understanding of who exactly counted as a regular soldier (deserving of the rights granted by the laws of war) and why. The prevailing wisdom said that a commission from a legitimate belligerent separated regular soldiers from partisan bands of illegal guerrillas. However, this understanding of the laws of war proved increasingly unsatisfying from the Union perspective, especially after the Confederate Congress approved the Partisan

Ranger Act in April 1862. The act empowered the Confederacy to commission preexisting guerrilla bands and thereby provide them with the status of regular soldiers. Yet the commissions often did little to change the actions of guerrillas who continued to plunder, rob, and murder in defiance of the laws of war.[60] These guerrillas had commissions like regular soldiers but behaved like lawbreaking marauders. Lieber believed the particular circumstances of the Civil War compelled him to think afresh about what exactly separated regular soldiers from unlawful guerrillas. He completed this task, as John Fabian Witt has argued, by setting aside "the formal question of whether a fighter had been commissioned" in favor of focusing attention instead on "functional considerations."[61] That is, Lieber shifted consideration from commissions and enlistments to a broader assessment of the distinguishing marks of a guerrilla.

What, then, were these defining characteristics and actions? Guerrillas carried on an "irregular war." Their irregularity "consists in [their] origins," for they were self-constituted or organized by the call of a single individual. As an impermanent body, they were "dismissed and called again together at any time." They remained disconnected from regular armies as to their "pay, provision, and movements." Lieber thought these "constituent ideas" defined guerrillas more than the absence of a commission. He also acknowledged other infamous yet somewhat secondary characteristics: guerrillas pillaged and destroyed private property, functioned under little or no discipline, typically dressed like noncombatants and rarely took prisoners of war.[62]

Still, that working definition of a guerrilla was not entirely adequate, Lieber believed. He proceeded to delineate ten specific forms of irregulars: "The freebooter, the marauder, the brigand, the partisan, the free corps, the spy, the rebel, the conspirator, the robber, and especially the highway robber, the rising en masse, or the 'arming of peasants.'"[63] Lieber devoted a lengthy portion of *Guerrilla Parties Considered* to outlining in meticulous detail these different categories and the punishments each deserved. They did not all deserve equal treatment. Lieber insisted Union armies should prudently determine what sort of irregular enemy they faced so that they could then decide the legitimate course of action.

Lieber intentionally offered little guidance on how to apply his understanding of irregular warfare and the laws of war into particular measures for quelling guerrillas. He admitted that there must remain a certain imprecision and flexibility in the application of these ideas. Policies could be refined and issued but the burden ultimately rested on officers in the field to use their best judgment in abiding by the laws of war in unique and unpredictable circumstances. "The application of the laws and usages of war to wars of insurrection or rebellion is always undefined," Lieber wrote, "suggested by humanity or necessitated by the numbers engaged in the insurrection." Lieber thought under certain circumstances a "relaxation or mitigation [of punishments imposed by the laws of war] would be likely to produce a beneficial effect upon an enemy." Sometimes the wisest action might be to not carry out a legitimate punishment. For all his legal expertise, that was not something Lieber could decide.[64]

Lieber's *Guerrilla Parties Considered* marked a culmination of Federals' early efforts to respond to the guerrilla problem in Missouri with measures both hard and humane. Lieber certainly sought to reconcile the two. His reworked understanding of the distinctions between guerrillas and regular soldiers empowered Union armies to strike vigorously against a class of commissioned guerrillas that continued to ignore the laws of war. Lieber also insisted on carefully distinguishing among different types of irregular combatants in the hopes that Union armies would not discard all discretion against its enemies.

The situation in Missouri hardly made it easy for Union forces to wage this kind of war. Guerrillas plundered, marauded, and murdered. Unionists, especially Jayhawkers in western Missouri, responded in kind. Chaos could rule the day. Yet the war in Missouri, earlier than in any other state, embodied the paradox that would come to define the entire Union war effort: as Federals embraced hard war measures, they also constructed military policies that imposed constraints. Federals in Missouri first envisioned how their armies might reconcile the hard hand of war with the limits to fighting imposed by the laws of war and common notions of civilized warfare. They came to believe a war effort both hard and humane was not a paradox but a necessity, the surest path to lasting peace, order, and victory. The necessity of precisely this kind of war effort became all the more apparent in mid-1862 as Union armies began to occupy some of the Confederacy's largest cities and interact directly with the civilians living there.

CHAPTER TWO

Not to Destroy but to Make Good
Occupying Cities

The gallows awaited William Mumford on a warm New Orleans morning in early June 1862. In accordance with a Spanish custom, his hanging would occur at the scene of his crime, in front of the New Orleans mint. The American flag that flew atop the mint's white-columned portico looked down on Mumford as he ascended the scaffold, protested his sentence, and then proclaimed he was prepared to die. Mumford committed his crime several weeks prior on the eve of the Union occupation of the city. He had gathered with other angry New Orleanians in front of the mint as Federals replaced the Confederate flag flying over the building with an American one. Mumford soon climbed the mint's roof, tore down the American flag, and dragged it through the streets before ripping it to pieces. Tall, black-bearded, and proud of his patriotic act, Mumford immediately won the admiration of the city's Confederates. But now he found himself back again at the mint. As the noose tightened around his neck, Mumford looked out one final time at the gathered crowd. The city's natives, Confederates and Unionists alike, could not quite believe this was Mumford's final fate. Many still expected a last minute reprieve. None came.[1]

Maj. Gen. Benjamin F. Butler, then in command of Union forces in New Orleans, approved Mumford's death sentence after a military commission convicted him of treason. The balding, potbellied, bag-eyed Butler was a shrewd Democrat from Massachusetts, a former Congressman turned political general. He had an uncanny knack for courting controversy, but *Frank Leslie's Illustrated Newspaper* still praised Butler soon after the occupation of New Orleans began as "an admirable administrator, and one who is not to be trifled with or tricked in any way or by anybody." Butler later claimed he received anonymous threats warning that he would lose his life if he refused to spare Mumford. The threats only hardened Butler's determination to proceed with the execution, for to him the central issue at stake was "whether law and order or a mob shall govern." Yankee rule in New Orleans seemingly had begun in merciless earnest. Cries of outrage and disbelief rang out across the Confederacy. President Jefferson Davis condemned Butler as an "outlaw and common enemy of mankind" who would face immediate execution if ever captured by Confederates. Sixteen-year-old Clara Solomon captured in her diary New Orleans Confederates' livid reaction: "Everyone is fired with indignation at the atrocious *wonder* of yesterday, the hanging of Mumford. . . . It is atrocious & oh! God, helps us to revenge it."[2]

By the summer of 1862, Union armies occupied many of the Confederacy's largest cities, including not only New Orleans but also Memphis, four hundred miles up the Mississippi River. Episodes such as Mumford's hanging make it easy to imagine life in the occupied South as a perilous reign of terror. "Beast" Butler in New Orleans sent men to the gallows. Maj. Gen. William T. Sherman commanded Federal troops in Memphis and surely reveled in the hellish war he inflicted on his enemies. Because Butler and Sherman are forever associated with the unremitting hard hand of war, historians have not neglected to detail the hardships endured by civilians in occupied New Orleans and Memphis—the shortages of food, the curtailment of freedoms normally enjoyed in peacetime, the sometimes-rash seizure and destruction of property, the thinly justified arrests and imprisonments.[3]

But why exactly were these early occupations important to the wider story of the Union war effort? The historian Steven V. Ash argues they helped cause a momentous change in Union military policy. Continued resistance by rebel civilians provoked a shift from "a conciliatory and conservative policy to a punitive and radical one that brought destruction, disruption, suffering."[4] Union officers and soldiers came to believe they could not afford to spare civilians from the horrors of war as long as unapologetic rebels like William Mumford threatened law and order and kept up the fight for Confederate independence.

However, this turn toward hard war was not the only effect that the occupation of New Orleans and Memphis had on Union military policy. As Federals faced difficult questions about how to treat Confederate civilians in occupied cities, they refined their thinking about the nature of justly waged wars. Benjamin Butler commanded the occupying Union force in New Orleans at roughly the same time William Sherman fulfilled similar duties in Memphis, from the summer to early winter of 1862.[5] Together, their tenures reveal how the initial occupation of the two major Confederate cities along the Mississippi River prompted Federals to refine a vision of just warfare premised on balancing hard war measures and humane restraints.[6] In his first weeks in New Orleans, Butler fully exemplified this approach in his treatment of civilians. He launched efforts to alleviate the hardships of poor New Orleanians. But he also censored newspapers, curtailed pro-Confederate religious expression, dismissed the municipal government, and seized property meant to aid Confederates. These and other similar actions won Butler bitter enemies in Louisiana and across the Confederacy. In contrast, Sherman's efforts to reconcile hard and humane warfare in the Memphis area centered on subduing guerrillas and regulating local commerce in a manner that would restore economic vitality but not aid the Confederate war machine. Both commanders consistently confronted similar just-war issues—for example, how thoroughly to protect civilian property, or how best to ensure order and foster loyalty to the Union. Perhaps most controversially, though, both Butler and Sherman had to face the moral and legal dilemmas of what to do with slaves who escaped to Union lines, even as official Federal policy on the matter remained in flux. As Butler and Sherman contemplated how exactly, if at all, to employ runaway slaves as laborers or soldiers in service of the Union cause, they inevitably also considered the nature of a just war.

If by the spring and summer of 1862 many Federals had grown skeptical of a conciliatory war effort, Union armies in occupied New Orleans and Memphis worked out a suitable replacement, one that traded conciliation for the hard hand of war while not ignoring the restraints imposed by the laws of war and notions of civilized warfare. Federals never unanimously agreed about how to prosecute this sort of war; opinions varied on where to draw the line between just and unjust conduct. Even so, taken together, the guerrilla war in Missouri and the Union occupations of New Orleans and Memphis in the initial eighteen months of the Civil War confirm that the early Federal military effort in the Mississippi River Valley was not simply the crucible of the turn toward hard war, but was also, at the same time, the crucible of early Union just-war policies.

Benjamin F. Butler's First Month in New Orleans

Flag Officer David G. Farragut's fleet made way for Butler's arrival in New Orleans on 1 May 1862. As Union armies entered the city, "both camp and street was a scene of wild confusion," remembered one New Orleans woman. Butler immediately declared martial law and publicly set forth the terms of the Union occupation. Federals entered New Orleans as conquerors but Butler assured civilians he "came here not to destroy but to make good, to restore order out of chaos, and the government of laws in place of the passions of men." Law and order, peace and harmony: These were the goals of the Union occupation, Butler promised. Citizens ready to turn from disloyalty and lawlessness and submit to the Union occupiers' yoke would find it gracious and mild. Those who refused faced swift punishment. Butler wasted no time in setting about to reconcile a terrifying show of force with a surprisingly generous and humane treatment of the law-abiders, the destitute, and the newly loyal.[7]

Butler's 1 May proclamation captured his vision of a hard yet humane occupation. He urged residents "to pursue their usual avocations" and to report Federal troops who committed "any outrage upon any person or property." Those who swore allegiance to the Union would receive "the safeguard and protection, in their person and property, of the armies of the United States." But few Federals expected the city to make a quick and widespread return to loyalty to the Union. One officer wrote in early May, "we do not deceive ourselves by thinking that this place can be held for the Union except by military force."[8] Another soldier, whose regiment bivouacked at Lafayette Square among a "numerous, bold, and insolent" crowd, was thankful his colonel emphatically commanded his men "to abstain from violence and verbal squabbling."[9]

Because Butler claimed he desired only "to preserve order and maintain the laws," he threatened harsh penalties for disorderly lawbreakers. In a none-too-subtle allusion to the Mumford episode, Butler guaranteed "severe punishment" for anyone who failed to treat the American flag "with utmost deference and respect." Martial law meant New Orleans residents could not expect all the robust constitutional privileges they once enjoyed. Butler swore to censor or shut down newspapers that sought "to influence the public mind against the Government of the United States." He forbade the free "assemblages of persons in the street" because they "tend to disorder." Butler promised to wield his power "mildly," but also "vigorously and firmly" whenever warranted.[10]

Butler tried with strong words to subdue the city's indignant rebel population. "I thought it necessary to make so large a display of force," he explained to Secretary of War Edwin Stanton, because he suspected there lurked in the city "a violent, strong and unruly mob that can only be kept under by fear." The *New Orleans Commercial Bulletin*, realizing they now answered to Butler as editor-in-chief, said of the proclamation, "some of its provisions are no doubt exceedingly stringent . . . while others are as fair and liberal as could be expected." The paper encouraged its readers "to quietly and gracefully submit." The *New Orleans Daily Crescent* similarly confessed that because it no longer possessed "that liberty which is essential to the satisfactory publication of a newspaper," it would instead "only act with common discretion in councilling quiet and order, and in advising our people to refrain from conduct which might inflame the hatred or excuse the brutality of an enemy." Butler, meanwhile, embarked on a series of measures "done in the emergencies called for by a new and untried state of things, when promptness and movement were more desirable than deliberation," he confessed to Stanton.[11]

Butler's first actions in New Orleans were his most humanitarian. He sought to end the city's disastrous food shortage, which disproportionately affected the poor. A volunteer in a Connecticut infantry regiment recounted the "astonishing" hunger and poverty endured by "rough and ragged beggars" who pleaded with the men of his regiment to spare some food. "The town is fairly and squarely in the point of starvation," the soldier wrote. "Unless work is soon found for these people, I do not see how famine can be averted."[12]

Butler acted quickly to prevent famine. On 3 and 4 May he issued a series of orders meant to ensure more food made it into the Crescent City. He guaranteed the safe passage of flour from Mobile. He required the directors of the Opelousas railroad to carry provisions (especially cotton and sugar) into the city to sell at market. He worked to make certain that "livestock, flour, and provisions" recently purchased by the city for poor relief were no longer held up at the junction of the Red and Mississippi rivers. He pledged to Louisiana planters that the occupying Federals would not destroy their cotton and sugar crops if they sent them to market in New Orleans. One "wife of a southern planter" curtly informed Butler her husband withheld their crops not because they mistakenly believed Union armies would burn them but because they "*detest* your government" and would make whatever sacrifices necessary to defeat it.[13]

Butler noticed that the city's lower classes suffered the most from the food shortage. He relished the opportunity to castigate "the wealthy and influential" of New Orleans, whom "this hunger does not pinch." Butler stridently attacked the city's well-to-do—"the leaders of the rebellion" who were "unmindful of their suffering fellow-citizens." *Harper's Weekly* echoed Butler's assessment in even more ominous terms. The hungry and ragged citizens who walked New Orleans' streets should appear to wealthy rebels as "dark forebodings of the terrible punishment that surely awaits them in another world."[14]

For Butler, these verbal attacks had a clear strategic objective. He sought to turn the city's poor against the wealthy and regain their allegiance to the Union. Butler took his appeal directly to the "mechanics and working classes" of the city: "How long, will you uphold these flagrant wrongs, and by inaction suffer yourselves to be made the serfs of these leaders?" Butler pledged to do all in his power "to feed the hungry and relieve the distressed." He later ordered his chief commissary to sell army provisions to the poor of New Orleans at heavily reduced prices.[15]

Butler acted in accordance with a fundamental yet mistaken idea that informed Union just-war thinking. He assumed the aristocratic slaveholding class had duped or coerced most poor white southerners into supporting the rebellion. Butler hoped not so much to punish these poor whites as to disenthrall them from their aristocratic overlords. Generously sharing portions of meat, flour, and sugar might be the best way to do so. The same rationale led Butler to argue for the reopening of the New Orleans port. "If we wish to bind them to us more strongly than can be done by bayonet," Butler wrote to Secretary Stanton, "let them again feel the beneficence of the United States Government as they have seen and are now feeling its power." Reopening the city's port would be more than merely a humane response to conquered Confederates' destitution. It also might effectively regain the loyalty of most white southerners.[16]

As the opening weeks of the Union occupation of New Orleans unfolded, Butler did not hesitate to unleash the power of Federal armies to stamp out disloyalty and disorder. Newspapers and churches quickly roused Butler's ire. Both continued to foster rebel sentiments in the hearts of their readers and parishioners, Butler believed. By mid-May he made good on earlier threats and shut down three newspapers, because one owner and editor was "a rebel now in arms," and the other two encouraged Confederate resistance. Throughout his time in New Orleans, Butler waged a determined war against the Confederate-sympathizing press, always demanding "self-censorship" and suppressing papers when he deemed it necessary.[17]

Butler similarly sought to curtail explicitly pro-Confederate religious expression in local churches. Some of the staunchest proslavery secessionist clergy resided in New Orleans. Benjamin Morgan Palmer, one of the South's leading Presbyterian ministers, had in a late November 1860 sermon exhorted his congregation to take up arms against the United States and do what the

Lord required: *"to conserve and to perpetuate the institution of domestic slav-ery."* One New York Unionist feared the churches of New Orleans were "a dangerous power in favor of despotism and rebellion." Among ministers, she continued, "treason lay like a dark pall upon their guilty souls." Butler agreed. On the same mid-May day he suspended three newspapers, he also forbade churches from observing the upcoming Confederate fast day pro-claimed by Jefferson Davis. For the rest of the war, Union forces and New Orleans ministers quarreled over where exactly freedom of religious expres-sion ended and overt acts of treason began.[18]

Butler's most infamous threat against the city's civilian population was his "woman's order" of 15 May. Federals in New Orleans found most women in the city strident in their loyalty to the Confederacy and hatred of Yankees. Clara Solomon, for one, vowed to continue the fight against the Union after the capture of her city: "Our *cause* is not *dead*," she wrote in her diary, "it is only *sick*." Solomon believed she and other women had an obligation to help revive it.[19] Many New Orleans women made known their distaste of the oc-cupying Federals. David Dixon Porter remembered some ladies "would not associate with the Union officers, drew the dresses close to them when they passed a Northern soldier, and some of the less refined spat upon the ground to show their contempt of their enemies." A Union private described to his brother how ladies often refused to walk on the same sidewalk as Federals. "We will humble them before long," the private promised. When John Bur-rud briefly traveled into the city with his New York regiment, he received nasty glances from women as he walked down the street, though he sarcasti-cally wrote home that the women thankfully were "kind enough not to spit on me." W. C. Corsan, an Englishman, witnessed similar episodes, though he claimed he "neither saw nor heard of any act of which any gentleman would take cognizance."[20]

Butler did take note. He warned if "any female shall by word, gesture, or movement insult or show contempt for any officer or soldier of the United States she shall be regarded and held liable to be treated as a woman of the town plying her avocation." Men and women across the Confederacy—and beyond—denounced Butler for vilifying the respectable women of New Or-leans and defaming their ladyhood. Butler equated the patriotic resistance of Confederate women with the sexual promiscuity of prostitutes, and he pledged to treat the two classes of women equally.[21]

The order ignited a firestorm of controversy. Confederate General P. G. T. Beauregard appealed to his countrymen to act: "MEN OF THE SOUTH: Shall our mothers, our wives, our daughters, and our sisters be thus outraged by the ruffanly soldiers of the North to whom is given the right to treat at their pleasure the ladies of the South as common harlots?" News of Butler's orders made it across the Atlantic Ocean, where from the British House of Commons, Lord Palmerston proclaimed no civilized person could read Butler's orders and not feel "the deepest indignation." The shameful order, Palmerston continued, only befitted "some barbarous race that was not within the pale of civilization." Butler immediately defended his actions to Edwin Stanton as "an absolute necessity from the outrageous conduct of the Secession women here, who took every means of insulting my soldiers and inflaming the mob."[22]

Several weeks later, Butler further justified his orders to a Boston resident as a measure meant to prevent abusive overreaction by Federal troops. The steady stream of "every opprobrious epithet, every insulting question . . . made by these bejeweled, becrinolined, and laced creatures calling themselves ladies" had reached near-intolerable extremes, Butler argued. He asked: "How long do you suppose our flesh and blood could have stood this without retort?" Butler claimed his orders sought to forestall unwarranted overreactions by offended Union soldiers. The infamous "plying her avocation" phrase had nothing to do with the character of New Orleans women and everything to do with how Union soldiers ought to interact with them: "You pass her by unheeded. She cannot insult you. As a gentleman you can and will take no notice from her. If she speaks, her words are not opprobrious."[23] Butler hoped in part to assure critics that his order certainly would not instigate sexual violence against Confederate women. Instead, in his characteristically sly manner, Butler insisted his order existed only to prevent retaliations by insulted Union troops; it did not offend the ladyhood of Confederate women, but protected it.

Despite all the criticism he garnered, and the failure of his justifications to quiet the criticism, Butler did have his defenders in the northern press. *Frank Leslie's Illustrated Newspaper* denounced the women targeted by Butler's order as ones who "discarded all feminine refinements and properties, and debased themselves in language and conduct to the level of the veriest drabs of their sex." Lest anyone mistake Butler's intention, the periodical insisted Butler's orders should not offend all women, only "women indulging in abusive and vulgar language and conduct." *Harper's Weekly* offered a different argument in defense: The order worked. Two illustrations of the "Ladies of New Orleans" before and after Butler's orders appeared in one edition of *Harper's Weekly*. In the before, the women appeared abhorrently disrespectful, spitting on an officer's face; in the after, the women were courteous and subdued. Sarah Butler, Benjamin's wife, thought her husband's orders made the "cruel and treacherous" people of New Orleans realize "there is a power here to sustain or crush them according as they merit protection from the government or deserve punishment for their traitorous deeds." Butler and his defenders believed his orders responded in a measured and legitimate fashion to the actions of hostile Confederate women.[24]

Well before controversy over Butler's "woman's order" erupted, tensions sharply escalated between Butler and the existing municipal government of New Orleans, especially Mayor John T. Monroe. The city council and Monroe had little faith in Butler's stated desire "to leave the municipal authority in the full exercise of its accustomed functions," namely the collection of taxes and administration of the local police force. Mutual distrust festered in the first two weeks of May. Occasions for open conflict soon appeared. Butler loathed Monroe for failing to implement "active, energetic measures" to clean up the city and ensure public health. Monroe's rumored overtures to a French fleet, presumably to retake New Orleans from the Union, only exacerbated the distrust and animosity. On 19 May, Butler gave up on the ill-fated cooperation with the plainly disloyal city officials. Butler arrested Monroe and the rest of the city council and directed his military commandant and provost marshal to assume most of the functions of the municipal government.[25]

With Monroe and the city council imprisoned, Butler took an even freer hand in managing the city's affairs. He turned immediately to cleaning up the city and removing any public health threats. Butler later remembered how much he feared a potential yellow fever outbreak, "the scourge of New Orleans, returning every summer with such virulence." Piles of filth on city streets only heightened Butler's fears. Local citizens had their fun inflaming these worries. Julia LeGrand noted in her journal how "people of the town are frightening [Union soldiers] terribly with tales about the yellow fever." Butler established a strict quarantine around New Orleans. Then he employed two thousand of "the unemployed and starving poor" to clean up the city, at a pay of fifty cents per day and a full soldier's ration.[26]

George Stanton Denison, a Unionist tax collector in New Orleans, noted in a mid-June letter to Treasury Secretary Salmon P. Chase that New Orleans "never was more healthy, and as yet there is no danger of the Yellow Fever." Denison then confessed he worried Butler's efforts were perhaps too humane: "I do not think the military rule here or elsewhere is severe enough. It ought to be more dangerous to be a secessionist than to be a loyal citizen . . . A real secessionist cannot be conciliated."[27] Denison did not say what exactly constituted a more severe war effort. Still, he voiced an emerging sentiment among many who closely monitored occupied New Orleans: as *Harper's Weekly* put it, that occupying Federals ought to bring about "The End of Gingerbread."

Harper's Weekly praised commanders such as Butler for inaugurating a new phase of the Union war effort that was "no longer gingerly" and did not "expect any thing but sullenness and hatred" from the Union's enemies. If Confederates howled that Butler's martial law proclamation was "pure despotism," they were right. They had no one to blame but themselves: "When the rebels invoked war they invoked despotism. War is the appeal to brute force. War reaches and maintains its ends by violence." God bestowed legitimate governments with the power of the sword, a power not to bear in vain. Once unsheathed it "was not an instrument to tickle with, but to kill with." The only effective and fair way to convince Confederates to abandon their quest for independence was "overwhelming superiority of force." *Harper's Weekly* praised Butler for attempting to salvage cotton and sugar crops and provide for the destitute of New Orleans. But it praised him even more for the fact that "his iron hand has not been covered with a silken glove."[28]

By the summer of 1862, rebel citizens of New Orleans certainly realized that Union armies had increasingly abandoned their "gingerbread" war effort. A string of notable executions and imprisonments hammered home the point. William Mumford's hanging was the most notorious example. When Gen. Robert E. Lee learned of Mumford's execution, he wrote a curt letter to Gen. George B. McClellan demanding an explanation. Lee warned that Confederates would retaliate in kind against "outrages of such a character." Because Mumford's "crime" occurred before the city officially surrendered, Lee considered the death sentence illegitimate, a mere "murder of one of our citizens." Henry Halleck assured—and subtly threatened—Lee that "this contest will be carried on in strict accordance with the laws and usages of modern warfare, and that all excesses will be duly punished." Butler believed the hanging was legal and effective in quieting disorderly rebels. The "peace and quiet which pervaded the city," Butler later wrote, was due in large part to a "belief which pervaded" among Confederates after Mumford's hanging: "nothing could be done there that I could not find out."[29]

But Mumford was not the only New Orleans resident sentenced to death or imprisoned in the summer of 1862. For example, two men were executed and another jailed for impersonating Union soldiers and plundering civilians. The crimes eliciting Butler's wrath were on occasion far less violent in nature. One man was sentenced to two years' hard labor for exhibiting a human skeleton in a public window, draping the label "Chickahominy" over it, and claiming they were the bones of a fallen Union soldier. Another man received the same sentence for fashioning a cross supposedly out of the bones of a Yankee soldier. Freedom of religious expression did not excuse outright treason, Butler believed, so he imprisoned three Episcopal clergymen for refusing to swear an oath of allegiance and continuing their "violent secessionist" preaching. Eugenia Phillips was imprisoned for purportedly "laughing and mocking" at a passing funeral procession of a Union lieutenant. Butler considered Phillips "a bad and dangerous woman, stirring up strife and inciting to riot," so he sent her to the Ship Island prison, where he allowed her to retain one female servant and guaranteed her a soldier's ration each day. Phillips fiercely denied the charges and fumed that in her native city, "Young girls were not safe for any indecent remark that reached Butler caused their arrest . . . So we lived, and the future seemed dark for us all."[30]

"War is tragical business," *Harper's Weekly* concluded in early July after reporting on several hangings ordered by Butler. "War is essentially brutal; it is the appeal to superior physical force. The amenities of war are the interpolations of humanity, because men can not be altogether brutes." War was tragic, perhaps irredeemable at its core, but *Harper's Weekly* held out hope that the destructive power of war did not altogether destroy a soldier's humanity. Sometimes "interpolations of humanity" broke through the killing and destruction and saved an army from utter barbarity. Federals could acknowledge the unavoidable brutality of war without embracing it wholeheartedly.[31]

Butler likewise endeavored to maintain rigid discipline among Union soldiers and prevent them from acts of plunder and abuse, even as he turned away from a "gingerbread" war. This often was no easy task, considering the animosity many Federal soldiers felt for local Confederate civilians. "And how I hate them," wrote one Union infantry regiment captain of the rebels he encountered in the New Orleans area, "their bitter, implacable, causeless enmity to their lawful government is enough to make one desirous of seeing them exterminated from the face of the earth."[32] On his first day in New Orleans, Butler reminded the soldiers under his command "amid the temptations and inducements of a large city, all plundering of public or private property . . . is hereby forbidden, under the severest penalties." But instances—and rumors—of plunder persisted. A Connecticut infantry captain stationed outside New Orleans wrote home to complain (with a touch of jealousy) of another Connecticut infantry regiment stationed inside the city that supposedly "seized on splendid houses, with costly furniture, and wine-cellars . . . and enjoying for once a luxury that they had never even looked at previously." The captain called the rumored "looting and foraging" a "disorder and a shame" that Butler must end. In late May, Butler proclaimed that no officer or soldier could seize private property without prior approval from the provost marshal, military commandant, or Butler himself. Several weeks later, Butler hanged two soldiers and sentenced another to hard labor as punishment for violating his orders and illegitimately seizing property.[33]

When it came to dealing sternly with Confederates, Butler favored no target more than the wealthy citizens of New Orleans. He acquired the names of wealthy residents who prior to the Union occupation donated a combined $1,250,000 to the Committee of Public Safety, a pro-Confederate organization aimed at bolstering the city's defenses. Butler believed the "need of relief to the destitute poor" exposed the "stupidity and wastefulness" of these donations. In early August he levied fines against contributors at roughly one-quarter the amount of their donation. Some paid as little as twelve dollars, others paid several thousand. Butler promised to divert the revenue raised from this tax on the wealthy to poor relief efforts: "Those who have brought upon the city this stagnation of business, this desolation of the hearth-stone, this starvation of the poor and helpless, should, as far as they may be able, relieve these distresses." Butler insisted this money would not line the pockets of greedy Union soldiers but would help feed the city's destitute, a problem of "alarming importance and gravity."[34] Butler could not imagine a more just and humane act by an occupying force.

Harper's Weekly, as always, came to Butler's defense with particularly overthe-top adulation in a mid-August editorial. After reviewing all the problems Butler faced in New Orleans—from a bitter civilian population to unsanitary conditions to a shortage of food to a hostile municipal government— the magazine concluded: "The historian will decide that General Butler's success in grappling with these unparalleled difficulties was so marked and so brilliant as to entitle him to the highest rank among statesmen." *Harper's Weekly* strayed even further from the truth when it proclaimed Butler had not "inflicted a single injustice upon the most rancorous of his enemies."

David Dixon Porter was surely more correct in concluding, "[Butler's] sys-tem was doubtless lacking in tact, and he would have saved himself a deal of trouble by not seeing too much."[35]

Given New Orleans's cosmopolitan character, Butler faced another unique variation on the issue of the treatment of noncombatants: determin-ing what do to with the foreign consuls living in New Orleans who appeared to support the Confederacy. How thoroughly could Butler subject foreign ci-vilians to the hard warfare he unleashed against rebellious American citizens? More often than not, though of highly questionable legality, Butler saw little reason to exempt Confederate-sympathizing foreign consuls from his hard yet humane war effort. If foreign residents in New Orleans supported the Confederacy, Butler tended to treat them like American-born Confederates guilty of the same offense. The consuls and their home countries appealed to international law to object to Butler's actions. Their conflict dramatized the potentially momentous diplomatic implications of deftly handling laws of war problems.

Butler's conflicts with foreign consuls began almost as soon as he arrived in New Orleans. At first, the squabbles seemed benign. French and Spanish consuls complained to Butler about the presence of Union troops surround-ing their consulates. Soon after, Butler grew incensed upon learning that a group of British subjects likely sent arms and uniforms to Confederate Gen. P. G. T. Beauregard. "I am content for the present to suffer open ene-mies to remain in the city of their nativity," Butler wrote to the acting British consul, but not "law-defying and treacherous alien enemies."[36] The first major controversy with foreign consuls concerned Butler's treatment of Amedee Conturie, consul of the Netherlands. In early May, Federals searched Conturie's store (which doubled as the consulate of the Netherlands) for a rumored stash of silver and found $800,000 worth in Mexican coins, along with a set of bank plates and dies, some used for Confederate treasury notes. Butler suspected Conturie hid the material for Confederates. Conturie complained that the search and seizure illegitimately infringed on the sover-eignty of his store as a consulate, but he did not persuade Butler. "Having prostituted your Flag to a base purpose," Butler wrote Conturie, "you could not hope to have it respected while so debased."[37] Conturie launched a pro-tracted and bitter effort to regain possession of the $800,000 in silver coins. He insisted, with good evidence, that an Amsterdam company entrusted the specie to his care and had made arrangements, prior to the Union oc-cupation, to ship the silver to Europe. Butler replied this did not explain the presence of the dies and bank plates, items that "could not by law be his property."[38] Conturie meanwhile rallied the support of other consuls living in New Orleans, and by late August the Lincoln administration intervened to resolve the diplomatic headache. Secretary of State William Seward said Lincoln sympathized with Butler's actions, given "the military necessity which manifestly existed for the most vigorous and energetic proceedings in restoring law, order, and peace." However, Lincoln and Seward still believed the search and seizure violated "the law of nations and of comity due from this country to a friendly sovereign State." They returned the $800,000 in silver to Conturie.[39]

Well before the controversy with Conturie ended, Butler also tried to compel anyone who claimed "any privileges of American citizens or protection or favor for the Government of the United States" to swear an oath of allegiance to the Union. His order initially extended also to foreigners living in America. Butler cared little about the absurdity of requiring a foreigner to swear loyalty to another country. He endeavored to root out and punish foreigners guilty of aiding the Confederacy by "furnishing arms and munitions of war, running the blockade, giving information, [and] concealing property."[40] Butler hoped that by his measure foreigners stubbornly supporting the Confederacy would soon feel the burdens of the Union's hard war. The consuls protested the action as contrary to the law of nations. They deemed it ridiculous for Butler to force them to swear allegiance to the United States and renounce "that true faith and allegiance which they owe to their own country only." Eventually, the Lincoln administration again sided with the consuls and ordered Butler to exempt them from his order. Seward chiefly worried about the diplomatic implications of the orders, so he thought it best for Butler to wait for the consuls to act overtly in support of the Confederacy.[41] Still, the ever-wily Butler soon hit on an alternative to his stymied plan. In mid-September, he ordered all "neutral" foreign residents to register with the nearest provost marshal and provide an assortment of information, including their home country, length of time in America, present residence and occupation, and names of immediate family members in the country. Butler said these orders made it easier to "distinguish the disloyal from the loyal citizens and honest neutral foreigners." The new approach still attempted to identify persons actively aiding the Confederacy. But the registration orders sought to circumvent the international law objections that doomed the loyalty oath effort, and largely proceeded as Butler wished.[42]

Throughout his tenure in New Orleans, Butler grew increasingly agitated with the seemingly unending complaints from consuls about his supposed violations of international law. Butler believed that the all-important goal of restoring order and subduing disloyalty in New Orleans rendered the consuls' complaints irrelevant. In Butler's vision of just warfare, noncombatants who actively supported the Confederacy deserved little protection from hard war measures. It mattered little to Butler whether the noncombatants were Americans or foreigners. Butler believed his treatment of the consuls remained consistent with his larger effort to occupy New Orleans in a hard yet humane manner. Butler did not dismiss the laws of war as a frivolous restraint so much as he chafed each time foreign consuls mistook hard war measures for violations of the laws of war.[43]

Injustices and illegitimate depredations inevitably occurred under Butler's command in New Orleans. Yet, even so, *Harper's Weekly* faintly grasped the significance of Butler's tenure in the city: "He has established safe and sound precedents," above all, for how to govern an occupied territory in keeping with the spirit of a hard yet humane war effort.[44] New Orleans remained a city ruled by martial law and not altogether shielded from the hard hand of war. Butler imposed sternly enforced limits on overt support for the Confederacy, a rebellion he believed Federals had to put down on the battlefront and home front. Residents of New Orleans, especially wealthy and resolute Confederates, could not expect to enjoy the same protections of property or free expression guaranteed in peacetime. Yet Butler acted not to devastate New Orleans but to restore order and loyalty. His public works programs and poor relief left the city cleaner and less disease ridden. He worked vigorously to stave off famine among the impoverished, which meant endeavoring to some degree to revitalize regular trade and economic activity. A widely feared potential yellow fever outbreak never occurred, which Butler credited to his stiff regulation of the New Orleans port. By the end of the first month of the Union occupation of New Orleans, one Connecticut soldier stationed there praised Butler's measures as "glorious successes" that resulted in the "quiet possession" of the city, the restoration of law-abiding order.[45] In the few short months Butler spent in command in occupied New Orleans, he modeled what it might look like for Federal armies to wage a hard yet humane war against Confederate civilians, a precedent that would in time characterize the entire Union war effort.

William T. Sherman in Occupied Memphis

Butler alone did not establish these "safe and sound precedents" for prosecuting a just war. Four hundred miles up the Mississippi River from New Orleans, William T. Sherman commanded the Union occupying forces in Memphis from late July to late November 1862. Sherman faced a variety of complicated problems in Memphis related to the treatment of civilian property, the regulation of cotton trade, the employment of slaves in Union armies, relations with the existing municipal government, and the subduing of guerrillas. In addressing these problems, Sherman also gradually worked out how Federals might reconcile hard war policies with humane restraint.[46]

When Sherman first arrived in Memphis, he later remembered, he found "the place dead; no business doing, the stores closed, churches, schools, and everything shut up." Before the outbreak of the war around twenty-three thousand people lived in Memphis, which had grown into a vital commercial city. Sherman set out to restore Memphis to an "active, busy, prosperous place" but he never doubted the vast majority of residents remained loyal to the Confederacy. A Union soldier stationed near the city agreed: "Memphis is quite a city," he wrote home, and "strongly secesh."[47]

Like Butler before him, Sherman asserted his authority in the city and established in detail the terms of the occupation. His initial actions ranged widely—from requiring military age men to swear a loyalty oath or leave Memphis, to establishing strict regulations for travel in and out of Memphis, to compelling businesses to reopen and thereby restore something of the spirit of the once "active, busy, prosperous" city. Some actions impinged more directly than others on questions of just conduct in war. When Sherman first arrived in Memphis and began rebuilding the fortifications at Fort Pickering, he forced families living inside the boundaries of the new fort to vacate their homes immediately. However, Sherman also assembled a three-person committee to assess the value of these homes, and then directed the chief quartermaster in Memphis to find displaced families a vacated home in the city of roughly equal value.[48] Military necessity demanded the confiscation of the homes within the fort, not the displacement to destitution of their occupants.

Sherman recognized the importance of cooperating with the Memphis municipal government. They might maintain some administrative responsibility in the city and thereby reduce the demands on Sherman's force. Butler also acknowledged as much, but his cooperative relationship with New

Orleans city officials proved dysfunctional and short-lived. Sherman assured the mayor of Memphis that he had "the most unbounded respect for the civil law, Courts & authorities," and would do all he could "to restore them to their proper use." Still, Sherman quite succinctly summarized the underlying philosophy of his attitude toward municipal government: "The Military for the time being must be superior to the Civil Authority but does not therefore destroy it." Sherman insisted Memphis' existing police force must remain responsible for the everyday arrests of citizens "for disorder or common crimes." In subsequent months, Sherman clarified the responsibilities assumed by the city government. He did not strip municipal authorities of their power, for doing so failed to prepare for the future: "The state of war is but temporary, and the time must come when the civil will resume its full power in the administration of justice in all parts of the country."[49]

One of Sherman's greatest challenges in Memphis was figuring out how to restore the Memphis economy without also thereby aiding the Confederacy. This challenge soon appeared in the trade of cotton for specie, namely gold, an issue that placed Sherman at odds with the Union high command. Though ultimately not allowed to pursue his preferred policy, the minor controversy over the cotton trade provided Sherman an occasion to refine his thinking about what a just war of hard yet humane measures looked like in practice.

As soon as Sherman arrived in Memphis, he sought to end the trade of cotton for specie. Although Sherman did not ban all trade for specie or all trade of cotton regardless of payment, he believed the trade of cotton for gold and silver aided the Confederate war effort. He hoped that by banning it he might deal a vital blow to the rebels without too adversely affecting the Memphis area economy. Secessionists selling cotton "had become so open in refusing anything but gold," which, Sherman believed, "has but one use—the purchase of arms and ammunition." So long as specie made its way into the Confederacy "it will not take long for Bragg and Van Dorn to supply their armies with all they need."[50] Henry Halleck noted disapprovingly that Sherman's policy contradicted Benjamin Butler's, who had done all he could to coax cotton planters to sell their crops and did not discourage payment in specie. After consulting with Edwin Stanton, Halleck asked Ulysses S. Grant to order Sherman to reverse his prohibition.

Sherman was not prone to insubordination, yet he still pleaded his case. To Secretary of Treasury Salmon P. Chase, Sherman argued that any reluctance to forbid payment of gold for cotton arose from a mistaken notion of the nature of the Union's war against the Confederacy—that is, a failure to recognize "all in the South are Enemies of all in the North." Southerners might "want Peace, and fear War," Sherman admitted, but they still "prefer a Southern Independent Government, and are fighting or working for it." One way they worked for it was selling cotton for specie. Sherman put the matter bluntly to Grant: "If we provide our enemy with money we Enable them to buy all they stand in need of. Money is as much contraband of war as powder." In a moment of frustration, Sherman complained to his brother John, senator from Ohio, that opponents of his prohibition threatened to prolong the war and imperil the lives of Union soldiers: "All the military men here saw at once that the Gold spent for Cotton went to the purchases of arms & munitions of war—but what are the lives of our soldiers to the profits of the merchant?"[51]

Sherman would never defy his superiors' orders, but Halleck still took time to justify the decision to Sherman—a decision, he admitted, motivated partially by a desire to maintain consistency with preexisting policies pursued by Butler and other Union commanders throughout the lower Mississippi River Valley. Halleck reminded Sherman he could always seize specie he had "good reason to believe [was] intended for the use of the rebel Government." Moreover, Halleck questioned Sherman's assumption that specie was somehow more valuable to the Confederate war effort than cotton itself, for "they can purchase military munitions with the latter as well as the former."[52] Sherman politely wrote back to Halleck letting him know he would "religiously carry out" Halleck's orders. Yet Sherman still believed his ban on the trade of cotton for specie was a model for the kind of military effort that crippled Confederates by vigorous yet restrained measures.

Whether or not Federals should prevent the trade of cotton for specie raised an even larger question: How should Union armies treat Confederate civilians living in the occupied city? Should Federals grant them something approaching the same rights and liberties normally afforded Americans in peacetime? Like Butler, Sherman believed in harsh punishments for the "disorderly secessionists" and those who still actively aided the Confederacy. But he also sought to deal humanely with the majority of civilians, and he put into place measures preventing unwarranted abuse.

"I will do nothing hastily," Sherman wrote in late July as he pondered what exactly to do with the obviously disloyal citizens still in his midst. An extreme response like expelling everyone hostile to the Union was obviously unreasonable; for one thing, it would mean "but few will be left" in the city.

A successful and just occupation demanded prudence to know when to show mercy and when not. On one point Sherman did not waver: "If any persons manifest any active hostility I will deal with them summarily." In this, Sherman aligned with Halleck's (and Butler's) vision of the war effort along the Mississippi. Halleck directed Grant in early August to handle "active sympathizers . . . without gloves." It was time, Halleck concluded, "that they should begin to feel the presence of war."[53]

Sherman did not take pleasure in subjecting Memphis civilians to the "presence of war." In a strikingly candid letter to his daughter Minnie, Sherman reflected on his complicity in the suffering occasioned by the war. "The People here look on us as invaders," Sherman wrote, but "we don't want their houses, their farms, their niggers, anything they have, but they don't believe us." This disbelief bred bitterness and hostility, which Sherman predicted would only intensify measures against civilians. He alluded to his recent orders displacing some civilians from their homes as indicative of where the war headed. "Think of this and how cruel men become in war, when even your papa has to do such acts." Sherman encouraged Minnie to pray every night for a speedy end to the war so that "our whole People may not become Robbers & murderers." Sherman believed war had its own terrible logic. It compelled actions from its participants they might find abhorrent in any other circumstance. It was hell and could not be refined. But that did not mean combatants should revel in war or not find ways to make it a bit more humane. Sherman expressed regret to his daughter about what war demanded of those who waged it, but he never doubted that the decisions he made were vital to victory and justified.[54]

As in New Orleans, interactions between occupying forces and Confederate civilians often centered on Federal soldiers' treatment of civilian property. Particularly relevant to the situation in Memphis was the proper confiscation and use of vacated property. Grant directed Sherman to take possession of all vacant stores and houses in Memphis and rent them out at reasonable rates. However, owners could regain control of their property on proof of their loyalty. When an assistant quartermaster wrote for guidance on implementing this directive, Sherman reiterated that every action ought to remain fully justified according to "the rules and laws of war." A few days later, a man wrote Sherman to claim possession of a vacated post office and theater in Memphis. Sherman said he would gladly return the building if the man swore an oath of loyalty to the Union. Sherman did not expect the man to do so: "I infer your desire is to secure your rents without this formality. This to me is simply ridiculous and unworthy a thought."[55]

In mid-September, Sherman issued another more thorough set of guidelines for the seizure of civilian property aimed at preventing abuses from soldiers under his command. Soon after his tenure in Memphis began, Sherman complained to his daughter that it "now requires all my energy to prevent our soldiers from robbing & plundering the houses & property of supposed Enemies." By the first week of August, Sherman set forth explicit rules governing Union soldiers' behavior, rules accompanied by stern punishments. Sherman insisted on "the quiet and good order of soldiers on the streets," and so he forbade noise, drunkenness, and fighting as a "military nuisance." Assistant provost marshals would now patrol places soldiers frequented and keep watch for any punishable behavior. Sherman placed new restrictions on travel. Soldiers wandering the city without passes would be arrested and sentenced to hard labor on the Fort Pickering fortifications for one week. The rules also prohibited plunder. When nearly two thousand dollars' worth of property was stolen from an elderly woman, presumably by Federal troops, Sherman threatened swift arrests and even executions if the thieves did not promptly return the money, which they soon did anonymously. In a letter to the *Memphis Bulletin*, Sherman promised that Federals guilty of senseless pillaging or "wanton waste" would receive the stiffest punishment afforded by law—execution. Sherman also pledged to investigate claims of abuse but he warned he would take seriously only detailed complaints, since "the Great mass of our soldiers would scorn to steal or commit Crime." Still, Sherman reminded readers of the *Memphis Bulletin* that these promises to monitor soldiers' behavior did not change the basic fact that "we are really *at war*." Many actions taken by Federals that seemed like wanton destruction might be essential to the Union war effort.[56]

Subduing guerrillas in the Memphis area inevitably raised these sorts of questions about what distinguished wanton destruction from actions essential to the war effort. Sherman issued fewer detailed guidelines concerning guerrillas and their abettors than did his counterparts in Missouri. Still, he came to embrace a key underlying rationale advanced by Federals in Missouri for waging a just and effective counterinsurgency—the principle of civilian responsibility, the idea that a civilian population could be held responsible for nearby guerrilla activity.

When Grant asked for a general report on the state of things in Memphis less than a month into Sherman's tenure, Sherman complained of the rampant

guerrilla activity: "All the people are now Guerrillas," he reported with obvious exaggeration, and they had grown skilled at targeting small bodies of
Union troops outside the city. As in Missouri, the guerrillas Sherman encountered deftly retreated into the surrounding civilian population, compli-
cating the task of identifying and punishing them; like Union commanders
in Missouri, Sherman threatened swift punishments for local communities
known to aid and harbor guerrillas. In an open letter to Memphis newspapers, Sherman promised retribution against local farmers or neighborhoods
who "encourage or even permit in their midst a set of Guerrillas." Sherman
reiterated it was "not our wish or policy to destroy the farmers or their farms."
But even if civilians claimed ignorance of particular guerrilla acts, it would
not necessarily override the fact that they had "become accessories by their
presence and inactivity to prevent murders and distruction [sic] of property." Sherman left vague the punishments civilians might face, but he made
clear his belief that "principles of war and common sense" justified retribution against civilians.[57]

Guerrilla activity continued throughout the summer and early fall of
1862. In late September, Sherman ordered an exceedingly harsh antiguerrilla
response against the village of Randolph, located north of Memphis along
the Mississippi River. Guerrillas lurking along the river banks near Randolph had recently fired upon a small vessel. Sherman presumed the real
culprits came "from the interior and depart as soon as the mischief is done,"
but that did not change the fact that Union forces had to punish Randolph
residents "to prevent a repetition." Sherman ordered his men to destroy the
village, "leaving one house to mark the place." He also wanted them to let the
people of Randolph know that while "we deeply deplore the necessity of
such destruction" it ensured the protection of travelers on the Mississippi.
Sherman gave the colonel in command of the expedition the authority to
spare more than one house "if any extraordinary case presents itself," but he
rejected anything else that might lessen the retribution for the guerrillas'
"acts of cowardly firing."[58]

Sherman eventually grew so frustrated with the guerrilla activity that he
complained to Confederate Maj. Gen. Thomas C. Hindman that the "guerrillas and partisan rangers" loosely connected to regular Confederate armies
committed "acts which you would not sanction." Guerrilla attacks on steamboats carrying provisions for civilians most infuriated Sherman. These
attackers did not deserve the "name or consideration of an honorable soldier," Sherman declared. More ominously, he warned he would soon strike

against the civilian population harboring these guerrillas. A short time later, when Sherman learned of guerrillas firing on two unarmed steamboats, he concluded they "must know and feel that not only will we meet them in arms, but that their people shall experience their full measure of the necessary consequences of such barbarity." Sherman warned Hindman that if he failed to tighten his control over these guerrillas "this war [will] become a reproach to the names of liberty and civilization." Sherman taunted Hindman for fighting not in a conventional fashion but by unmanly guerrilla tactics. Sherman boasted he and his superiors "know what civilized warfare is and has been for hundreds of years." The guerrillas, and Hindman in tolerating them, deviated dramatically from it, Sherman concluded. He believed if the guerrilla activity continued, normal "restraints of discipline" among regular soldiers would crumble.[59]

While in Memphis, Sherman reflected at length on the proper nature of the Union military effort. By late summer 1862, he decided conciliatory polices intended to woo southerners back to the Union were naïve and fated to fail. "We have finished the first page of this war in vainly seeking a union sentiment in the South," Sherman wrote in mid-August, "and our Politicians have substantially committed suicide by mistaking the Extent and power of the Southern People & its Government." Sherman worried that while "the whole South is in deep intense earnest we of the north still try reconciliation." Victory and peace would only come once the northern people mustered the "patriotism" necessary to "the task of subjugating the whole South." The very "self existence" of the Union demanded it.[60]

Even though Sherman believed "nothing more is left us but force" to defeat the Confederacy, he also affirmed, as he wrote to a group of New Yorkers, that Federals must unleash that force with "a wise and united purpose." Sherman implied that the Constitution and orders from "our constituted authorities" placed limits on how Union armies waged war. The fact remained that the war proved more demanding and all-encompassing than many had assumed in the early spring of 1861: "Thousands will perish by the bullet or sickness; but war must go on—it can't be stopped. The North must rule or submit to degradation and insult forevermore. The war must now be fought out."[61] In the months ahead, Union forces had to reconcile hard war policies that vigorously "fought out" the war with earnest efforts to impose restraints on the fighting's death and destruction. As Butler and Sherman implemented their hard yet humane occupation measures, another issue emerged that posed particularly controversial and problematical challenges to waging a just war: emancipation's place in the Union war effort.

The Just-War Quandary of Emancipation

Butler and Sherman alike confronted one of the most vexing and controversial just-war questions of the first eighteen months of the war: What should Union armies do with the slaves who made daring flights to Federal lines? Could Federals harbor runaway slaves and put them to work in service of the Union war effort? Or must they return some fugitives to their former masters, especially masters who remained loyal to the Union? Should the Union officially commit itself to destroying slavery, and if so, how should that destruction proceed? While Butler and Sherman commanded occupying forces, northern society engaged in bitter debates about emancipation's place in the Union war effort. The loyal citizenry hardly agreed that a justly waged war could destroy slavery. Amid debates over the Second Confiscation Act and Lincoln's preliminary Emancipation Proclamation, Butler and Sherman contemplated how to justly wage a war against Confederates that threatened their slave property. Doing so inevitably meant also considering the character of a hard yet humane war and the proper role of military emancipation within it. Both commanders came to see targeting slavery as both just and immensely valuable to the Union war effort. Yet in this season of ambiguity in official Union policy on emancipation, they both remained conflicted about the legitimate extent to which the Federals army could act as a liberating force, especially when it came to emancipating the slaves of ostensibly loyal southerners. As Butler and Sherman struggled (not altogether successfully) to determine how military emancipation ought to proceed, they also in the process contemplated the character of a hard yet humane war.

Butler had faced emancipation-related just-war questions as soon as the conflict began when he was stationed in Maryland and Virginia. Because Maryland remained loyal to the Union, Butler vowed to uphold the Constitution and protect slavery. But in Virginia, which had abandoned the Union and the Constitution, Butler felt no such obligation to protect slave property. When three slaves escaped to Fort Monroe in Hampton, Virginia, Butler proclaimed that the fugitives were "contraband" of war and refused to return them to their former masters. Louisiana posed trickier problems. It seceded like Virginia, but some slaveholders swore loyalty to the Union after the Federal army's arrival. Butler wondered if he ought to extend the same protection to their slave property as he did in Maryland.[62]

Butler soon found himself embroiled in an open conflict over these issues with one of his subordinates in the Department of the Gulf, Gen. John W. Phelps, an abolitionist from Vermont. In May 1862, while stationed at Camp Parapet, four miles north of New Orleans, Phelps resolved to offer safe harbor and freedom to runaway slaves who made it to his lines.[63] One soldier serving under Phelps recalled him insisting, "We owe it to justice and humanity to proclaim the immediate abolition of slavery," but the soldier himself added that the runaways who made it to their lines were "mainly a burden."[64] When Butler learned that Phelps harbored an escaped enslaved boy whose former master had tried to retrieve him, the blunt advice he gave offended Phelps's abolitionist sentiments: "If you have any use for him, use him," Butler wrote, "if not, is he not like any other vagrant about the Camp." Later that month, when a Louisiana slaveholder traveled to Phelps's camp to retake three slaves, Phelps refused to let the slaveholder search the camp. Meanwhile, runaway slaves continued to arrive. One June morning, soldiers at Camp Parapet awoke to find 150 or more fugitive slaves waiting outside. Phelps wanted to feed, shelter, and free the fugitives, and he complained again to Butler of the Union's continued "course of undecided action" against slavery, "determined by no policy but the vague will of a war-distracted people."[65]

Phelps believed wartime emancipation was morally and constitutionally justified. The Constitution required the United States to secure a republican form of government, and slavery and republicanism were antithetical, he reasoned. Like President Lincoln, Phelps reasoned that the president's power as commander in chief, coupled with the demands of military necessity, offered the sturdiest justification for wartime emancipation, for "amidst the clash of arms the laws of peace are silent."[66] Yet even before Lincoln issued the preliminary Emancipation Proclamation, Phelps refused to take any action that might risk returning refugees in his camp to their masters, regardless of a master's supposed loyalty to the Union. When word came that a levee just north of Camp Parapet desperately needed to be repaired, Butler directed Phelps to send some runaways who had escaped from that general area to help with repairs. Phelps refused. Butler responded by directing Phelps to exclude from his camp "all unemployed persons, black and white," in short, runaways whose labor Phelps did not need. Phelps again ignored the order.[67]

Phelps's insubordination frustrated Butler, but so too did the lingering ambiguity in official Union policy on the matter. In late May 1862, Butler asked Secretary of War Edwin M. Stanton to clarify when exactly Federals could legitimately confiscate, harbor, or employ escaped slaves. Butler wanted to know if the Lincoln administration thought Phelps's actions contradicted the demands of just warfare. Butler told Stanton he had no qualms about confiscating the slaves of persons "actively in arms" against the Union. But he still wondered if doing so was entirely justified when "no military necessity" existed. Moreover, he asked for more precise direction on what to do with the slaves owned by southerners who had remained "passive rather than active in the rebellion." Was their slave property—like the Maryland slaveholder's—unquestionably protected by the "inviolability of the rights of property" under the Constitution? If not, Butler asked Stanton why it was not "manifestly unjust to make a virtual confiscation of this particular species of property" when other types of property went untouched by Union armies. Put another way, what exactly made slavery, as a "particular species of property," uniquely yet legitimately susceptible to confiscation, especially when not immediately demanded by military necessity?[68]

Phelps believed that only an unashamedly emancipatory war was a just war. Butler agreed that slavery was "a curse to a nation," but in the absence of a clear and thorough policy, he worried over how exactly to justly prosecute a war against slavery. As with any other kind of property, Federals could confiscate slaves in an illegitimate and unjust manner, Butler believed, so he pressed Stanton to endorse or repudiate Phelps's actions. Stanton evaded the query. He told Butler he thought it was not "necessary or wise to fetter your judgment by any specific instructions." He only asked Butler to deal with the matter with great discretion and avoid "any serious embarrassment" to the Lincoln administration.[69]

Even after the passage of the Second Confiscation Act and the Militia Act in July 1862, the conflict between Butler and Phelps over the nature of a just war of emancipation continued. In accordance with the Militia Act, which authorized President Lincoln to enlist "persons of African descent" in service of the Union war effort, Phelps sought to raise three regiments of former slaves. He appealed to Butler to supply the regiments with the arms and equipment needed for combat. Butler instead instructed Phelps to employ the freed slaves behind the lines cutting down trees. Butler promised to send all the axes and tents needed. Phelps furiously replied that he refused "to become a mere slave driver" and resigned in defiance. Butler concluded to his wife, "Phelps has gone crazy . . . He is mad as a March Hare on the 'nigger question.' "[70] Phelps gambled that he and not Butler had a better read on northern public opinion and President Lincoln's ultimate intentions. He hoped Lincoln would eventually support his defiant stand against Butler. But Lincoln did not intervene and Butler soon accepted Phelps's resignation.[71] Their protracted conflict over confiscating, harboring, and arming of former slaves revealed profound confusion and disagreement over how to justly wage war against slavery, and over wartime emancipation's legitimate place in a hard yet humane war effort.

In Memphis, Sherman similarly ruminated on emancipation's place in the Union war effort and the role of Federal armies as agents of emancipation in a just war. As late as mid-June, Sherman gladly complied with the "well-settled policy of the whole army . . . to have nothing to do with the negro."[72] Yet in the wake of the Second Confiscation Act, Sherman increasingly put to work hundreds of fugitive slaves in service of the Union war effort. He promised to pay them one pound of tobacco per month and provide them shoes and clothing. By the end of July, Sherman employed as many as eight hundred escaped slaves to repair the fortifications at Fort Pickering. Even so, prior to the preliminary Emancipation Proclamation, Sherman suspected escaped slaves might one day have to return to their former masters. He therefore kept precise records of the enslaved persons employed and the names of their masters so that "a fair and equitable settlement may be made at the end of the war."[73]

Sherman remained somewhat unsure about the just limits of the Union army's liberating activity. He confessed it was "neither his duty nor pleasure to disturb the relation of master and slave." He also feared what some interpreters of the laws of war warned, that if "Negroes are liberated either they or masters must perish." Even by early September 1862, Sherman had not changed his mind. Yet his antipathy toward slaveholding Confederates increasingly outweighed his misgivings about emancipation. Sherman accepted that Federal armies could justly target the slave property of active supporters of the Confederacy. Their right to slavery "only exists by force of that very Constitution they seek to destroy," Sherman argued. As he explained to a southern slaveholder, "The Constitution of the United States is your only legal title to slavery." By making war against the Union and the Constitution, Confederates forfeited their only legitimate legal guarantee of the right of slaveholding. Moreover, Sherman came to believe that waging hard war against Confederate civilians justly necessitated a direct strike against slavery.

"You know I don't want your slaves," Sherman told the same slaveholder, "but to bring you to reason I think as a Military Man I have a Right and it is good policy to make *you all* feel that you are but men." The "simple laws of War" fully justified this course of action toward Confederate slave property, Sherman argued.[74]

Still, the more difficult just-war questions concerning emancipation remained. Like Butler, Sherman hesitated to apply this same logic to patently *loyal* slaveholders and their slave property. By what authority could Federal armies legitimately seize the slaves of southerners who remained loyal to the Union? Perhaps military necessity offered one justification—for example, a dire need for fugitive slave labor to rebuild fortifications. But what should happen to the escaped slaves once this military necessity lapsed? Should Federals promptly return the fugitives to their loyal masters? As Sherman wrestled with these questions in the weeks prior to the preliminary Emancipation Proclamation, he also confronted what he considered innumerable practical problems over how to implement the Second Confiscation Act. In late September, Sherman asked his brother John in exasperation, "Are we to free all the negroes, men women & children? Whether there be work for them or not?" Sherman complained also of the costly "incumbrance" it would place on his army to provide food, clothing, and other provisions to the escaped slaves.[75] Not surprisingly, Sherman responded tepidly to President Lincoln's preliminary Emancipation Proclamation. He thought the proclamation "can do no good & but little harm." After all, Lincoln guaranteed "no machinery by which such freedom is assured," Sherman wrote, except the advance of Union armies, which already had the practical effect of liberating slaves.[76]

Even as Sherman and Butler became convinced that a hard yet humane war could not afford to leave the institution of slavery unscathed, the summer of 1862 remained a time of great confusion about emancipation's place in a just war. The clarity in official Union policy on emancipation provided by Congressional acts or Presidential proclamations remained somewhat limited. The task still remained for Federal officers and soldiers to discern how exactly to fulfill such policies in a truly just and legitimate manner. To proclaim that the war to save the Union would also be a war to end slavery did not immediately resolve all the innumerable just-war quandaries surrounding the carrying out of wartime emancipation.

The Union occupations of New Orleans and Memphis convinced many Federals of the foolishness of a conciliatory war effort and the necessity of embracing hard war measures. Yet these early occupations—like Union army encounters with guerrilla warfare in Missouri—also prompted Federals to consider the nature of a justly waged war. Federals did not always agree about how to wage a just war, and Union soldiers did not always act in accordance with official policies governing just conduct. Still, the Federal experience of occupying New Orleans and Memphis proved influential in shaping the wider development of the Union military effort. By the end of 1862, Federal forces commanded by Butler and Sherman pursued a vision of just warfare that sought to reconcile a hard hand with humane restraints.

This style of warfare came to define the Union military effort against the Confederacy in the final stages of the conflict. It first took root during the opening months of war in the Mississippi River Valley, from guerrilla-ravaged Missouri to occupied Memphis and New Orleans. By late 1862, the task of refining this manner of waging just war into rules for all Union armies soon passed to Francis Lieber.

CHAPTER THREE

The More Vigorously Wars Are Pursued, the Better It Is for Humanity

Francis Lieber and General Orders No. 100

Francis Lieber believed the Union did not have to choose between the hard hand of war and humane restraint in its conflict with the Confederacy. A just war possessed both in equal measure. How could Federal armies reconcile two seemingly antithetical approaches to warfare—one determined to devastate and destroy an enemy into submission, the other committed to curtailing carnage? Lieber's code offered a simple and alluring answer: "The more vigorously wars are pursued, the better it is for humanity." Hard wars *are* humane wars. If the Union waged war vigorously, it could conquer the Confederacy quickly; by restoring peace as rapidly as possible, the Union could limit the conflict's total suffering and destruction.[1] This fundamental idea constituted the heart of Lieber's moral vision of warfare—that is, his most basic beliefs and assumptions about war's moral dimensions. His certainty that vigorous wars were humane and just is nearly ever present in the code's articles.

Lieber's code reconciled hard and humane war in theory, and also translated this moral vision of warfare into detailed military rules and guidelines. Lieber assumed most Union soldiers shared his conviction about the necessity and humanity of a vigorously waged war. But this logic, taken to an unwarranted extreme, might seemingly justify nearly any action in combat. Therefore, soldiers needed practical and intelligible instructions for how to wage a war vigorous in its prosecution but still mindful of certain inviolable restraints imposed by the laws of war. This is what Lieber's code sought to provide soldiers.

On 24 April 1863, President Lincoln promulgated the code as General Orders No. 100, known also as "Instructions for the Government of Armies of the United States in the Field." Lieber formally began work on the code in late December 1862, during a long winter of discontent in the Union war effort.[2] In the Eastern Theater, Gen. George B. McClellan had forged the Army of the Potomac into an imposing force but proved less adept at wielding it for decisive victory along the James and York and Potomac rivers. McClellan failed to capture Richmond in late July and thereby speedily end the war. Then came the ghastly carnage at Antietam in September. Exasperation with McClellan mounted, and in the wake of the 1862 midterm elections, President Lincoln finally replaced him with the decidedly uneager Ambrose Burnside. Lincoln and the northern public craved strong offensive action, so off again toward Richmond went the Army of the Potomac. But Burnside led his army to another demoralizing defeat at Fredericksburg, Virginia in mid-December, where Union causalities neared 13,000, a staggering toll equivalent to the losses at Antietam.

Two days after Fredericksburg, General in Chief Henry Halleck and Secretary of War Edwin Stanton finally relented to Lieber's pleas and formed a special committee to draft his code. Given the disheartening setbacks of the previous months, this was not a particularly auspicious moment to produce rules meant to constrain Federal soldiers and guarantee the humane treatment of their enemies. But the sobering news from Fredericksburg did not demoralize Lieber as much as it invigorated him to finish his code and ensure that the Union's hard war did not descend into utter barbarity and indiscriminate destruction.[3] Scholars of Lieber's code tend to analyze the document not chiefly within its immediate historical context, the American Civil War, but within the wider history of international law or modern just-war thinking. Yet this angle on the code risks underemphasizing the remarkable fact that the code appeared when it did, amid a demoralized Union war effort tenuously sustained by the loyal citizenry.[4]

Lieber's inspiration to draft the code came from fears that the opening months of the war revealed widespread ignorance and misunderstanding of the laws of war. Events on the battlefield had posed many perplexing problems that Union officers appeared ill equipped to resolve. Although Federal soldiers embraced the spirit of hard yet humane warfare they still needed practical guidance for how to act in particular situations when facing difficult and controversial dilemmas. The issues that most worried Lieber—guerrilla warfare, prisoner exchanges, and the parole—might not now seem particularly important, but they inspired him to draft his code and profoundly shaped its character. Without an accurate understanding of the code's inspiration, it is impossible to comprehend correctly the code's content.[5]

The spirit of hard yet humane warfare embodied in Lieber's code first appeared in earnest among Union armies in the greater Mississippi River Valley, especially Missouri, Memphis, and New Orleans. Lieber endeavored to refine this spirit of warfare and inculcate it among Union forces in every theater of the war. The code's promulgation made the spring of 1863 a moment of clarity, not confusion, in the Union military effort, not least on the all-important question of how Federal armies should prosecute its war against the Confederacy. The Union had abandoned an earlier spirit of conciliation. Lieber's code crystallized an alternative: a moral vision of hard yet humane warfare that would define Union military strategy and policy for the rest of the war.[6]

It is difficult to assess the extent to which Lieber's code actually shaped the conduct of Union soldiers. Even so, at the very least, Federal officials and soldiers widely embraced the moral vision contained in the code, affirming the morality of hard yet humane war. What Lieber offered in General Orders No. 100 was a blueprint for waging a just war in accordance with this moral vision of warfare. In doing so, Lieber sought to vindicate vigorously waged wars as the most moral wars.

Francis Lieber: A Life Charged by War's "Moral Electricity"

Long before the outbreak of the American Civil War, or the Battle of Fredericksburg, or the drafting of General Orders No. 100, war captivated young Francis Lieber. It shaped the formative experiences of his early childhood and in due time engrossed his intellectual interests as an ambitious scholar. For a young boy born in Berlin who came of age during Napoleon's conquests, he could easily have grown to feel utter revulsion toward war. Lieber remembered weeping in bitter dismay as Napoleon's armies marched through Berlin after Prussian defeats at Jena and Auerstedt. Yet the young Lieber grew only more fascinated by the art and grandeur of war. A deep-seething hatred of the French took hold of Lieber, and after Napoleon's return from exile in 1815, he and his brothers enlisted in the acclaimed Colbert regiment. After the Battle of Waterloo, as his regiment pursued the retreating Napoleon outside the village Namur, Lieber "suddenly experienced a sensation as if my whole body were compressed in my head, and this, like a ball, were quivering in the air." He was shot through the neck. As he lay helpless on the battlefield, he was shot again in the chest. He begged a fellow soldier to end his life as an act of mercy but the soldier refused. It seemed that Lieber's final moments would end like countless other soldiers, in unimaginable pain, powerless to prevent local peasants from plundering the few possessions he carried. But death relented before it took Lieber. He survived to tell of the exhilarating horrors of the battlefield. If the horrors were immense—which Lieber never denied—so too were their terrible glory, he believed. Lieber had experienced it for himself, and he sought it again five years later when he fought on behalf of the Greeks for their independence from the Ottoman Empire.[7]

Lieber soon traded the life of a soldier for that of a scholar. Never fully at home under the reactionary Prussian regime of his native land, Lieber relocated to London in 1826 after receiving a doctorate in mathematics from the university in Jena. He managed to acquaint himself with some of England's most prominent intellectuals, including John Stuart Mill and Jeremy Bentham. Though he met his future wife in England, Lieber never secured the teaching post he coveted. Within a year Lieber uprooted to Boston to run a gymnasium styled after the Friedrich Ludwig model. The gymnasium venture failed but the personal connections Lieber made in Boston helped launch his professional scholarly career. Joseph Story, jurist and later Supreme Court justice, once wrote that Lieber would likely die "for want of a rapid, voluminous, and never-ending correspondence," and it was while living in Boston that Lieber cultivated acquaintances and friendships with many of New England's leading men, from John Quincy Adams to Henry Wadsworth Longfellow to Charles Sumner. Lieber soon joined the publisher Mathew Carey in the production of the multivolume *Encyclopaedia Americana*, a runaway success. Copies of the *Encyclopaedia* made it all the way from Andrew Jackson's White House to the law office of an enterprising Illinois lawyer named Abraham Lincoln. Even so, the *Encyclopaedia* did not win Lieber the teaching appointment at Harvard he desired. In search of secure employment to provide for a wife and sons, Lieber migrated again, this time to the near opposite of Boston, the Midlands of South Carolina. For the next twenty years, the antislavery-inclined Lieber taught history and political economy at South Carolina College in Columbia.[8]

Although Lieber's intellectual interests ranged widely, he loved nothing more than contemplating the morality of war. Lieber believed war contained "the spark of moral electricity." It possessed an ennobling yet destructive power that could inspire both moral vigor and immoral desolation. War revived noble and virtuous characteristics in soldiers just as easily as it unleashed the base passions of their nature. Lieber insisted that while war was "not of an ethical nature, so far as the physical force goes, it is not immoral on that account." He therefore devoted much of his life's work to explaining why a people might justly enter a state of war, and, having entered it, how they might justly prosecute the war to victory. Lieber forever believed in the possibility of channeling war's power toward truly righteous ends—the promotion of virtue, the protection of civilization, the pursuit of justice.[9]

Though a student of war, Lieber was no warmonger. He opposed the Mexican-American War as "bad, thoroughly so . . . an unrighteous war." Yet on the eve of that conflict, he scorned the strident pacifism of men like future Massachusetts senator Charles Sumner. In a 4 July 1845 speech in Boston, Sumner, anticipating the Mexican-American War, thundered: "In our age there can be no peace that is not honorable; there can be no war that is not dishonorable." Lieber heard Sumner's harangue in person, which he later dismissed as a poorly reasoned pacifist rant. He told Sumner as much. Their friendship deteriorated soon thereafter, and they eventually ended altogether their two-decades-long correspondence. Lieber criticized Sumner for assuming all wars were immoral. As he explained at the time to Sumner's law partner George Hillard, "though an economist, who knows that war can never increase wealth; though a publicist who knows that peace is the normal state of man; though a Christian that knows the message of the energizing love of the gospel, I am no vilifier of war under all circumstances." A just war still possessed the spark of moral electricity. Lieber sought to harness that spark, for he thought a great war could preserve and perfect true civilization. Marathon, Tours, Leipzig—each battle, Lieber believed, testified to a central truth about warfare: "Blood is occasionally the rich dew of history."[10]

Not long after the Mexican-American War, as the sectional crisis intensified, the Liebers left South Carolina for New York City. A faction of prominent South Carolinians thwarted Lieber's candidacy for the presidency of South Carolina College (they rightly doubted his unwavering commitment to state's rights and proslavery orthodoxy). By 1857, Lieber took a position at the expanding Columbia College, again teaching history and political economy. When the chaos of secession unsettled his adopted country in late 1860, a fierce nationalist ardor for the Union swelled in Lieber, who voted for Abraham Lincoln in the 1860 election. "God has given us this great country for great purposes," Lieber wrote to Attorney General Edward Bates, and it therefore "must be maintained at any price under any circumstances." As war loomed, Lieber penned patriotic poetry to rouse the young men of Columbia College to take up arms against the Confederacy and defend the Union: "Our Flag! The Red shall mean the blood / We gladly pledge; and let the White / Mean purity and solemn truth, / Unsullied justice, sacred right." Lieber loved the Union as a beacon of free and enlightened civilization, a land of opportunity in a world of tyranny and oppression. He came also to believe that a justly waged war against the Confederacy would vindicate the loyal citizenry's highest claims about the exceptional moral character of the Union and its people.[11]

Lieber's thinking about the laws of war and the morality of military conflict at the outset of the Civil War are well presented in a series of public lectures he delivered at the Columbia law school from late October 1861 to February 1862. Lieber addressed particular issues at length in the lectures— from retaliation, to flags of truce, to spies, to the use of poisons, to prisoners of war, and so forth—but taken together, the lectures revealed his three core convictions about warfare. First, as he had said to Sumner during the run-up to the Mexican American War, Lieber insisted that wars could have positive moral effects. Lieber did not deny that the brute force and violence inherent in war was often immoral and illegitimate. But when he reflected on the *outcomes* of war, he rejected the idea that war was sheer immorality. A war waged for righteous reasons by just means possessed "a moral character—I mean in its effects," Lieber argued. These effects included the "tendency to invigorate public spirit and to unite selfish individuals." If warfare always remained utter amorality, Lieber asked, why did wars sometimes produce morally beneficial outcomes? Second, Lieber affirmed repeatedly that peace is humanity's natural condition and its restoration should be the goal of any war. "Peace is the normal state of civilized society. War is the exception," Lieber reminded his listeners. For that reason, "Peace of some sort must be the end of all war . . . They who would carry on war for its own sake are enemies to civilization and to mankind."[12]

Finally, most important, Lieber argued that vigorously waged wars were typically the most humane ones, an argument at the heart of his moral vision of warfare. "War being an exceptional state of things," Lieber reasoned, "the shorter it is the better; and the intenser it is carried on, the shorter it will be." Vigorous wars usually ended quickly and therefore reduced the total suffering and destruction occasioned by war. Lieber again thought the history of warfare supported his moral argument: "The gigantic wars of modern times are less destructive than were the protracted former ones, or the unceasing feudal turbulence," he insisted, precisely because the violence of the distant past was *protracted* and *unceasing*. If an army wanted to wage war humanely it should wage war "intensely," and thereby sooner restore peace. Lieber's logic here often seemed to lead him inevitably to authorize unrestrained warfare. He concluded in his lectures: "All means to injure the enemy so far as to deprive him of power to injure us or to force him to submit to the conditions desired by us are allowed." Yet after setting forth this axiom, Lieber also immediately affirmed that "religion and civilization" placed some limits on it. "All means" did not exactly mean *all*. There still remained certain restrictions on what armies could do in war, because "man can never divest himself of his ethical character."[13]

Lieber's call for a vigorous war came tinged with personal turmoil. As America plunged headlong into war, Lieber's family stood at the precipice of irreparable division. "Behold in me the symbol of civil war," Lieber wrote as the conflict raged. Francis's oldest son, Oscar, had spent nearly his entire life in South Carolina and remained there when the Liebers moved to New York. Tensions between father and son escalated alongside the sectional crisis. Francis's decision to vote for Lincoln in 1860 effectively ended what was left of their relationship. Caught up in the secession fever sweeping South Carolina, Oscar joined Hampton's Legion, led by Wade Hampton, and chose country over family.[14]

Hamilton Lieber, Francis's middle son, enlisted instead in an Illinois regiment. The fighting at Fort Donelson in February 1862 left him without a left arm; doctors amputated it three inches below the shoulder days after the battle. "This is a grave and grievous period in our lives," Francis wrote to Norman Lieber, his youngest son, as Hamilton recuperated from his injuries. At the time, Norman served in the Army of the Potomac in Gen. George McClellan's Peninsula Campaign. "Everyone here feels very anxious about you," Francis wrote Norman in mid-April. But death had its eye instead on another Lieber boy on the Virginian peninsula. Oscar died from particularly grisly wounds suffered at the Battle of Williamsburg in May 1862. Oscar's death left Francis anguished but no less devoted to the Union cause. Reflecting to Henry Halleck on the loss endured by his family in 1862, he could only conclude: "Civil War has thus knocked very loudly at our door."[15]

Lieber's three sons marched off to war. One returned maimed, another never returned. Lieber worked to constrain the death and destruction of the Civil War not simply as a scholar but also as a father. As Lieber's finest biographer explains, "The stress and strain of following his three sons in battle endowed Lieber with a realistic approach to the international law of war; even more, it developed in him a strongly humanitarian feeling."[16] Lieber had many reasons for translating the laws of war into a useable code to govern the conduct of Civil War armies. But the dull grief and anxiety of one reason burned deep and steady unlike any other: The war had come to Lieber's doorstep and taken his three sons.

The Wartime Origins of the Lieber Code

War ravaged the Lieber family in 1862. That year also witnessed a steady transformation in the Union military effort, in how Federals waged war against the Confederacy. Historians have described this transformation as a shift from "conciliatory" to "hard war" policies and measures. Lieber supported this evolution. As it unfolded, he conceived and drafted his code. In fact, General Order No. 100 offered to a Federal army that had abandoned conciliation a set of guidelines for how it might wage a hard yet humane war. As Lieber observed how Union soldiers and military and political leaders handled certain problems concerning the war's prosecution, he came to believe that most Federals inadequately understood the laws of war. This conviction inspired Lieber to draft his code. To understand the content of Lieber's code, it is essential to appreciate its immediate origins and inspirations. General Orders No. 100 became internationally influential, but its articles and underlying moral vision remained so thoroughly the product of one particular national conflict. The story of the wartime genesis of the Lieber code is the story of a man coming to terms with the moral, legal, and strategic dilemmas facing the Union as it waged a war for national survival.

At the outset of the Federal war effort, especially in the Eastern Theater, Union armies generally adhered to a military strategy of conciliation against Confederates, treating lightly civilians and their property. The conciliatory strategy assumed most southerners did not enthusiastically support the Confederacy and might abandon their tenuous loyalty to the rebellion if dealt with mildly and shielded from the war's worst devastation. Lieber always opposed this strategy. As he explained to his son, he thought it foolishly "let the enemy class off with impunity!" Increasingly after Gen. George B. McClellan's failure to capture Richmond by the early summer of 1862, more and more loyal citizens and Union officials agreed with Lieber and questioned conciliation's effectiveness as a path to victory. Confederate resolve seemed to demand something sterner. "They have fought the rebels with the Olive branch," Frederick Douglass said of the Lincoln administration. "The people must teach them to fight them with the sword. They have sought to conciliate obedience. The people must teach them to compel obedience." In embracing hard warfare over conciliation, Union armies acted strategically to subject southern society to the war's hardship and destruction, although usually never indiscriminately. Federals eventually worked in wide-ranging ways to implement the spirit of hard war; this approach to the war's prosecution included many particular policies and actions. But most importantly, as 1862 unfolded, an ever-greater number of Union officials affirmed that the turn toward hard war above all else required the Union to strike vigorously against Confederate slavery.[17]

Congress acted first. Since December 1861 it had debated Illinois Republican senator Lyman Trumbull's new confiscation act, which proposed the confiscation of all property, including slaves, held by persons in Confederate armies or actively aiding the Confederate war effort. Some northerners denounced the bill as unconstitutional and indiscriminate in its attack on southerners; others complained that it did not do enough to hasten emancipation. Regardless, the passage of the act in mid-July 1862 signaled a hardening war against slavery. On the same day Congress also passed a militia act that authorized President Lincoln to enroll "persons of African descent" for "any war service for which they may be found competent." In theory, this included service as soldiers in combat.[18] As Congress considered these acts, Lieber completed a memorandum commissioned by Secretary of War Edwin Stanton on "the great service which the coloured people might render our cause." Lieber's memorandum defended what the militia act authorized. He suggested that "able-bodied negroes" should mostly fulfill noncombat duties as members of "Armed Working Companies." But Lieber did not advise restricting all black soldiers from combat. He argued Federals eventually should use the ablest companies for "higher military purposes in the field." Lieber also adamantly insisted that the laws of war plainly guaranteed the freedom of any slave employed in the Union war effort. If Federal officials openly promised freedom the Union ranks would swell with runaways, Lieber predicted, and "we should derive essential benefit from them."[19]

The Union's ever-hardening war against slavery quickly came to involve far more than the confiscation of Confederate-owned slaves or the enlistment of African American troops. In late July, President Lincoln informed his cabinet of his intention to issue a proclamation declaring free all slaves in the rebellious states. Lincoln had become convinced this was necessary after McClellan's failure to capture Richmond in the Peninsula Campaign, but he was persuaded to delay his proclamation until Union military fortunes improved, lest the revolutionary act reek of desperation. After his victory at Second Manassas in late August, Robert E. Lee advanced into

Maryland, assuming that the sustained presence of the Army of Northern Virginia in the loyal state might result in significant strategic gains: access to bountiful resources to feed and fuel his army, the chance to further shatter northern morale, and perhaps even the opportunity finally to win foreign recognition. Emboldened by news of Thomas J. "Stonewall" Jackson's anticipated capture of Harpers Ferry, Lee gathered his outnumbered army near Sharpsburg. Lee's army met McClellan's on 17 September in a battle that resulted in more than 23,000 casualties. After the sobering shock of the toll at Antietam, McClellan did not pursue Lee's badly wounded Army of Northern Virginia as it escaped back into Virginia. But Lincoln still seized the opportunity to issue a preliminary Emancipation Proclamation, slated to take effect on 1 January 1863. In the short term, the action exacerbated disagreements over what exactly Federals fought for. "I am well enough suited with soldiering if it was in and for another purpose," said a New York cavalryman bitter over the Emancipation Proclamation, "but to be made a fool of by this d—n administration does not go down so easily." Lieber, however, heartily approved of Lincoln's decision, which he welcomed as the final deathblow to the conciliatory military policy. Only an unwavering hard war effort that targeted slavery could defeat the rebellion. To Lieber, the conflict boiled down to one question: "Shall the North conquer the South or the South conquer the North?"[20]

As this turn from conciliation to hard war and emancipation unfolded, Lieber contemplated as never before the demands of the laws of war and the nature and limits of a moral war. However, he was not alone in working to define a just war and explain how and why Union armies should wage one. Many northern ministers addressed the same topic, especially on the fast day observed near Thanksgiving 1862, mere weeks after Lincoln issued his preliminary Emancipation Proclamation. While they did not possess Lieber's technical knowledge of the laws of war, and so contemplated the question of just conduct in war from a different perspective, these northern ministers envisioned just warfare in terms strikingly similar to the hard yet humane moral vision of war that defined Lieber's code.

In their 1862 Thanksgiving fast day sermons, many northern ministers affirmed God's providential control over the unfolding war and echoed Lieber in not denouncing war as utterly lacking beneficial moral consequences. The most common metaphor ministers used to describe war was a purifying fire. A Connecticut minister insisted the war would end once God "sufficiently purified us in the furnace of this great calamity," and finished "cleansing us with his own baptism of fire." Another thought the war was good for "bleeding us of our moral and political malady." A New York Dutch Reformed minister likewise labeled the war a "fatherly chastisement . . . by which we shall be sanctified." This bloody furnace of purification and sanctification would instill in the loyal citizenry "great lessons of public spirit, of self-sacrifice, of loyalty to principle and to the powers ordained of God." A New York minister rejoiced "in the ascendancy the war has given to moral and spiritual ideas over material interests." Another minister praised life in the army for instilling in soldiers, "prompt attention to duty, of self-denial and sacrifice . . . the aroused sense of dependence on an unseen Power."[21] As a purifying fire, the qualities war could foster in combatants chiefly included self-sacrifice, honor, discipline, and a concern with ultimate spiritual matters over base material interests.

Ministers also insisted that the Union's war differed fundamentally from the wars of the past, which further accounted for why it could purify Americans of their iniquities. Albert Barnes, one of the nation's leading theologians, criticized European wars of the recent and distant past as waged by means "that, as a Christian and civilized people, we could not but regard as barbarous and cruel." The Union, he continued, had thus far resisted "waging a fearful, a bloody, and a horrid war." Unlike history's innumerable wars "of conquest and ambition," proclaimed a Baptist minister, the Union waged war for loftier reasons and by nobler means. It did not revel in "pride and subjugation of the weak." The minister appealed to his listeners to "compare this war in these respects with any other war of history"—wars waged by Alexander, Xerxes, Alaric, Tamerlane, Napoleon—for, if they did so, they would discover the Union's war was uniquely righteous in its purpose and prosecution, a war waged in "true Washingtonian spirit," the Baptist minister concluded. A New York Presbyterian agreed that the Union's war was "righteous" because it rejected "lust of conquest" and "self-aggrandizement." Another minister insisted that Federals should not wage war "in any spirit of malignant vindictiveness . . . nor for vengeance, nor for any needless destruction."[22] This vindictive, unwarranted destruction defined barbaric wars of the past, ministers proclaimed; the Union's present war, in contrast, had been thus far (and should remain) a war truly Christian and civilized in its aims and means.

Although northern ministers usually did not discuss explicitly the laws of war, or even the intricacies of the Christian just-war tradition, they still advocated a Lieber-style hard yet humane war effort. "We have put up, for seventeen long months," Henry Ward Beecher complained, "with the dilatoriness of conservatism" in the prosecution of the war. But "people have found out that there is no wisdom in conservatism, and that radicalism is what we want," a radicalism that did not spare Confederate civilians, especially their slave property. Another minister agreed, and called for "manly courage, unflinching resolve," in this new hard war. One pastor admitted that this type of war at times might be "dreadful in its nature," yet he insisted it was necessary to preserving a lasting peace and forestalling future suffering and destruction. Continued conciliation, a Philadelphia minister feared, would result only in "the annihilation of all hope of peace till the nation has bled to death." This newly "terrible war" should replace earlier policies of "mistaken tenderness," a New York Presbyterian concluded, because "enduring peace would be simply impossible," if the Confederacy won its independence.[23] Not to wage a hard and vigorous war was to invite greater violence and devastation in the present conflict and in future wars.

Although "severity is beginning to mingle itself with the war," a Baptist minister noted, an element of clemency remained: "It is a war of patience which resents injury—a war of calmness which avenges affronts—a war of forbearance which demands a submission, not to curse but to bless." Wars were "too sad, and too exhausting," another minister argued, for armies to abandon this humanitarian impulse. A New York minister suggested that Union armies fought to advance the Lord's will, since it was "His honor that we are commissioned to vindicate, not our own." Federal soldiers, he concluded, must put away "vengeance" and endeavor instead, while prosecuting the war, to "keep it just."[24]

Many northern ministers also agreed with Lieber that war was not sheer amorality but might well produce positive moral effects. One Presbyterian minister looked to the history of war on the American continent to support this idea. British colonists waged three wars in America—against Native Americans, then the French, and then their British homeland. Out of each victory, the minister insisted, "God has sent a great blessing upon the land"—Christianity over paganism, Protestantism over Catholicism, liberty over tyranny.[25] War, he believed, whatever its horrors, might also preserve and advance American civilization's highest ideals.

Not long after northern pulpits rang out with fast day sermons that pondered the morality of the Union war effort, Ambrose Burnside and his subordinates bungled the battle on the Rappahannock River at Fredericksburg. Delays in crossing the river set Federals at an ominous disadvantage against

Robert E. Lee's hastily secured elevated position. Federals succeeded in crossing the river and wreaking havoc in Fredericksburg, but mismanaged assaults against Lee's army ended in defeat, not to mention the particularly ghastly slaughter of Federals at the base of Marye's Heights. Burnside withdrew his army on 15 December. "The Nation will stand aghast at the terrible price which has been paid," the *New York Times* predicted. No one felt more sorrow and despair than President Lincoln. "If there is a worse place than Hell," he confessed, "I am in it." Nine months earlier, the loyal citizenry hoped soon to celebrate the fall of Richmond and the collapse of the Confederacy. Instead, they now marched toward another year of war—battered, demoralized, and fearful of the uncertain horrors that might lie ahead. "Times are sad—too sad," Lieber wrote his wife after Fredericksburg. "I am one of the very few among those I see who say: Do not give up."[26] When Lieber wrote these words from Washington D.C., he had recently begun work on his code. With one son dead, another wounded, and the Union war effort badly demoralized, a hopeful Lieber endeavored to reconcile the hard hand of war with humane restraint—to set forth in clear and compelling detail rules for an effective vigorously waged war against the Confederacy.

A lifetime of study prepared Lieber to draft the code he completed in late 1862 and early 1863. But the immediate inspiration to do so came from fears that Union officers and military and political leaders inadequately understood the laws of war. During the first eighteen months of the war, Lieber grew concerned about the extent and consequences of this confusion. He watched with worry and frustration as Federals responded to certain dilemmas that arose from the battlefield and that revealed the need for a useable guide to the laws of war. But what exactly were these specific dilemmas, the issues that inspired Lieber to draft the *Instructions for the Government of Armies of the United States in the Field*? Lieber answered this question soon after President Lincoln issued General Orders No. 100. In a letter to Charles Sumner in late May 1863, Lieber sketched the "genesis" of the code:

> The genesis of this little tablet with my name is this: When the war broke out, our government hesitated to exchange prisoners of war fearing that it would amount to an acknowledgement of the rebels. I wrote an article in the Times, to show that this was not the case. At the same time I concluded the lecture on the law of war in the law school. Then came the abuse of flags of truce, the arrogant pretensions of the enemy to lay down absurd rules of the law of war, and then the 'guerrilla'

business and confusion of ideas. Gen Halleck called upon me, after my correspondence with him, to write a pamphlet on guerrillas, which I did. The fearful abuse of paroling, becoming a premium on cowardice, went on. The Harpers Ferry affair happened. At last I wrote to Halleck that he ought to issue a Code on the Law of Nations so far as it relates to the armies in the field. I was approached, and here is the thing.[27]

In this brief paragraph, Lieber candidly explained what compelled him to produce his code. Lieber's writings and correspondence from April 1861 through December 1862 confirm that concerns related to three major issues mentioned in this letter primarily prompted him to lobby for the creation of a useable guide to the laws of war: prisoner exchanges, guerrilla warfare, and the parole.[28]

Leading off Lieber's explanation of the "genesis" of his code was an issue that appeared as soon as the war commenced and became an urgent problem after the First Battle of Bull Run in July 1861: What should Federals do with captured Confederate soldiers? Should the Union exchange prisoners with the Confederacy? The question raised fundamental issues concerning the legal status of the Confederacy and the relevancy of the laws of war to the Union's struggle against the seceding states. Put simply, were Confederates engaged in a *criminal* act of rebellion or a legitimate act of *war*? Were Confederates criminals or enemies? President Lincoln insisted secession was unconstitutional; therefore, the so-called Confederacy was not a legitimate nation. He hoped this argument might in part dissuade foreign powers from intervention on behalf of the Confederacy. However, this seemingly arcane debate about the legal status of the Confederacy affected far more than wartime diplomacy. It also impinged on how the Union would conduct its war against the Confederacy.[29]

If the Confederacy was not a legitimate belligerent, then perhaps Federals did not need to abide by the laws of war in resolving the conflict. Existing criminal law would suffice to subdue the lawbreakers, not the laws of war, which only governed conflict between equally legitimate belligerents. But would Federals really attempt a person-by-person trial, conviction, and punishment of all the lawbreakers in seceding states who had engaged in the illegal act? Surely prudence required Federals to subdue the rebellion in the same way it would deal with any other war, by abiding by the laws of war as it conquered enemy armies and territories. But if the United States adhered to the laws of war might that amount to tacit recognition of the Confederacy as a nation, something the Lincoln administration sought to avoid? The choice before Federals seemed undesirable either way: insist on the illegitimacy of the Confederacy and thereby raise the specter of a conflict waged in disregard of the laws of war, or abide by the restraints imposed by the laws of war and thereby implicitly acknowledge the Confederacy as a legitimate belligerent.[30]

This dilemma moved quickly from the abstract to the concrete soon after the shooting began and the Union captured Confederate soldiers. Lieber tackled the issue in an editorial published in New York newspapers in August 1861. He sought to reassure Union leaders they could have it both ways. They could abide by the humanitarian restraints of the laws of war without thereby extending de facto recognition to the Confederacy as a nation. "The exchange of prisoners involves no question of acknowledgement of right, but is a simple recognition of fact and reality," Lieber argued. Acknowledging the "fact and reality" that these men acted like legitimate soldiers and should be treated as such had no bearing on the status of the Confederacy as a nation. Important reasons might exist for not exchanging prisoners but Union leaders need not worry that exchanges amounted to recognition of the legitimacy of the Confederacy.[31] Writing this editorial first sparked Lieber's interest in a more comprehensive work on the laws of war. When he passed along to Charles Sumner a copy of the editorial, Lieber confessed his "desire to write a little book on the Law and Usages of War, affecting the combatants," a task, Lieber expected, that would require great effort because "nothing of the sort [had] ever been written, so far as I know."[32]

When the "guerrilla business" confronted Federals early in the war, Lieber also sought to bring clarity to the "confusion of ideas" it occasioned. Wherever Federals confronted guerrillas the underlying question remained the same: What exactly distinguished the regular soldier from the unlawful guerrilla? As George Hillard said to Lieber: "It is difficult to say where the regular army ends and the guerrilla band begins." Amid this confusion, Lieber sought to explain why a combatant qualified as a regular soldier instead of an unlawful guerrilla deserving swift punishment as a marauder and murderer. Conventional wisdom held that a commission or enlistment from a legitimate belligerent distinguished the two groups. But during the Civil War, especially following the Confederate Partisan Ranger Act of April 1862, preexisting guerrilla bands newly commissioned by the Confederacy seemed to continue to act as they always had. Their commissions did not change their behavior, so should Federals still treat these enemy bands as unlawful guerrillas?[33]

In late July 1862, Lieber told Henry Halleck he had begun to study "the very important question" of guerrillas and the laws of war. The news pleased Halleck. He agreed it had "now become a very important question in this country," and insisted no one could answer it as well as Lieber. Eager as always for his work to achieve maximum influence, Lieber asked, "Can there be such a thing as being called upon by high authority, by you for instance, or Secretary Stanton, to give my views?" Halleck liked Lieber's suggestion. When Lieber finished the 6,000-plus-word essay *Guerrilla Parties Considered with References to the Laws and Usages of War*, Halleck distributed 5,000 copies to Union officers. Lieber soon received praise for his work. George Hillard complemented Lieber for dealing with the guerrilla problem "as well as it is possible to deal with a subject so essentially vague as that is." Another admirer thought Lieber did "a good work to unmuddle a difficult subject," which meant a Union officer "can now—after a perusal of your tract—talk intelligently on the matter."[34]

Lieber's chief goal was to explain what distinguished someone like John S. Mosby from someone like William C. Quantrill, and how Federals ought to combat both categories of enemies. Mosby commanded a Confederate cavalry battalion infamous for its elusive and effective guerrilla-like strikes on Union forces. Quantrill led a self-organized, loosely affiliated band of guerilla fighters separate from regular Confederate armies, most notoriously known for leading a raid on Lawrence, Kansas in August 1863. In Lieber's parlance, Mosby was a *partisan*, the commander of a regularly constituted force that acted "separate from that of his own main army," most often to attack in "rapid and varying movements" meant to disrupt an enemy's "lines of connection and communication." Still, a partisan like Mosby remained "part and parcel of the army," and deserved the privileges of the laws of war. Quantrill and his force were *guerrillas* proper, "self-constituted sets of armed men . . . who form no integrant part of the organized army." Lieber detailed their defining features: Among other things, they were not on the army payroll, they "take up arms and lay them down at intervals," and generally give no quarter to prisoners. Lieber insisted self-constituted bands of guerrillas deserved none of the privileges afforded to soldiers by the laws of war. But he left officers considerable latitude to decide the proper and effective means for actually subduing guerrillas.[35]

A less obvious inspiration for the code came from the "fearful abuse of paroling." A parole occurred when an army released a captured enemy soldier after he swore never again to take up arms in the present conflict. In the opening year and a half of the war, the Confederacy often paroled large numbers of Union soldiers in the aftermath of battle. Confederates hoped paroling might neutralize Federals' vast manpower advantage and relieve them of the responsibility to imprison and provide for an immense prisoner of war population. Lieber feared paroling posed disastrous consequences for the Union. He advised Charles Sumner in late August 1861 that the government ought "to proclaim that no man, in arms for his country against rebellion, and having taken a solemn oath to that effect, has a right to invalidate that oath by his own parole." Paroled Union soldiers abandoned their solemn pledge to defend the Union. Lieber did not object to the *exchange* of prisoners, but he vehemently opposed paroling. Yet Confederates continued to parole captured Federal soldiers. A particularly prominent example occurred in September 1862, when on the eve of the Battle of Antietam, a Confederate force led by Stonewall Jackson captured the arsenal and garrison at Harpers Ferry. More Federals surrendered there than at any other time in the war. The terms of the surrender, finalized by Maj. Gen. A. P. Hill, paroled more than eleven thousand Union soldiers.[36]

The problem that irked Lieber in August 1861, then, still persisted by the following summer. As late as November 1862, Lieber complained to Halleck of the continued practice of paroling: "Never was a thing in a more deplorable confusion and that the same time in a more disastrous state of expansion." Lieber took a keen interest in ending paroling not simply to forestall any advantage Confederates might gain from it, but because he thought the act violated a soldier's solemn obligations. Lieber believed no soldier had a right to accept a parole and prematurely end his responsibilities to his nation. As he told Charles Sumner, paroling "put a fearful premium on cowardice." Lieber worried some soldiers, knowing the possibility of parole existed, might eagerly surrender, offer themselves up for capture, and soon return home paroled. Lieber suspected the practice continued because of a misunderstanding of the laws of war.[37]

By late fall 1862, all the issues Lieber mentioned in his letter to Sumner had convinced him that Union armies needed a useable guide to the laws of war. Although Lieber had envisioned something like his code since the start of the war, in November 1862 he refused to put off work on it any longer. Lieber suggested to Henry Halleck that President Lincoln "ought to issue a set of rules and definitions . . . in which certain acts and offences (under the laws of war) ought to be defined and, where necessary, the punishment be stated." As he did for the rest of his life, Lieber also insisted on the originality of a document of this kind: "I do not know that any such thing as I design exists in any other country, but in all other countries the Law of War is much more reduced to naked Force or Might, than we are willing to do it, especially now, perhaps, in this Civil War."[38] Federals stood at a crossroads in their war: acquiesce in limitless violence or abide by the laws of war. Halleck initially said he had no time at the moment to consider Lieber's proposal. Eventually, after more pleading from Lieber, a committee was officially formed in mid-December to draft the code. Its members included Maj. Gen. Ethan Allen Hitchcock, commissioner of Prisoner of War Exchange; Maj. Gen. George L. Hartsuff, lately wounded at Antietam; Maj. Gen. George Cadwalader, recent military commander in Maryland; Brig. Gen. John H. Martindale, military governor of Washington, D.C.; and Francis Lieber, the committee's only civilian but the member with the greatest knowledge of the laws of war.

In early December, Lieber traveled to Washington to begin work on the first draft of the code. He completed the work in Washington and New York as a demoralizing chill lingered over the Union war effort. When Lieber finished a first draft in late February he submitted copies to his fellow committee members, key Union political and military leaders, and a handful of prominent loyal citizens for their scrutiny and suggestions. "I have earnestly endeavoured to treat of these grave topics, conscientiously and comprehensively," Lieber wrote to Halleck.[39] The committee did not hesitate to edit Lieber's code on style, organization, and the particular phrasing of certain articles. Halleck also offered substantive suggestions, namely to include sections on the nature of rebellion and civil war and the impermissibility of perfidy. By and large, though, the code survived as Lieber first envisioned it, barring one exception. Lieber wanted to include lengthy notes with the code explaining each article in detail. These notes would have made the code much longer, and perhaps also made specific articles clearer in their practical application, but, ultimately, the notes were not included in the final draft disseminated to Union armies.[40]

On 24 April 1863, President Lincoln officially promulgated the code as General Orders No. 100. Secretary Stanton made plans to distribute 3,000 copies to Union armies. It consisted of 157 articles, many as brief as a sentence or two, that addressed a wide array of topics—from martial law to retaliation to prisoners of war to private property to spies to flags of truce to irregular warfare to armistice and capitulation, among many others. The goal always remained to inform Union soldiers and civilians of the essence of the laws of war. "Our people as well as our army are very ignorant of the laws of war, and required to be educated on the subject," Halleck wrote Lieber soon after the code's promulgation. "I think this is the time and mode for beginning the education."[41]

The Lieber Code and Its Moral Vision of War

General Orders No. 100 contained far more than pithy and practical rules for just conduct. Lieber's code also possessed a distinct moral vision of war. Some people beheld war's manifold evils—the suffering, destroying, hating, and killing it unleashed—and concluded war was wholly immoral. Lieber sought to vindicate just wars from this charge. He tried not simply to show that morality could exist in wars, even in ones vigorous and uncompromising in their prosecution; his code also made an even more provocative claim: "The more vigorously wars are pursued, the better it is for humanity. Sharp wars are brief."[42] The lodestar of the moral vision of Lieber's code was the idea that wars waged in terrible earnest are the *most* humane wars.

Lieber scoffed at overly sentimental restraint in war because he believed mild conciliatory wars only prolonged suffering and destruction. He assumed that the surest way to reduce suffering caused by war was to end it as quickly as possible, and the surest way to end a war as quickly as possible was to wage it with sharp fury. But what if an army succeeded in waging a sharp war and still failed to make it short, only magnifying suffering and destruction? The closest Lieber came to addressing this dangerous possibility was to affirm that even the most vigorously waged wars must abide by certain limits. As the code proclaimed, "Men who take up arms against one another in public war do not cease on this account to be moral beings, responsible to one another and to God."[43] Lieber hoped soldiers would understand that in waging a vigorous war in a just manner they would best fulfill their moral obligations.

Central also to the code's moral vision of war was Lieber's understanding of military necessity. The code defined military necessity as "measures which are indispensable for securing the ends of the war, and which are lawful according to the modern law and usages of war."[44] The two clauses of this definition are equally important; measures taken by an army necessary to achieve its ends must remain authorized by the laws of war. Lieber did not hesitate to describe what military necessity might entail. Armies could destroy all "life or limb of *armed* enemies, and of other persons whose destruction is incidentally *unavoidable*." They could demolish public and private property and essential lines of travel and communication. They could withhold "sustenance or means of life." They could appropriate from the enemy countryside whatever they might need for their "subsistence and safety." Military necessity could compel armies to act in ways that intensified civilian suffering in war. While lamentable, Lieber insisted this was justified. Individual civilians were an inextricable part of a wider whole. The fate of nations and their civilians remained tied together: They "bear, enjoy, and suffer, advance and retrograde together, in peace and in war." Enemy civilians could not expect total protection from war's hardship and devastation.[45]

Lieber's thinking about the nature of military necessity points toward one important way he criticized leading Enlightenment-era authorities on the laws of war, chiefly Emmerich de Vattel, the eighteenth-century Swiss jurist that Lieber mocked as "Father Namby Pamby." Lieber thought Vattel erred in failing to weigh what an army *did* in light of what it aimed to *achieve*, a critical component to assessing properly the limits of military necessity, Lieber assumed. Vattel and other like-minded thinkers divorced means and ends by insisting that the laws of war applied equally to belligerents regardless of their goals. While Lieber did not deny that certain restrictions should apply universally in every war, he was often more inclined to judge the permissibility of means in relation to a warring nation's ends. For this reason, Lieber's writing sometimes seems reminiscent of Carl von Clausewitz, the Prussian military theorist and general. Unlike most mid-nineteenth-century Americans, Lieber read and was influenced by Clausewitz. He embraced Clausewitz's well-known dictum that war is the continuation of politics by other means. "The destruction of the enemy in modern war, and, indeed, modern war itself, are means to obtain that object of the belligerent which lies beyond the war," the code explained. Lieber believed that anyone who followed Vattel and judged the means used by a nation at war apart from that belligerent's ends engaged in a deeply flawed moral evaluation of warfare.[46]

While this way of thinking about means and ends might lead someone to appeal disingenuously to military necessity to justify any heinous action as "indispensable for securing the ends of the war," Lieber did not go to this extreme. His code regretfully noted that ever since war "has come to be acknowledged not to be its own end, but the means to obtain great ends of state . . . no conventional restriction on the modes adopted to injure the enemy is any longer admitted." Lieber could not consent to this rejection of restrictions, because the laws of war still imposed "many limitations and restrictions on principles of justice, faith, and honor."[47] As such, even though the code insisted, "To save the country is paramount to all other considerations," it also identified specific measures *never* justified by military necessity, even under the direst circumstances. Military necessity did not allow armies to inflict suffering "for the sake of suffering or for revenge." It did not allow the use of torture to extort confessions. It did not allow the use of poison "in any way." It forbade the "wanton devastation" of an area and disclaimed all acts of perfidy. The code also suggested that no action pursued in the name of military necessity should undermine the "ultimate object of all modern war . . . a renewed state of peace." Some actions might undermine a lasting peace with a former enemy (such as the assassination of its political leader), which is why the code forbade them.[48] In Lieber's vision of military necessity, even if a warring nation fought to achieve the most righteous of ends, it still had to adhere to certain absolute constraints imposed by the laws of war.

A closer look at the code's 157 articles reveals a fairly comprehensive, albeit abbreviated, guide for justly handling specific issues usually faced in war. One useful way to begin to better understand the code's content, and see how its articles embodied Lieber's moral vision of war, is to recall Lieber's letter to Charles Sumner explaining the code's genesis. The issues Lieber raised in his letter—prisoner exchange, paroling, guerrillas, and flags of truce—also figured prominently in his code.

Lieber devoted five articles to the exchange of prisoners, which he labeled an "act of convenience," not something required of a nation at war. "No belligerent is obliged to exchange prisoners of war," he wrote, but, if they did, Lieber set forth a few key rules to govern the exchanges. Lieber began with a general rule: Exchanges should occur "number for number— rank for rank—wounded for wounded." Then he proceeded to outline exceptions to this rule, for example, instances when a sizeable number of prisoners of lesser rank might be exchanged for a handful of prisoners of greater rank. When the prisoner exchange conundrum confronted the Union early in the war, it did so in the context of questions about the precise legal nature of the Confederacy. Lieber revisited this question, at Halleck's prompting, in nine articles at the code's conclusion. He carefully defined insurrections, civil wars, and rebellions, concluding that the Confederacy constituted a rebellion. As he did earlier in the war, Lieber insisted that treating Confederates according to the laws of war in no way acknowledged the legitimacy of their plainly illegitimate rebellion: "When humanity induces the adoption of the rules of regular war toward rebels, whether the adoption is partial or entire, it does in no way whatever imply a partial or complete acknowledgement of their government, if they have set up one, or of them, as an independent and sovereign power." The United States could continue to treat the Confederacy as it would a normal legitimate belligerent without fearing that doing so somehow "establishes an acknowledgement of the rebellious people."[49]

As for paroling, Lieber insisted that it was "the exception," and release of prisoners by exchange was "the general rule." As with exchanges, a belligerent had no obligation to parole captured enemy soldiers. Those disclaimers aside, when Lieber outlined rules to govern paroling, the events at Harpers Ferry in September 1862 still clearly lingered in his mind. Two of Lieber's strictest rules prohibited paroling on the battlefield and paroling "entire bodies of troops after a battle." Lieber frequently said he opposed paroles because they put a premium on cowardice. He feared the possibility of a parole would tempt soldiers to surrender too quickly. The code tried to prevent this possibility by declaring, "No non-commissioner officer or private can give his parole except through an officer." Commissioned officers themselves could swear parole only after receiving a superior's permission. If Lieber could not have his way completely on the parole issue, he at least sought to ensure as best as possible, through this system of oversight, that the parole did not become a quick crutch of cowardice.[50]

Lieber distilled his *Guerrilla Parties Considered* into five succinct articles on irregular warfare. The code denounced the plunder and marauding of men "without commission, without being part and portion of the organized hostile army, and without sharing continuously in the war." These articles did not depart in any substantive way from the ideas Lieber developed in his earlier essay. They sternly warned that because irregular guerrillas were not soldiers, Federals would treat them "summarily as highway robbers or pirates," the stern fate they deserved.[51]

The "sacred character" of flags of truce made their misuse a grave violation of the laws of war, the code said. The worst abuse occurred when a bearer of a flag used it "for surreptitiously obtaining military knowledge," the work of a spy punishable by death. Even though this abuse remained "an especially heinous offense," the code insisted on showing "great caution" in convicting abusers of a flag of truce as spies. Lieber also attempted to lay down realistic expectations concerning the protections afforded to bearers of flags of truce *during* a battle. A belligerent need not immediately cease a battle if an enemy sent forth a bearer of a flag of truce. If the bearer was killed or wounded, it furnished "no ground of complaint whatever."[52]

Beyond the issues Lieber singled out to Charles Sumner as essential to explaining the genesis of the code, three other topics addressed in the code deserve attention: slavery, the treatment of prisoners of war, and the treatment of an enemy civilian population. The code's articles on these three topics also capture its overarching moral vision of a hard yet humane war.

Lieber matter-of-factly declared that the laws of war did not protect slavery. He had said as much since the beginning of the Civil War. If Union armies intentionally or incidentally destroyed slavery, Confederates had no recourse in the laws of war. Escaped slaves "coming into our lines must be and are by that fact free men," Lieber told Sumner. Similarly, in the late summer of 1862, in his memorandum on African American troops, Lieber again argued that the laws of war acknowledged the "justice of employing the slaves of the enemy, and thereby of course making freedmen of them." The many interpreters of the laws of war hardly spoke with one antislavery voice as Lieber implied. But the code boldly declared otherwise: "The law of nature and nations has never acknowledged [slavery]," which existed only according to "municipal law or local law." Therefore, the code concluded, slaves who "come as a fugitive under the protection" of Union forces are thereby "immediately entitled to the rights and privileges of a freeman."[53] Within the just terms of a hard yet humane war, the Union could strike vigorously against Confederate slavery and thereby undermine its war effort. To Lieber, this was a settled question in the laws of war needing no elaborate explanation. While the code's articles on slavery broke sharply with a long tradition within the laws of war that denounced wartime emancipation as barbaric and unjust, Lieber's chief motivation for drafting the code was not to refashion the laws of war to justify the Union's emancipation-related measures, above all, Lincoln's Emancipation Proclamation.[54] Only two articles in the code explicitly addressed slavery and emancipation, far less than the attention devoted to many other topics, including the treatment of prisoners of war and civilians.

The code's section on the treatment of prisoners of war began with a generous answer to an essential question: Who deserves the protections afforded to prisoners of war? Lieber sought to ensure that no one arguably deserving the laws of war's privileges would fail to receive them. The code explained that a prisoner of war was "a public enemy armed or attached to the hostile army." This included all soldiers and many sorts of citizens usually accompanying armies, especially "sutlers, editors, or reporters of journals, or contractors," as well as the leaders of an enemy government, its diplomatic agents, and anyone else "of particular and singular use and benefit to the hostile army or its government." The code offered a general principle for the humane treatment of such prisoners: Captors must never inflict "any suffering, or disgrace, by cruel imprisonment, want of food, by mutilation, death or any other barbarity." Confinement and imprisonment must never degenerate to "intentional suffering or indignity." In practice this meant that a captor must provide prisoners "plain and wholesome food," and could not plunder prisoners or use violence to extort information from them. An even more heinous violation of the laws of war was "to resolve, in hatred and revenge, to give no quarter" to enemy soldiers.[55] Lieber did not provide a comprehensive list of unjustified actions toward prisoners of war. Instead, he trusted Union army officials to take the general principle he set forth—to avoid the intentional infliction of suffering or indignity—and apply it in particular circumstances.

Recent controversies surrounding African American troops in Union armies shaped many of the articles on prisoners of war. In the section on no quarter, Lieber said Confederates had no right to deny quarter to particular soldiers, especially African Americans. "No belligerent has a right to declare that enemies of a certain class, color, or condition, when properly organized as soldiers, will not be treated by him as public enemies," the code claimed, an implicit condemnation of Confederate promises to treat captured black soldiers as insurrectionary slaves and their white officers as instigators of slave rebellion. The code's declaration that belligerents had no right to treat some men in arms as less than regular soldiers because of "class, color, or condition" was well meaning but also potentially ineffectual. Confederates felt no obligation to abide by this Union-drafted code. Therefore, in the article that followed, Lieber tried to compel Confederate compliance. If Confederates failed to treat captured black Union soldiers as normal prisoners of war, "it would be a case for the severest retaliation" against captured Confederate soldiers, in this case, death.[56]

Retaliation was "the sternest feature of war," the code said, but still on occasion a legitimate measure. Even when justified, Lieber found nothing pleasant in retaliation; a nation ought to resort to it "cautiously," only after all other efforts to remedy the offense failed. Lieber remained wary of retaliation because it made a speedy and lasting return to peace more difficult. "Reckless enemies" often leave an opponent no other way of "securing himself against the repetition of barbarous outrages," but retaliation must occur not for "mere revenge" but for "protective retribution." Still, any belligerent who embraced retaliation should remember that it "removes the belligerents farther and farther from the mitigating rules of a regular war, and by rapid steps leads them nearer to the internecine wars of savages." Retaliation was sometimes necessary, but all things permissible by the laws of war were not always advisable, certainly not as a first recourse. This call for prudence aside, even though Lieber sought to ensure the humane treatment of prisoners of war, he still maintained that captors, if necessary, could subject prisoners to the harsh "infliction of retaliatory measures."[57]

This same hard yet humane spirit also defined the code's articles on the treatment of enemy civilians. Early in the code, Lieber called for sparing civilians from war's hardships as much as possible. In Lieber's retelling, modern warfare did not mark the end of longstanding distinctions between soldiers and civilians. In fact, the opposite occurred. Modern war witnessed the widespread recognition of "the distinction between the private individual belonging to a hostile country and the hostile country itself, with its men in arms." Lieber welcomed this development. Everyone should rejoice that armies no longer "murdered, enslaved, or carried off" enemy civilians. The code insisted "the unarmed citizen is to be spared in person, property, and honor as much as the exigencies of war will admit."[58]

Federal soldiers simply could not commit certain actions against civilians: "wanton violence . . . all destruction of property not commanded by the authorized officer, all robbery, all pillage or sacking, even after taking a place by main force, all rape, wounding, maiming, or killing of such inhabitants." For these and similar crimes, the code authorized severe punishment, in many instances, death. Lieber also affirmed that armies did not have to show the same humane restraint toward all categories of noncombatants. Union officers should distinguish loyal from disloyal civilians in enemy country; moreover, Federals should classify disloyal civilians by those who actively "give positive aid and comfort" to enemy armies and those who do not. Armies should spare loyal citizens as much as possible from "the common misfortune" of war, and instead "throw the burden of war" on disloyal citizens.[59]

Lieber's attempt to shield at least some civilians always came with an important disclaimer: "as much as the exigencies of war will admit." The real challenge remained to balance the humanitarian obligation to protect civilians with the relentless demands of military necessity. While soldiers should never resort to certain actions against civilians—wanton violence, pillage, rape, or maiming—Lieber insisted that military necessity sometimes compelled armies to subject civilians to great hardship and suffering. This was the consequence of "the overruling demands of a vigorous war." For example, while the Union should "acknowledge and protect" private property, its armies could seize it "by way of military necessity, for the support or other benefit of the army."[60] Lieber's justification of subjecting civilians to wars' hardships rested on his larger vision of a moral war. The harsh treatment of civilians sometimes proved necessary to end war as quickly as possible, the most moral and humane thing a belligerent could do. To induce civilian suffering in war was never desirable, Lieber believed, but it might be a harrowing path to the most moral of wars: stern and short.

Lieber's friends and acquaintances sent him many letters of approval and admiration soon after the code's official release. Theodore Dwight Woolsey, president of Yale College, praised the code as "excellently well drawn up." Alexander Dallas Bache, West Point graduate and army engineer turned science professor, appreciated its "plain, terse, and lucid" style. A Union officer who left his legal practice at the war's outbreak considered himself "much instructed and charmed" after reading Lieber's work. Northern newspapers soon reported on the code, though they tended simply only to summarize the essential details of the code's articles, and did not engage in lengthy editorial reflections. George Hillard, Lieber's longtime Boston correspondent, effusively praised the code for its "exhausting fullness" and "ample learning." Hillard also commended its "benignant spirit of humanity and Christianity by which the rigor of war is now tempered and mitigated."[61] The rules and restraints that Lieber codified were partially indebted to the precepts of Christianity, Hillard suggested, namely the faith's basic respect for human life and its abhorrence of violence.

Confederates officials who took note of the code saw nothing Christian in it—no spirit of benign humanity, no attempt to temper war's devastation. They claimed the code offered only a self-serving, immoral justification of a war waged with little restraint. "The enemies of our cause have naturally assailed me furiously," Lieber rightly wrote in June 1863.[62] James A. Seddon, Confederate secretary of war, delivered the closest thing to an official Confederate response in a public letter to Robert Ould, then chiefly responsible for administering prisoner exchanges. Seddon's vitriolic response insisted that the code's ambiguous "military necessity" provision undermined its effort to impose any constraints on Union armies. Seddon lambasted the code as a "confused, unassorted and undiscriminating compilation from the opinion of the publicists of the last two centuries, some of which are obsolete, others repudiated." Furthermore, he thought that while the code's articles supposedly fostered "principles of justice, faith, and honor" in the conduct of war, in reality, given the military necessity articles, it just as easily authorized "conduct correspondent with the warfare of the barbarous hordes who overran the Roman Empire, or who, in the Middle Ages, devastated the continent of Asia and menaced the civilization of Europe." Federals claimed to set forth the rules of civilized warfare, but in reality their rules only unleashed the horrors of barbaric warfare. But the key reason Seddon responded so harshly to Lieber's code was the fact that he adamantly believed Federal soldiers did not abide by the code's articles. The gap between Union army actions and official policies was so great, Seddon claimed, that it rendered Lieber's code a hypocritical sham.[63]

While Lieber did not deny that Federal soldiers sometimes failed to act in accordance with his code, he also cared relatively little about Confederate criticisms of the document. He devoted much more attention to reiterating that the code should attain international influence. "It is a contribution to the state of common civilization," he said soon after the code's issuance. He insisted time and again that the document was without parallel in international law and would likely serve as a model for other nations. Lieber called the code "one of the prominent products of our war." No country had anything of the kind, he said, and in the future it "will be the basis of many." This, Lieber confessed, was "one of my objects in drawing up this code." Ethan Allen Hitchcock, for one, affirmed Lieber's grandest hopes. "The Code must gradually become the law of the civilized world in war—if this is not a contradiction," he wrote to Lieber.[64]

Lieber's code influenced much of the subsequent history of the laws of war and international law. As Lieber hoped, other nations turned to the code to govern the actions of its own armies—beginning as early as 1870 when the Prussian army adopted it in the Franco-Prussian War, and subsequently in military manuals revised by France, Great Britain, Italy, and Spain. The influence of Lieber's path-breaking work appeared also in the major moments of international law throughout the next half-century, from the Brussels Conference of 1874 to the Hague Conventions of 1899 and 1907, and even, if more distantly, the Geneva Convention of 1949. One scholar has rightly called Lieber's code the "Ur-text of the modern laws of war."[65]

Whatever international influence the code eventually achieved, Lieber's work still had a more proximate objective: to instruct Union armies in how to wage a just war. The code appeared in a moment not particularly promising for achieving this goal, a season of bitter disappointment and demoralization that forced northerners to confront the horrifying toll that their war exacted. It was by no means inevitable that in this moment Federals would commit to waging a hard *and humane* war. After all, defeats and setbacks might just as easily have turned Federals toward a war utterly devoid of restraint in which their intractable and hated enemy suffered the full horror of the hard hand of war. What emerged instead was an effort to set forth in clear detail how Union armies might wage war justly in accordance with the laws of war. Lieber marshaled all his intellect and energy to distill the laws of war into a set of rules that earnest and intelligent Federals could understand and follow.

When Union officials distributed General Orders No. 100 in late April 1863, another two years of war awaited—two years of death on a scale once unimaginable, two years full of moments when victory seemed a faint hope. Uncertainties abounded as Federals embarked on the final stage of the war, not least in *how* Union armies would wage war. Would they abide by the spirit and letter of Lieber's code? Could they reconcile hard and humane warfare?

CHAPTER FOUR

The Sternest Feature of War
Retaliation against Confederate Soldiers

Francis Lieber's code labeled retaliation "the sternest feature of war." The laws of war sanctioned retaliation as "protective retribution," punishment meant to prevent an enemy from repeatedly committing atrocities. But Lieber insisted Federals should not resort to retaliatory measures in vengeance or haste.[1] Although the laws of war allowed for retaliation, they did not justify every retaliatory act, so in practice retaliation wavered precariously between just and unjust conduct. When and how to retaliate were some of the more vexing and controversial questions Union officials faced throughout the war. How they handled retaliation-related controversies revealed a great deal about their basic assumptions about the nature of a justly waged war.[2]

Federal political and military leaders were not alone in contemplating the justness of retaliation. It attracted wide attention from the northern citizenry as well, especially after the massacre of African American troops at Fort Pillow in April 1864. Like many northern newspapers in the weeks after the massacre, William Lloyd Garrison's *The Liberator* condemned the Confederate atrocity and mused at length over how the Union should respond. Some northerners called for retaliation *in kind*, the execution of an equal number of Confederate prisoners of war, but *The Liberator* did not. "Every fair-minded man must concede that retaliation for such barbarities would be an act of justice," Garrison's newspaper granted, "but there are many grave objections in the way of it."[3]

What were these grave objections, these reasons for restraint? Retaliation in kind stood contrary to "our civilization, our self-respect," the *Liberator* argued. It violated the moral values that supposedly defined the Union as an exceptionally free and enlightened civilization. Although technically justified by the laws of war, retaliation no longer stood "in consonance with an enlightened age and country." America would tarnish its international reputation if it pursued formal retaliation, which remained "terrible in the eyes of the world." Federals should remember "the perpetrators stand low in the scale of civilization" and retaliation in kind merely imitated their unjustified "barbarism." To these moral considerations, *The Liberator* added the practical one that retaliation would not end Confederate atrocities but only spur "counter retaliation" and more "cold blooded slaughter." While the Union had a sacred obligation to protect African American soldiers, *The Liberator* concluded retaliation in kind did not fulfill that obligation in a moral and effective manner.[4]

Many key members of the Lincoln administration, U.S. Congress, and Union army also shared Francis Lieber's view of retaliation as war's sternest feature. Like him, they believed the laws of war justified retaliation as sometimes necessary. But they remained wary of resorting to it too quickly, and to support their views these Union leaders appealed not only to the laws of war but also to the moral demands of Christianity, the so-called enlightened values that distinguished civilized societies, and retaliation's mixed record in actually altering Confederate behavior. This is not to suggest that Federals *never* authorized retaliatory acts contrary to the spirit of the Lieber code. However, the Union political and military leaders most intimately involved in major retaliation-related controversies tended to reject systematic retaliation in kind as official policy. Even as these Union officials refused to do away entirely with retaliation, they also largely resisted resorting to it in an indiscriminate and extreme manner. Ultimately, their attitudes toward retaliation embodied the same hard yet humane spirit that many Federals assumed made for a justly waged war.[5]

To see this vision of just war in action requires examining in close detail not only instances of retaliation carried out as threatened; important also are moments when Federals debated and decided against retaliatory measures, as well as occasions when they partially implemented threatened retaliations. In the final two years of the war a significant number of retaliatory episodes occurred that fell roughly into one of these three categories. What follows is not a comprehensive account of these episodes but a detailed study of the more important and revealing ones. These particular episodes drew close attention from leading Union military and political officials. They lasted for fairly prolonged periods of times, often several months or more, and therefore were not easily resolved. Perhaps most importantly, they spurred explicit reflections on retaliation's place in a justly waged war. Historians have pointed to some of these episodes as proof of the Union's ominous formal embrace of a vicious policy of retaliation in kind. In fact, careful attention to how these episodes unfolded and ended suggests the opposite. While Federal leaders hardly rejected retaliation outright, they also imposed restraints on its implementation in an effort to wage a hard yet humane war.[6]

Common Arguments against Retaliation in Kind

Federals hesitant to support retaliation in kind marshaled a wide array of arguments, as William Lloyd Garrison did after the Fort Pillow massacre. These arguments appeared frequently throughout the major retaliation controversies, even though the circumstances surrounding each controversy varied significantly. The most common argument denounced retaliation in kind as a mode of warfare unchristian and uncivilized, and therefore antithetical to the values that defined America. "*Retaliation in kind* belongs to savages," one New Yorker wrote, and was "shocking to every Christian sentiment and . . . cultured people." Garrison's *The Liberator* agreed that if Americans ("who call ourselves Christians") resorted to retaliation in kind they would in effect "return to that Jewish law which Christ denounced and superseded eighteen hundred years ago, and begin a course of infliction of burning for burning, wound for wound, stripe for stripe." Even worse was pursuing retaliation only to satisfy base desires for vengeance. Charles Sumner believed that if retaliation "proceeded from vengeance alone" it would "degrade the national character and the national name." Abraham Lincoln affirmed the same point to Edwin Stanton after the Fort Pillow massacre: "Blood cannot restore blood, and government should not act for revenge." Retaliation for revenge's sake stoked what the *New York Herald* labeled "all the worst passions and . . . brutal propensities" in a people at war. It also stood at odds with retaliation's legitimate purpose as a way to compel just conduct from an enemy.[7]

A related argument insisted that even though Confederates committed atrocities, Federals should not do so in return. Nothing good could come from imitating barbaric behavior. *Harper's Weekly* made this argument with a revealing comparison in early January 1865: "If we were at war with cannibals who ate alive the prisoners whom they took from our armies, we could not retaliate in kind. If we were fighting Indians who burned their captives at the stake, we could not retaliate in kind. We are at war with men whom the long habit of enslaving other men has imbruted and barbarized," therefore Federals must not resort to savage Confederate tactics. The *Army and Navy Journal* put the matter even more bluntly. Union officers in charge of prisoner of war camps who imitated Confederate mistreatment of prisoners "would be scorned as unfit to associate with gentlemen."[8]

Retaliation in kind might also betray the best of what the Union embodied in the minds of loyal citizens as an enlightened Christian civilization in the moral vanguard of human history. For that reason, many Federals feared certain acts of retaliation would tarnish America's international standing. When John B. Henderson, U.S. senator from Missouri, argued in early 1865 against retaliatory measures that would have subjected Confederate prisoners to near-starvation, he asked his Senate colleagues: "Do we, by it, do anything else than disgrace ourselves in the eyes of the civilized world?" A Boston newspaper agreed midway through the war that "measures of retaliation are justly looked upon with so much suspicion by the world at large . . . [for] the result is so shocking to our humane feelings."[9]

Federals also opposed retaliation because of practical concerns about its effectiveness. Some like the *New York Times* assumed Confederates would never abandon unjust atrocities: "Are we to wait for these people to change their disposition? Absurd. They cannot change." In fact, according to this argument, retaliation usually spurred only counterretaliation and greater bloodshed. This possibility weighed heavily on Lincoln's mind as he resisted calls to retaliate in kind for Fort Pillow. Frederick Douglass recalled Lincoln saying retaliation was a "terrible remedy, and one which it was very difficult to apply," adding that there was "no telling where it would end."[10] Lincoln assumed that if retaliation would not likely achieve its stated end—compelling one's enemy to alter an unjust behavior—then a civilized belligerent had no legitimate reason to retaliate.

Some argued that retaliation unfairly punished Confederates not guilty of a particular atrocity. As Indiana's Democratic senator Thomas A. Hendricks argued, in opposition to a proposed retaliation measure against Confederate prisoners, "Reach the men that are in fault, strike them if we can; but where is the propriety, where is the Christianity of starving a man to death against whom we can lay no fault except that perhaps he has been compelled to obey the demands of the rebel government?" Hendricks assumed the South's slaveholding elite had compelled Confederate soldiers to take up arms; therefore, the soldiers should not endure extreme Federal retaliation. An Ohioan opposed to the same retaliatory measure similarly asked Charles Sumner: "[W]hy inflict upon those we have in our power who are not responsible for the cruel treatment of our soldiers the very wrongs of which our friends in Southern prisons complain?" Some Federals also worried that too much retaliation undermined the Union's ultimate goal of a just and lasting peace. Senator Hendricks reminded his colleagues that Federals ought to adhere strictly to the laws of war "so that when the war is over there may be mutual respect and confidence, that the ancient relations of commerce and trade may return unimpaired ... [and] make us once more one Government and one people with one destiny."[11]

Despite all these arguments, most Federal political and military leaders believed retaliation sometimes remained a just and effective response to Confederate atrocities. Henry Halleck thought "summary retaliation" was necessary if Confederates continued to act in "deliberate and systematic violation of the usages of civilized warfare." As *Harper's Weekly* put it, "Reprisals and retaliation are a legitimate method of war." Although Francis Lieber worried about its misuse, he still argued that certain circumstances warranted retaliation. After all, Lieber believed, Confederates acted with "callous cruelty and fiendish ferocity," rejecting all conventional rules of warfare and instead embracing mere "moral madness."[12] Yet Lieber still insisted that even in a war against an enemy driven to "moral madness," the Union must not resort to retaliation in careless haste or vengeance.

Lieber's code justified retaliation only as a method of protecting against "the repetition of barbarous outrage." When a belligerent fought a "reckless enemy," sometimes retaliation alone prevented atrocities. This meant retaliation could not proceed for "mere revenge," but only for "protective retribution." Even then, Federals should resort to retaliatory measures "cautiously and unavoidably," after a careful inquiry into the "character of the misdeeds that may demand retribution" and after all other options to forestall the repeated misdeeds failed. Lieber vehemently disagreed with northerners who deemed retaliation unjust because it punished an innocent person for someone else's offense. "Retaliation is no punishment for a crime committed by the victim," he explained to Halleck, who hardly needed the lesson on the laws of war. Instead, retaliation was "a measure of defense and repression in which the opposite party is treated as a unit, as in all international affairs." A just retaliation did not seek punishment for a particular crime; instead, it remained an act of "protective retribution" against an enemy, a means of preventing further atrocities. This grim fact disheartened Lieber: "It is this very thing which makes retaliation so awful." Lieber did not explain in his code exactly what form retaliation could take, but he believed it "must have its limits in simple death."[13] Northerners who called for retaliation in kind in the form of near-starvation or exposure failed to abide by the laws of war.

Lieber acknowledged that retaliation, once begun, could quickly unleash a vicious cycle of counterretaliation. "If one belligerent hangs ten men for one," he wrote to Halleck, "the other will hang ten times ten for the ten, and what a dread geometrical progression of skulls and cross bones we would have!"[14] Or, as Lieber said in his code, even justified retaliation leads "nearer to the internecine wars of savages." This made permanent peace with a former enemy all the more difficult. Lieber believed the only way to avoid the bloody arithmetic of savage warfare was to adhere closely to the rules he set forth in General Orders No. 100: Retaliate only to prevent "the repetition of barbarous outrage," and, even then, do so cautiously as a last resort. If Confederates subjected Union soldiers to "barbarous outrages," the challenge for Federals was deciding when and how to retaliate. In the war's final year, Federals were often confronted with this question. Each time, the central problem remained the same: Could Federals reconcile wariness over retaliation in kind with a zealous commitment to protecting Union troops?

Retaliation for Atrocities against African American Soldiers

Confederate atrocities against African American soldiers certainly confronted Union officials with this dilemma. Rebels refused to grant African Americans, especially former slaves, the full rights and protections of legitimate soldiers. On many notorious occasions, Confederates committed heinous atrocities against black troops. Some historians have castigated the Lincoln administration for its seemingly lackluster response to these atrocities. As one concluded, "Lincoln and his generals took no concrete action to stop the slaughter of their black soldiers," even though Union officials often quickly retaliated in response to atrocities against white soldiers. According to this argument, Federal officials (whether inspired by sinister racism or coldhearted political calculations) responded to atrocities against black troops with tepid threats but no substantive action.[15] This is true in part. The most infamous atrocity against black troops, at Fort Pillow, did not ultimately elicit a retaliatory response from the Lincoln administration. Yet Lincoln and other Federal officials responded to these atrocities not out of racist indifference but in keeping with their generally cautious attitude toward retaliation. Even as these Union leaders insisted on equal protections for African Americans in uniform, their deeply ingrained wariness over ineffective retaliation tempered their reprisals to atrocities against black soldiers.

Soon after the war began, Federal officials faced the question of how exactly, if at all, they would employ African Americans in Union armies. As Federals advanced into the Confederacy and crippled the institution of slavery, escaped former slaves increasingly contributed to the work of the Union military. In Memphis, for example, William T. Sherman employed escaped slaves in noncombat roles such as rebuilding the city's fortifications; outside New Orleans, John W. Phelps, without authorization, unsuccessfully tried to organize fugitive slaves into new army companies. Soon after President Lincoln issued the Emancipation Proclamation, Federals moved toward enlisting black soldiers in Union armies. By May 1863, the War Department established the Bureau of Colored Troops to organize these new black regiments. All told, nearly 180,000 African American soldiers served in Union forces by the war's end.[16]

Confederates looked upon these tens of thousands of African American men in uniform as proof of the radicalism and barbarity of the Union war effort. Confederate secretary of war James A. Seddon denounced the enlistment of former slaves as "an abandonment of the rules of civilized warfare," for it amounted to inciting "servile insurrection." Confederate officials warned they would not recognize black Union troops as legitimate enemy soldiers. In May 1863 the Confederate Congress passed a resolution threatening to even execute captured white officers commanding African American soldiers.[17]

President Lincoln insisted the "law of nations and the usages and customs of war as carried on by civilized powers, permit no distinction as to color in the treatment of prisoners of war as public enemies." If Confederates treated black Union troops as anything less than legitimate soldiers they would simply "relapse into barbarism." Lincoln's June 1863 "Order of Retaliation" warned that for every Union soldier, regardless of color, "killed in violation of the laws of war," Federals would in kind execute a Confederate soldier. For every Union soldier "enslaved by the enemy or sold into slavery," Federals would place a Confederate soldier "at hard labor on the public works" until the Union soldier was released.[18]

The coming months tested Lincoln's resolve in fulfilling these threats, but he was not alone in professing his commitment to protecting black Union soldiers from Confederate atrocities. Francis Lieber similarly thought Federal officials had a solemn obligation to guarantee African Americans received the same rights and privileges afforded white soldiers. "If we lead [black troops] into battle and even place them in its path, and then permit them to be butchered when captured and held as prisoners, the world will fully denounce our conduct as both criminal and cowardly," Lieber wrote to Joseph Holt not long after Lincoln issued his retaliation order. Federals ought to respond to the murder of captured or surrendered black soldiers with "instantaneous and unsparing" retaliation. *Harper's Weekly* also called on Union officials to compel from "the rebel ringleaders an explicit guarantee of the same treatment that all our soldiers in their hands receive," otherwise African Americans would soon realize the foolishness in fighting "for a flag which does not protect [them]." The Union should respond with "swift, sure, and deadly" retaliation for atrocities against black troops, *Harper's Weekly* declared. If Federal officials failed to protect African American soldiers, then the Union was "simply unworthy of success."[19]

Not long after the enlistment of black soldiers in Union armies came grim occasions for Federal leaders to prove their worthiness of success. From the summer of 1863 onward, Confederates committed repeated atrocities against African American troops, at places such as Milliken's Bend, Olustee, and Poison Spring. These events followed a terribly familiar script. After a relatively small-scale engagement, Confederates gave no quarter to black soldiers, killing many as they surrendered or soon after. Confusion sometimes shrouded these instances of no quarter, so Federals often responded as Ulysses S. Grant did after reports of the murder of black soldiers at Milliken's Bend. He warned Confederate Maj. Gen. Richard Taylor that because "colored troops are regularly mustered into the service of the United States," Confederates had to offer "the same protection to these troops that they do to any other troops." Still, no formal retaliation followed. By the spring of 1864, despite warnings from Federals, the atrocities continued. They not only called into question the power of Union leaders to protect their troops, but also seemingly confirmed, in Lieber's words, that Confederates had abandoned "the track of common justice, fairness and honor."[20]

The most infamous atrocity occurred on 12 April 1864, when Confederates commanded by Nathan Bedford Forrest captured Fort Pillow. The fort sat on a bluff in Tennessee along the Mississippi River roughly forty miles north of Memphis. In the aftermath of the fort's fall, Forrest's men massacred part of the Federal garrison, comprised in substantial part of African American soldiers. Confederates killed well over two hundred Federal soldiers, white and black, after they surrendered. President Lincoln had promised one year prior to retaliate each time Confederates killed a

Federal soldiers, regardless of his race, "in violation of the laws of war." Now it came time to see if he would fulfill his threat.[21]

Lincoln first publicly commented on the massacre less than one week later in an address at a Sanitary Fair in Baltimore. He reaffirmed his commitment to protecting black troops from Confederate atrocities. The Union resolved "to use the negro as a soldier," Lincoln declared, so it must ensure they received "all the protection given to any other soldier." This obligation weighed heavily on Lincoln: "I am responsible for it to the American people, to the Christian world, to history, and on my final account to God." Yet the responsibility to guarantee equal protection for black soldiers was easily acknowledged but not easily fulfilled. "The difficulty is not in stating the principle, but in practically applying it," Lincoln said. For the time being, Lincoln resisted an immediate reaction. "We do not to-day *know* that a colored soldier, or white officer commanding colored soldiers, has been massacred by the rebels when made a prisoner. We fear it, believe it, I may say, but we do not *know* it," Lincoln reminded his audience. He confessed he believed the rumors but still needed to thoroughly investigate them before responding. "To take the life of one of their prisoners, on the assumption that they murder ours, when it is short of certainty that they do murder ours, might be too serious, too cruel a mistake," Lincoln said. Once Federals "conclusively proved" the massacre, it would remain "a matter of grave consideration in what exact course to apply the retribution." Still, Lincoln promised retaliation "must come."[22]

Northern newspapers denounced Confederates for the savagery at Fort Pillow. Many also insisted on equal protection for black soldiers and did not hesitate to opine on the "grave consideration" of how to respond to the atrocity. *Frank Leslie's Illustrated Newspaper* condemned the massacre as "savage in conception, savage in execution, and savage in its bold endorsement by the rebels." The *Christian Advocate and Journal*, a leading Methodist publication, denounced the atrocity as "the work of absolute demons," while the *New York Times* labeled it "Devilish Atrocities of the Insatiate Fiends." The *Chicago Tribune* predicted news of the atrocity would shock "the whole civilized world." Other newspapers likewise assumed Confederates had resorted to the savage tactics. The *New York Herald* called the incident "one more step in [the Confederacy's] degeneration towards mere barbarity... The Chinese and the Sepoys have become the chosen models of Southern men." *Harper's Weekly* concluded the "annals of savage warfare nowhere record a more inhuman, fiendish butchery."[23]

These same northern newspapers also advised the Lincoln administration on how it should respond to the atrocity, even though their proposals lacked specificity and did not really grapple with the problem in all its complexity. *Harper's Weekly* admitted the question before the Lincoln administration was a difficult one. While the Union utterly refused "to allow its soldiers to be butchered in cold blood," *Harper's Weekly* acknowledged it "is not easy to say" exactly how best to retaliate. The magazine avoided offering a specific solution other than to declare, "Let the action of the Government be as prompt and terrible as it will be final." The *Chicago Tribune* insisted that unless Confederate officials immediately disavowed the massacre, the Union ought to resort to "retaliation *in the same circumstances and of the same kind.*" This meant, simply, "what the rebels do to black men wearing our uniform, we will do to white ones wearing theirs." But not all newspapers called for immediate retaliation in kind. After all, it was in this moment that Garrison's *Liberator* set forth its "many grave objections" to it. The *New York Times* warned that if Federals did not do all within their power to prevent future atrocities against black soldiers, "Heaven and history will hold us responsible." But it also remained wary of true retaliation in kind: "It would certainly be very hard for us either to counsel or to witness the execution in cold blood of this number of Confederate prisoners who have had no share in this bloody deed." While these prisoners were "technically answerable" before the laws of war for the massacre at Fort Pillow, the *New York Times* deemed their retaliatory execution "something which no Christian man at the North likes to face, if it can possibly be avoided." The execution of "Forrest's butchers," however, would bring "intense satisfaction," the newspaper confessed.[24]

The most vigorous initial response to the Fort Pillow massacre came not from northern newspapers but from the congressional Joint Committee on the Conduct of the War. Nearly as soon as word reached Washington, D.C., of what happened at Fort Pillow, Radical Republicans set in motion plans for a formal investigation, which Congress eventually authorized. Senator Benjamin F. Wade of Ohio and Representative Daniel Gooch of Massachusetts conducted the investigation, interviewing several dozen witnesses and survivors. Wade, Gooch, and other like-minded Republicans in Congress saw in the investigation an opportunity to demonstrate again that the slaveholding South desperately needed a radical reconstruction after Union victory. Without it, they warned, horrors unimaginable—far worse even than Fort Pillow—would inevitably follow.[25]

The committee's eventual report intentionally attempted to generate anger toward the barbarities of slaveholding society. The report contained infamous and incendiary stories of the atrocities committed by Forrest's men. Some within the Union high command looked with skepticism on the report, certain it contained misleading exaggerations. The committee insisted its investigation definitively proved that what occurred at Fort Pillow was "cruelty and murder without a parallel in civilized warfare, which needed but the tomahawk and scalping-knife to exceed the worst atrocities ever committed by savages." Confederates perpetrated nothing less than "indiscriminate slaughter."[26]

The responsibility of deciding how to respond to the atrocity still rested with President Lincoln alone. In early May, he turned to his cabinet for advice. He received written opinions from six senior cabinet members: Edward Bates, Montgomery Blair, Salmon Chase, William Seward, Edwin Stanton, and Gideon Welles. Wells likely spoke for the entire cabinet when he confided in his diary the difficulty of answering Lincoln's request. He doubted he could ever reach a firm conclusion "on so grave and important a question": "The policy of killing negro soldiers after they have surrendered must not be permitted . . . But how is this to be done?"[27]

The cabinet members tentatively proposed possible courses of action, some more stern or specific or practical than others. But everyone agreed on two important points, both contained also in the Lieber code. First, they all affirmed that the Union had an inviolable obligation to protect its troops, white and black alike. To fail to fulfill this obligation "would be a crime and a national dishonor," as Bates wrote. For this reason, everyone assumed some sort of retaliatory punishment should eventually occur, either against the Confederates guilty of the atrocities or against randomly chosen captured rebel soldiers. Stanton believed a formal response was necessary "to compel the rebels to observe the laws of civilized warfare." Bates agreed, and reiterated that any retaliation must occur for "the sole purposes of punishing past crimes and of giving a salutary and blood-saving warning against its repetition."[28]

Second, the cabinet members all opposed resorting to retaliation *in kind* in response to Fort Pillow. They ultimately agreed with the Lieber code that retaliation in kind, while often justified and necessary, was not always effective, rarely desirable, and ought to be used cautiously, as a last resort. Blair believed retaliation in kind in this instance "would not be just in itself or expedient." Bates likewise wrote that the Fort Pillow controversy presented

"not a question of law, but questions of prudence," because the "consequences" of resorting to retaliation in kind tended to be "so terrible, in their
results." Seward similarly advised Lincoln to act "with prudence and frank-
ness as well as with firmness."[29]

On 17 May, Lincoln informed Confederate officials they had until 1 July
to offer an ironclad assurance that a massacre like the one at Fort Pillow
would never again occur, and that captured Union soldiers of all races would
always be treated "according to the laws of war." If Confederates failed to offer such assurances, formal retaliation for Fort Pillow would follow.[30] The
first of July came and went. Confederate officials offered no promises as demanded, and Lincoln did not carry out the threatened retaliation.

Lincoln and his cabinet largely agreed that the decision of whether to retaliate was a choice between two evils. Should they retaliate and potentially
unleash a vicious cycle of counterretaliations? Or should they not retaliate
and fail to protect Union soldiers by avenging Confederate atrocities? Lincoln believed African American troops deserved the same rights and protections that white soldiers received. Yet he also assumed, like Lieber, that
retaliation was not always prudent or wise, even when justified. Lincoln suspected that retaliation in this instance would not accomplish what legitimate retaliations had to likely accomplish: to compel a belligerent to abide
by rules of warfare it had disregarded. Having assumed that Confederates
would never accept African Americans as legitimate enemy soldiers, and
that no amount of retaliation likely would convince them otherwise, Lincoln saw the dilemma before him largely as one of effectiveness: If retaliation
for Fort Pillow would not alter Confederates' behavior, and in fact might
only spur them to commit greater atrocities against black soldiers, why should
the Union retaliate?

The Union's May 1864 Retaliatory Ration Reduction

If atrocities against African American soldiers spurred talk of retaliation, so
too did Confederate treatment of white Union prisoners of war. As news of
the Fort Pillow massacre spread across the North, tensions had escalated for
nearly seven months over the conditions of prisoner of war camps in Virginia,
especially in and near Richmond. The diseased and decimated bodies of
Union prisoners in these camps infuriated northerners and appeared to
prove that captured soldiers endured malicious maltreatment at the hands
of Confederates. In late May 1864, Federal authorities officially reduced the

rations provided to Confederate prisoners of war. Some historians have pointed to the action as a coldhearted retaliatory response to perceived mistreatment of Union prisoners.[31] In fact, this reduction in rations was not as extreme as some historians have suggested. Neither did it mark an ominous turn toward a war defined by vicious and vengeful retaliation. Given the seven-months-long conflict with Confederate officials over the treatment of Federal prisoners near Richmond, not to mention the bitter passions sparked by reports of the suffering endured by captured Union soldiers, the ration reduction of May 1864 was surprisingly minimal. In light of all that northerners believed had happened to their captured troops, Federals officials might easily have resorted to a far more drastic response.

In late October 1863, almost two hundred sick and wounded Union prisoners arrived from City Point, Virginia, to Camp Parole in Annapolis, Maryland. William Hoffman, the Union's commissary general of prisoners, received word from an officer at Camp Parole that the Federal soldiers arrived "in a pitiable condition of mind and body, having experienced extreme suffering from a want (apparently) of proper food," which left them reduced to "invalids." When Ethan Allen Hitchcock, then still the Union's commissioner for the exchange of prisoners, learned of the condition of these former prisoners of war, he demanded an explanation from Robert Ould, his Confederate counterpart. Hitchcock inquired specifically about the precise rations provided to Union prisoners and subtly threatened that Ould's reply would guide Federal authorities "when the question of retaliation shall be forced." Yet Hitchcock initially advised Edwin Stanton not to retaliate in kind immediately against Confederate prisoners, if for no other reason than that "it would result in an uprising of the prisoners against their guards . . . Human nature would not endure such treatment."[32]

Union officials collected more information about the conditions of Confederate prisons in the Richmond area. At the same time, northern newspapers began denouncing the treatment of prisoners there as unchristian and uncivilized. A delegate from the U.S. Christian Commission who visited the camps told Hitchcock that Federal soldiers lived in conditions "in the highest degree uncomfortable and threatening to their health." He feared thousands would soon die of disease, and pleaded with Hitchcock and the Union government to "do something for humanity's sake." A Connecticut chaplain who temporarily visited the same prisons likewise informed Hoffman that the Belle Isle prison was "a perfect slaughter pen" which reduced soldiers "to such weakness and exhaustion as would unfit them for military service."[33]

After reporting on the conditions of these camps, the *New York Times* lamented the terrible fates of the "woe-begone, miserable, starving men" trapped there. "They were starved to the verge of the grave," the newspaper insisted, "and what was left of them was nearly devoured by vermin." The paper concluded that Confederate "diabolism will never abate as long as it is in their power to exercise it," for slaveholders were "reared to cruelty." The *Christian Advocate and Journal* condemned Confederates for working "deliberately to kill or ruin the constitution of every prisoner . . . Our brave soldiers who fell into the hands of these barbarians were killed by inches, starved to death." *Harper's Weekly* concluded that Confederate behavior belonged to an earlier age of uncivilized warfare in which belligerents "drag [prisoners] away to starve in loathsome dungeons."[34] Still, many northern newspapers also called for a restrained response. The *Chicago Tribune* thought Confederate treatment of prisoners would "shine in hellish lustre at the inverted pinnacle of man's inhumanities," but it also rejoiced that the Lincoln administration had not resorted to "swift and instant retaliation in kind." Doing so would only "increase the odium these acts of [Confederates] must bring them in all coming time." The *New York Herald* hoped the Union's prosecution of the war would "remain Christian in spite of every provocation." The *New York Times* also called upon Union leaders "not to treat [Confederate] prisoners as our prisoners have been treated by them—though this would be in strict accord with the laws of war."[35]

Union officials faced the difficult task of reducing the suffering of Federal prisoners without imitating what they deemed unjustifiably cruel actions by Confederates. Ethan Allen Hitchcock and his subordinates did not hastily resort to retaliation in kind against Confederate prisoners. Instead, they first tried to provide prisoners in Richmond with additional provisions donated by northerners, and then tried to secure their exchange.

The United States Christian Commission had earlier sent food and other provisions to Federal prisoners in Richmond. In mid-November, Hitchcock directed Sullivan Meredith, a commissioner for prisoner exchanges, to ensure that the provisions actually made it to imprisoned Union soldiers. Hitchcock told Robert Ould that in giving this task to Meredith he sought only "to relieve our prisoners from suffering inflicted upon them contrary to the claims of both humanity and the laws of war."[36] Ould did not yet block northerners' efforts to provide additional provisions to their soldiers, but he denied the "infamously false" rumors about the condition of Richmond prisons. "We recognize in the fullest form our obligation to treat your prisoners with humanity and to serve them with the same food in quantity and quality as is given to our own soldiers," Ould wrote. Hitchcock thought the emaciated bodies arriving at Camp Parole discredited Ould's promises.[37]

Meanwhile, Hitchcock also publicly explained to the loyal citizenry why Union authorities acted as they had thus far to protect captured prisoners in Richmond. In a letter published in early December in the *New York Times* and other northern newspapers, Hitchcock addressed a pressing question on the minds of many northerners: Federal prisoners in Richmond endured "extreme sufferings . . . contrary to the usages of war and the dictates of humanity," so why were they not *exchanged*? The first and most important reason, Hitchcock argued, was that Confederates stubbornly refused to recognize African American troops as legitimate soldiers deserving all the rights and protections afforded by "the laws of civilized warfare." To engage in large-scale prisoner exchanges with Confederates who denied the legitimacy of black troops "would manifest the most stupid blindness on our part," Hitchcock continued, because it would undermine the Union's "most solemn obligation" to protect all its soldiers.[38] Moreover, the Union currently held nearly 40,000 prisoners, while the Confederacy held around 13,000. This imbalance also complicated any attempt to negotiate an exchange. Robert Ould suggested that the two sides formally exchange the same number of prisoners and also *parole* the remaining captured Confederates. Hitchcock scoffed at this proposition; he rightly assumed some of the paroled rebels would soon rejoin Confederate armies. In late November, Meredith attempted to convince Ould to exchange 12,000 prisoners, but Ould still demanded the parole of the remaining rebel prisoners. Hitchcock did not want to risk allowing tens of thousands of paroled soldiers to rejoin Confederate armies because doing so would ignore a fundamental fact about the war: "This rebellion is to be put down by organized armies in the field."[39]

Hitchcock worked to alleviate captured Federal soldiers' suffering by providing additional provisions and securing their exchange because he remained hesitant to resort to retaliation in kind. But by mid-December, even the effort to supply Federal prisoners with additional provisions turned futile. Ould forbade prisoners in Richmond from receiving food and clothing from the North on account of the "misconstruction and misrepresentation . . . much vilification and abuse," concerning Confederate treatment of prisoners. Ould's action seemingly made more likely a promise Stanton made to Lincoln several days earlier: "If it should become necessary for the protection of our men, strict retaliation will be resorted to."[40] After a winter of failed attempts to negotiate an exchange of prisoners, another round of nearly four hundred recently paroled prisoners arrived to Camp Parole in May 1864. The long-simmering controversy erupted again. As Walt Whitman looked upon these soldiers he wondered, "Can these be *men* . . . these little, livid brown, ash-streaked, monkey-looking dwarfs? Are they really not mummied dwindled corpses?" On orders from Stanton, William Hoffman traveled to Maryland to report on the soldiers' condition, which he described as "a very sad plight, mentally and physically." The men appeared "wasted to mere skeletons . . . and dispirited by their many privations." Hoffman recommended "retaliatory measures be at once instituted" by subjecting captured Confederate officers to "a similar treatment."[41]

Stanton passed along Hoffman's report to Ohio senator Benjamin F. Wade, chairman of the Joint Committee on the Conduct of the War. "The enormity of the crime committed by the rebels toward our prisoners . . . cannot but fill with horror the civilized world," Stanton wrote to Wade. "There appears to have been a deliberate system of savage and barbarous treatment and starvation."[42] As Wade's congressional committee completed its report on the Fort Pillow atrocity, it also launched an investigation into the treatment of captured Federal soldiers by Confederates. Eventually, the committee published the two reports together as evidence of Confederate barbarity and the wisdom of Radical Republican plans to remake the South. The report on the treatment of prisoners of war contained lengthy interviews with former prisoners, all confirming that Confederates "deliberately and persistently" mistreated Federal soldiers in a manner "which no language we can use can adequately describe." The prison camps' shanty dwellings and meager rations were intended "to reduce our soldiers in their power . . . that those who may survive shall never recover so as to be able to render any effective service in the field."[43] The report also contained some of the most infamous images of the war, recently released prisoners who looked like Whitman's "mummied dwindled corpses." *Harper's Weekly* reprinted these images as proof of "the work of desperate and infuriated men whose human instincts have become imbruted by the constant habit of outraging humanity."[44]

When in late May Union officials decided to reduce the rations provided to Confederate prisoners, they did so not as a rash response to a congressional report and the public outrage it inspired. The reduction instead marked the culmination of a nearly seven-months-long conflict with Confederates over the treatment of captured Federals in the Richmond area. It was a final attempt to compel better treatment for captured Union soldiers. A close look at the extent of this reduction in rations reveals a surprisingly modest change given all that Federals believed about the supposedly barbaric treatment of Union prisoners.

William Hoffman, as commissary-general of prisoners, took the lead in establishing official prisoner rations. In late April 1864, those rations were: "Hard bread, 14 ounces per one ration, or 18 ounces soft bread, one ration; corn-meal, 18 ounces per one ration; beef 14 ounces per one ration; bacon or pork, 10 ounces per one ration; beans, 6 quarts per 100 men; hominy or rice, 8 pounds per 100 men; sugar, 14 pounds per 100 men; R. coffee, 5 pounds ground, or 7 pounds raw, per 100 men, or tea, 18 ounces per 100 men." On 19 May 1864, Hoffman recommended reducing the rations issued to prisoners. He believed the reduction would not deprive prisoners "of the food necessary to keep them in health." Hoffman suggested reducing rations in three of nine categories of provisions: corn meal, sugar, and tea. The corn meal ration would decrease from 18 to 16 ounces, the sugar ration from 14 to 12 pounds per 100 men, and the tea ration from 18 to 16 ounces per 100 men. Hoffman also suggested an increase in the rations of "soft bread" from 14 to 16 ounces. Henry Halleck argued for the elimination of the tea, coffee, and sugar rations entirely but the surgeon general insisted that they should remain available to sick and wounded prisoners, a compromise that Union officials accepted.[45] By late May, Stanton approved this reduction. The average healthy Confederate prisoner would in theory no longer receive tea, coffee, and sugar and would also have to survive on two fewer ounces of corn meal.

Although Union leaders reduced the rations provided to Confederate prisoners, the May 1864 reduction did not institute a vengeful retaliatory policy of deliberate near-starvation. For seven months in late 1863 and early 1864, Federal officials and citizens read chilling accounts of what Union soldiers endured in prisons near Richmond. Even if the most sensational newspaper reports risked mischaracterizing the true conditions of the Richmond prisoner camps, many northerners still came to believe that captured Union soldiers suffered barbaric and unjustifiable cruelty at the hands of Confederates. Yet, after other possible solutions failed, Federals responded in May 1864 with a remarkably mild retaliation. The official reduction in rations came nowhere close to true retaliation in kind. The Union officials involved in the decision desired to protect captured Federal soldiers. But their prevailing attitude toward the issue largely remained prudent caution, for fear that a hasty and extreme retaliation in kind would unleash a vicious cycle of unthinkable horrors.

The Sawyer, Flinn, and Lee Episode

Federal officials sometimes threatened retaliation to compel an action from Confederates despite having little intention or desire to follow through with the threat. In one such instance, Federals held captive the son of Robert E. Lee and threatened to execute him if Confederates did not release two Union soldiers slated for execution. The fact that none of the executions occurred suggests that Federals could quickly resort to the stern rhetoric of retaliation even as they remained uneager to carry out a threatened retaliatory measure.

This particular incident of unfulfilled threats began with two executions. In April 1863, two Confederate cavalrymen, William Corbin and T. Jefferson McGraw, recruited fellow Kentuckians to join the Confederate army. Corbin and McGraw's actions directly violated Union Gen. Ambrose E. Burnside's warning that anyone found within Union lines who committed "acts for the benefit of the enemies of our country" would be tried as spies or traitors and if convicted face execution. A military commission in Cincinnati found Corbin and McGraw guilty of recruiting in Union-held areas and sentenced them to death. The men were executed in mid-May 1864 at Johnson's Island, a Union prison camp in Ohio.[46]

The execution of McGraw and Corbin infuriated Robert Ould. In an angry letter to William Ludlow, Ould denounced McGraw's and Corbin's deaths as a "cruel barbarity." The two cavalrymen were "duly authorized" to recruit in Kentucky, Ould protested, and so their unjustified execution deserved a fitting retaliation. Ould warned that in the near future Confederates would select two captured Federal captains for execution. This retaliatory measure might send events further into an "awful vortex," Ould predicted, but God would judge Federals as responsible for "the initiation of this chapter of horrors."[47]

Ould's threats did not intimidate Ludlow. Nor did Ludlow doubt that Federals had acted justly in executing McGraw and Corbin. In fact, Ludlow returned Ould's threat with one of his own: "For each officer so executed one of your officers in our hands will be immediately put to death." Confederates would violate basic rules of warfare, Ludlow continued, if they "barbarously put [Federal captains] to death in retaliation for the just punishment of spies." Ethan Allen Hitchcock agreed that Ould's proposed retaliation was "not simply an offense against the laws of war but an outrage upon civilization and humanity." Ould showed no immediate signs of backing down in the face of Ludlow's counterthreats, for, as he explained to Ludlow, "The Confederate Government is too well satisfied of the justice of its proceeding in this matter to be in any manner deterred."[48]

By mid-July, Federal officials learned Confederates had chosen for execution H. W. Sawyer of the First New Jersey Cavalry and John M. Flinn of the Fifty-First Indiana Volunteer Regiment. Ludlow soon set in motion plans to select two captured Confederate officers to execute as retaliation if Flinn and Sawyer were killed. The unfolding controversy lasted nearly eight more months. The northern press kept the home front updated on the fates of Flinn and Sawyer. *Harper's Weekly* repeatedly lauded the two soldiers as heroes of the Union cause. The *New York Times* did the same, and sought to evoke anger and dismay among the northern citizenry when it ran a letter Sawyer wrote to his wife soon after learning of his fate. "My situation is hard to be borne," Sawyer said, "and I cannot think of dying without seeing you and the children . . . I have no trial, not jury, nor am I charged with any crime, but it fell to my lot."[49]

Sawyer's wife and a family friend from Philadelphia eventually secured an audience with Lincoln and Stanton. Lincoln and his cabinet took the matter seriously. After hearing from Sawyer's wife, they spent the better part of the afternoon and evening of 14 July searching for a solution. By the following morning, they decided on a response that would either defuse or exacerbate immeasurably the standoff.[50]

Several weeks earlier, Federals had captured Confederate Brig. Gen. William Henry Fitzhugh "Rooney" Lee, second son of Robert E. Lee. At the moment of his capture, Rooney Lee was recuperating at a Hanover County, Virginia, farm estate from injuries suffered at the Battle of Brandy Station. Lincoln and his cabinet decided the surest way to save Sawyer's and Flinn's lives was to threaten to retaliate in kind against Rooney Lee and another Confederate captain, even though some cabinet members worried about the wisdom of actually following through with the threat. As Ethan Allen Hitchcock later explained, Federal officials believed these sorts of threats against high profile prisoners were the only way "to secure such treatment to our troops as may fall into rebel hands as the laws of war entitle them to." On 15 July, Lincoln ordered Halleck and Ludlow to place Lee under close confinement and to inform Confederates if they executed Sawyer and Flinn, Federals would retaliate against Lee.[51]

Weeks, then months, passed without the execution of Sawyer and Flinn. The retaliatory crisis reached an impasse. The four officers slated for execution remained in a precarious position but death no longer seemed imminent. By early October all four had been removed from isolated confinement and returned to the general prisoner of war population. By early 1864, Federal and Confederate officials began negotiations to end the standoff. While the Dix-Hill cartel, which governed prisoner exchanges earlier in the war, had collapsed, an exception was made in this case. Federals and Confederates worked out plan to trade Sawyer and Flinn for Lee and the other Confederate officers identified for possible execution. Negotiations began in early February 1864, and proceeded with no real difficulties. On 14 March 1864, the prisoners were exchanged at City Point, Virginia.[52] Federal and Confederate officials stepped back from the brink of a vicious cycle of retaliation. Despite all the portentous talk from Federals about retaliation as retribution for Confederates' uncivilized warfare, a prudent reluctance to resort to the war's sternest feature won the day. Federals ultimately acted under the assumption that the *threat* of retaliation—perhaps even more than an act of retaliation itself—could prove remarkably effective in peaceably compelling certain actions from Confederates.

A Retaliation-in-Kind Showdown in Charleston Harbor

Three months later, another retaliation crisis embroiled Federal officials. It too was long on stern threats and indignant accusations but short on reckless bloodshed. Although both Federals and Confederates in this instance embraced a form of retaliation in kind, they also worked to curtail its worst effects. The standoff developed in Charleston harbor when Federals were more than a year into a renewed bombardment of the city from nearby Morris Island. On 1 June 1864, Confederate Maj. Gen. Samuel Jones, whose command included Charleston, requested his superiors send fifty Union prisoners of war, including one general, to confine in parts of Charleston "under the enemy's fire." Jones hoped this would lessen the Federal bombardment of the city, which lately was "endangering the lives of women and children." Eventually, President Jefferson Davis approved Jones's request. By the second week of June, the fifty Union officers arrived in Charleston.[53]

When Maj. Gen. John G. Foster, then Federal commander of the Department of the South, learned of the strategic placement of the Union prisoners of war in Charleston, he lashed out against Jones for the "indefensible act of cruelty." Foster disbelieved Jones's claim that he acted to protect defenseless women and children. Federals gave ample warning to the city's residents that the bombardment would commence, leaving them plenty of time to escape harm. Jones cloaked his real motivations in this humanitarian hypocrisy, Foster charged. "That city is a depot for military supplies," Foster wrote, but Jones tried to prevent Federals from destroying the military targets in Charleston "not by means known to honorable warfare, but by placing unarmed and helpless prisoners under our fire." Foster decried Jones's decision to place fifty Union prisoners in places exposed to Federal fire as an unjust and illegitimate action beyond the rules of civilized warfare.[54]

Jones vehemently denied these charges. He countered that the Federal bombardment of Charleston rained down indiscriminately on the city "in a spirit of mere malice and cruelty." Jones also promised that the Federal officers received "all the consideration due to prisoners of war." Their "commodious and comfortable quarters" remained among "the houses occupied by our wives and children," far from *military* targets. Jones insisted that as long as Federals directed their fire against legitimate targets and not noncombatants then the Union prisoners of war would remain "in no danger whatever from the effects of your shot." If Federals shelled the city like an "honorable foe," they would not harm their own officers.[55]

Foster still believed that the "cruel determination" to expose captured soldiers to Federal fire reflected nothing more than "vindictive weakness" by Confederates. The *New York Times* agreed in its reports on the developing situation, labeling Jones's actions as another example of "rebel barbarity." Foster advocated to Henry Halleck for retaliation in kind against "this wicked work and cruel act." Foster requested an equal number of captured Confederate officers to place "under the enemy's fire as long as our officers are exposed in Charleston." In the meantime, Foster promised, the bombardment of the city would continue.[56]

Halleck agreed with Foster's recommendation. He directed Hoffman to send fifty officers to Charleston harbor and ordered Foster to treat the Confederate prisoners "in precisely the same manner as the enemy treat ours." Foster followed Halleck's orders by asking Jones for more information about where exactly the Federal prisoners were held and "the degree of exposure to which they are subjected." Foster also requested that Jones allow one general officer and one field officer to provide a detailed written summary of the food they received and "the comforts afforded to them in the way of beds, bedding, [and] blankets." There was no ulterior motive to these requests, Foster assured Jones, for he sought only to ascertain "the exact manner in which these officers are treated, that I may treat in the same manner a like number of your officers."[57]

Even as Foster sent this request to Jones, despite all the threats and condemnations they previously traded, plans quickly emerged to exchange the prisoners. On 24 June, Jones raised with Confederate Gen. Samuel Cooper the possibility of negotiating a prisoner exchange with Foster. Jones defended his recent actions to Cooper as both legitimate and expedient, but inquired if the Confederate War Department would authorize him to negotiate with Foster to exchange the fifty officers each side held. One week later, Jones proposed the exchange to Foster. He did so by passing along a letter from five Federal brigadier generals imprisoned in Charleston pleading with Union authorities to secure their exchange. "I fully concur in opinion with the officers who have signed the letter that there should be an exchange of prisoners of war," Jones wrote to Foster, even though, he admitted, he was not yet technically authorized to enter into such negotiations. Jones pledged to secure this authorization from Confederate authorities if Foster desired to negotiate "just and honorable plans" for exchanging the officers. Jones confessed he "should be glad to aid in so humane a work."[58]

Foster accepted Jones's offer. He requested from Halleck the authority to conduct the proposed exchange. Halleck authorized Foster's request on 12 July, and the negotiations began in earnest. After a minor squabble over Jones's refusal to inform Foster of the exact location of the Federal prisoners, the negotiations proceeded smoothly. By 1 August, the imprisoned officers were exchanged, little more than one month after Jones first raised the possibility with Foster. Northern newspapers closely followed the situation in Charleston, and many approvingly reported on its resolution. The *Brooklyn Daily Eagle* rejoiced that the exchange occurred and hoped that more like it would occur in the future, "until the rebel prisons are entirely relieved of our suffering Union soldiers." Other newspapers argued the entire ordeal confirmed that a stern policy of retaliation produced its desired effect. "The wisdom of a prompt and effective system of retaliation on our part," the *Chicago Tribune* opined, "is shown in the recent exchange of prisoners at Charleston . . . Nothing but prompt and exemplary retaliation will humanize a war with slaveholders educated to barbarism from their infancy." As *Harper's Weekly* put it succinctly, "The retaliatory measure adopted by the Government was perfectly successful."[59]

Although Foster and the other Federal officials did not hesitate to resort to retaliation in kind, they still ultimately welcomed the opportunity to avoid doing so. The threatened retaliation was meant only to protect endangered Federal officers. When Jones presented an opportunity to secure their safety through exchange, Foster quickly abandoned the original retaliatory plans.

As soon as this first crisis ended another began, born mostly of misunderstanding. In late July, against Jones's wishes, Confederate officials arranged to send six hundred additional Federal prisoners of war to Charleston in an effort to move them away from Union armies advancing into the Deep South. The decision to send the new prisoners to Charleston infuriated Jones. "The presence of so many prisoners in Charleston will complicate negotiations for exchange of those now here," he complained to Cooper. Jones rightly feared Foster would decry the action as dishonorable and deceptive, and promptly abandon the tenuous exchange agreement.[60] Foster and other Federal authorities did not learn of the new influx of prisoners to Charleston until after finalizing the release of the original fifty officers each side held. But when Federals discovered that six hundred new prisoners would soon arrive to Charleston, they quickly planned to retaliate in kind.

Halleck and Stanton agreed to send six hundred new Confederate prisoners to Foster "to be confined, exposed to fire, and treated" like the six hundred Federals in Charleston. Foster then confronted Jones about the rumored arrival of the new Union prisoners. He responded precisely as Jones feared. "I am surprised at this repeated violation of the usages of humane and civilized warfare," Foster wrote, "as I had hoped that the exchange of our prisoners formerly exposed would have ended the cruel treatment on your part." Foster then informed Jones of his plan to retaliate in kind, "unless the prisoners are removed from Charleston."[61]

Jones tried to clear up the misunderstanding but remained defiant in his response to Foster that Confederates did nothing inhumane or illegitimate in sending more prisoners to Charleston. "You are mistaken if you suppose those prisoners have been sent here for the purpose of being placed in positions where they may be reached by your shot," Jones told Foster. Confederate authorities simply sent the prisoners to Charleston temporarily because "it is found more convenient at present to confine them here than elsewhere." Moreover, Confederates did nothing "cruel and inconsistent with the usage of civilized warfare" in sending the prisoners to Charleston. Only

Federals were guilty of truly cruel and uncivilized action toward captured enemy soldiers, Jones concluded.[62]

Even as he traded stern words with Foster, Jones worked to have the six hundred prisoners removed from Charleston. He desired to avoid another retaliation standoff and sought to convince Cooper and Secretary of War Seddon to move the prisoners. In early September, Jones stressed how "very inconvenient and unsafe" it was to keep the prisoners in Charleston. Cooper bluntly replied that the prisoners "cannot be removed." Jones then appealed to Seddon twice directly, arguing that he lacked sufficient manpower to guard the new influx of prisoners. This failed to sway Seddon. By late September, Jones even tried to convince Cooper that the yellow fever scare in Charleston made removing the prisoners an urgent necessity. More and more prisoners (mostly from Andersonville and Macon) arrived in the city throughout September, as many as 7,000 total, Jones estimated. This vastly exceeded the number of Confederate prisoners arriving on Morris Island in the Charleston Harbor. Despite Jones's best efforts to remove the prisoners, he did not waver in matching Federals' retaliation measures. Foster placed Confederate prisoners in the line of Confederate fire on Morris Island, and Jones pledged to Cooper that he would do the same with Federal prisoners.[63] Jones and Foster seemed poised to plunge across the retaliatory precipice they had narrowly avoided weeks prior.

When the Confederate prisoners arrived at Morris Island, Jones inquired about the conditions of their imprisonment. Foster replied at length about the types of tents the prisoners stayed in and the rations they received. "I deeply regret being compelled to resort to retaliatory measures," Foster informed Jones. "I shall continue them only so long and to such an extent as your treatment of our officers and soldiers in your hands demands." Until then, Foster pledged it would be his "pleasant duty as an act of humanity" to show the Confederates in his custody any "leniency" Jones presently extended to the Federal prisoners in Charleston. When the *New York Herald* reported on the prisoner conditions on Morris Island, it emphasized that Confederate prisoners received exactly the same treatment and rations that Federal prisoners received in Charleston. Conditions on the island conformed "to precisely the same standard adopted by the rebel authorities in their treatment of our officers," the newspaper concluded, which was a key reason the Federal retaliation remained just.[64]

What Foster did not tell Jones in his report about the prisoners' conditions on Morris Island was that the prisoners were in no serious danger from Confederate fire. Foster had earlier informed Halleck that the prisoners "have little fear of their own shells, which they watch with interest." Many of the soldiers imprisoned on Morris Island later confirmed Foster's claim. As one prisoner put it, "Shells from the Confederate batteries were thrown with great precision . . . passing immediately over our pen." Another imprisoned Virginian agreed: "The first evening and night the shelling was very heavy but none of us were killed. It seemed our guns got the range and fired over us."[65] If Foster's retaliation was supposed to seriously threaten the lives of rebel prisoners, it failed miserably; this, in fact, was precisely what Foster intended.

Foster's intention was all the more remarkable given his opinions about the treatment of prisoners of war in Charleston and across the Confederacy. One of the more revealing letters of this crisis came from Foster to Halleck in late September, in which he described at length his perception of the treatment that Federal prisoners routinely faced—"deplorable in the extreme," he called it. Prisoners in Charleston endured a "miserable plight," Foster said, and most other captured Federals were "ill fed, destitute of clothing, and rapidly sickening and dying." Foster reiterated to Halleck his hopes for a general exchange of prisoners, for he believed only it could alleviate their suffering.[66]

Foster's vivid description of prisoner of war conditions offers an important reminder that outrage over Confederate treatment of prisoners did not automatically lead to rash vengeful retaliation. Federals could loath Confederates for their presumed mistreatment of prisoners and also remain reluctant to resort hastily to retaliation in kind. Although Foster denounced Confederates for their deplorable and inhumane treatment of captured Federals, when he resorted to retaliation he minimized the likelihood of serious injury or death among Confederate prisoners.

This second retaliation standoff in Charleston harbor ended peacefully by late October. With little fanfare, Lt. Gen. William J. Hardee, who had recently replaced Jones, informed Foster on 13 October that the Federal prisoners formerly in Charleston had been moved elsewhere. "It is hoped the communication of this fact," Hardee wrote to Foster, "will cause the removal of the Confederate prisoners of war from Morris Island to a place of greater security." Foster promptly worked to remove all Confederate prisoners on the island "to a corresponding place of safety." By the end of October, all the Confederate prisoners from Morris Island had arrived to Fort Pulaski, Georgia.[67]

What happened to the six hundred Confederate prisoners chosen to endure the Union's retaliation? Forty-two never made it to Morris Island: Thirty-nine remained instead at Hilton Head, two escaped en route to the island, and one died during the voyage. Of the remaining 558, three died while on Morris Island from disease or malnourishment. Two more suffered injuries by Union guards. Not a single prisoner died or sustained serious injuries from Confederate shells fired at the island.[68]

Foster and the other Federal officials involved in the retaliation crisis in Charleston harbor spoke in stern and uncompromising terms about the barbarity and inhumanity of Confederate treatment of prisoners. They threatened to retaliate in kind, and did not fail to carry out these threats. Yet these same Federal leaders also ultimately worked to temper the worst effects of retaliatory measures. Retaliation remained a means, not an end. Northern newspapers recognized the wisdom and efficacy of this approach. After the resolution of the first prisoner of war crisis in Charleston, the *New York Times* denounced retaliation in uncompromising terms: "Its employment in a conflict such as this, increases existing animosities, ministers to a general spirit of vengeance, brutalizes the feelings of those who have partaken in the conflict, proclaims the irreconcilable nature of the struggle, and bars even the most distant approach of the evangel of peace." But the newspaper praised Federals for how they handled the situation in Charleston Harbor, which it deemed an example of prudent military leaders avoiding the worst terrors of retaliation. The *Boston Daily Advertiser* agreed: "nothing succeeds so well with the rebels as a resolute course of just retaliation, when they undertake their characteristic barbarities." The newspaper believed this "resolute course" rarely should result in extreme retribution: "It is never necessary actually to go very far in the retaliation," the paper concluded, "for [Confederates] always give way when they see that on our part there is a determined will."[69]

The U.S. Senate's 1865 Retaliation Debate

Well into the war's final months, Union politicians continued to debate how thoroughly they should turn to retaliation in response to Confederate atrocities. The United States Senate took up this debate in earnest in early 1865 when it considered a resolution calling for retaliation in kind against Confederate prisoners of war. The Senate's prolonged debate over the resolution mirrored divisions in northern society concerning when—if at all—retaliation could be part of "Christian" and "civilized" warfare.

Despite all the furious condemnations of Confederate savagery, the opponents of the retaliation in kind measure prevailed and passed a significantly watered-down resolution. Once again, Federal authorities, this time in the Senate, opted not to embrace an official policy of near-starvation and extreme depredation justified as retaliation in kind. Religious arguments suffused both sides of the debate. Senators of all persuasions appealed frequently to Christianity; so too did constituents who wrote to senators to express their views. The thoroughly religious character of the arguments reveal how distinctly Christian ideas informed what many northerners thought about just conduct in war, especially the justness of retaliation. Moreover, the debate again revealed how loyal citizens linked considerations of just conduct in war with concerns over preserving the exceptional moral character of the Union as a beacon of enlightened civilization.[70]

The debate began in late December 1864 when Minnesota Republican Morton S. Wilkinson introduced a resolution denouncing Confederates' "cruel and barbarous" treatment of Federal prisoners and calling for retaliation in kind—a reduction in "rations, clothing, and supplies" provided to captured Confederates equal to that provided to captured Federals. Wilkinson believed the retaliation was needed to "induce the rebel authorities to pursue a more humane policy." Wilkinson's resolution stalled in committee, but when Senate business resumed in early 1865, Benjamin Wade introduced a similar retaliation-in-kind resolution. Wade's resolution won immediate support from Indiana Republican Henry Lane, who denounced Confederates for disregarding "all their obligations to God as Christians and all their obligations to the world to abide by the laws of civilized war." Eventually, the Committee on Military Affairs and the Militia crafted a new resolution, denominated S.R. 97, adapted from Wilkinson and Wade's proposals. It too demanded retaliation in kind in the form of a reduction in rations, clothing, and supplies to captured Confederates. However, the resolution's authority remained limited. The most senators could do, S.R. 97 admitted, was "advise" President Lincoln on how to act, not "limit or restrict" his authority.[71]

The six days of debate over the resolution in late January amounted to a substantive and religiously informed consideration of the justness of retaliation in kind.[72] Wade rose first to speak in support of S.R. 97 when debate began on 23 January. He defended the retaliation called for by the resolution as the only means "to insure the observance by the insurgents of the law of civilized war." Wade also tried to silence critics who rejected retaliation in kind as an affront to Christian morality. "Where is the Christianity of starving a man to death," a skeptical Thomas A. Hendricks, Democrat from Indiana, asked Wade. With characteristic bluntness, Wade replied, "I do not understand that there is very much Christianity in war. If you go to war you have departed from the great principles laid down by Christ and His followers . . . and if you go to war you must not only depart from those principles, but you must follow out that departure." An alternative ethical and legal framework governed legitimate conduct in war, Wade argued, a framework that justified the proposed retaliation in kind.[73] Wade's arguments hardly satisfied opponents of the resolution who criticized it as leading inevitably toward the same unchristian and uncivilized warfare practiced by Confederates. Charles Sumner, Radical Republican from Massachusetts, rejected S.R. 97 as "impracticable, useless, immoral, and degrading." He explained: "We cannot be cruel, or barbarous, or savage because the rebels whom we are now meeting in warfare are cruel, barbarous, and savage." Democrat Reverdy Johnson from Maryland argued that if Federals implemented the proposed retaliation measures, the Union would "no longer have the support of the God of justice." The Union ought to dissolve, Johnson suggested, if saved "only by a resort to savage methods." Thomas A. Hendricks agreed that S.R. 97 would "bring our fair fame and good name as a civilized and Christian people down." Hendricks concluded that by avoiding the "inhumanity, barbarism, and cruelty" of retaliation in kind, Federals ensured a just and lasting peace with Confederates after Union victory. However, supporters of S.R. 97 could also turn to Christianity to defend the proposed retaliation in kind. Michigan Republican Jacob M. Howard, for one, believed America had a duty "as a Christian nation . . . to punish these barbarities and to make it necessary for the rebels, if they intend further to protract this war, to submit to the code governing civilized nations."[74]

Although S.R. 97 had staunch defenders, it ultimately elicited opposition too wide ranging, from senators opposed to retaliation in nearly all circumstances as well as from senators open to retaliation but displeased with the terms of S.R. 97. Even Francis Lieber penned an editorial in the *New York Times* opposing the resolution as contrary to the terms of General Orders No. 100. "It is too sickening, too vile," Lieber wrote of S.R. 97, a line that Charles Sumner quoted on the Senate floor.[75] Eventually, an amended and far milder resolution passed the Senate on 31 January. The revised resolution only appealed to President Lincoln "to retaliate upon the prisoners of the enemy in such a manner and kind as shall be effective in deterring him from the perpetration in the future of cruel and barbarous treatment of our soldiers."[76] The effort to institute retaliation in kind, including the near-starvation of prisoners, as official Union policy failed. Federals again avoided a thoroughgoing embrace of the sternest feature of war.[77]

Many northern newspapers reported on the Senate's debate, and they did not shy away from editorial commentary on the proposed resolution. The most commonly voiced opinion granted that retaliation was sometimes necessary and justified, yet also expressed misgivings about the retaliation in kind of the original S.R. 97. Although the Unitarian *Monthly Religious Magazine* lamented that a "mawkish and bastard charity" toward Confederates had cost Federals "thousands of precious lives," it still opposed the proposed retaliation in kind. The *Boston Daily Advertiser* also dismissed the resolution as "far beyond the proper scope of the rules which should govern a civilized belligerent." The *Chicago Tribune* insisted that only formal retaliation "will have the slightest effect in relieving the conditions of our prisoners," yet it too worried that S.R. 97 could lead to an unjust retaliation in kind that would expose captured Confederates to "starvation, scurvy, small pox, rats, lice, fleas, or filth."[78] Still, a hesitancy to resort to extreme forms of retaliation scarcely tempered denunciations of supposedly barbaric Confederates. "We are at war with a people that have been half barbarized by slavery," the *New York Times* declared, which it reckoned put Federals at a decided disadvantage. As the "civilized power," the Union faced "the most difficult dilemma": "whether to submit to the worst outrage or also to act the savage." Ultimately, the *New York Times* concluded that to "act the savage," by which it meant resort to stern retaliation in kind, was not a suitable response. *Harper's Weekly* similarly proclaimed that while slavery had left Confederates "imbruted and barbarized," Union officials should reject resorting to "the slow agony of starvation and exposure.[79]

Another intriguing source of public reaction to the Senate's debate are found in letters northern citizens wrote to prominent senators regarding the proposed retaliation resolution. Charles Sumner in particular received a significant number of letters on the issue from soldiers and civilians alike. Admittedly, these letters surely do not capture the full range of northern public opinion on retaliation in kind. But the letters did arrive not only from residents of Massachusetts but also from other northern states. As with the Senate debate itself, the letters reveal the ways many citizens turned to Christianity and its ethical commands to build an argument against the style of retaliation in kind proposed by S.R. 97.[80]

The northerners who wrote to Sumner widely agreed that while the re-ported conditions of Confederate prisons constituted barbaric behavior, Fed-eral officials should not respond by authorizing equally barbaric retaliation in kind. John Maxwell, from Ann Arbor, Michigan, compared Confederates who mistreat captured soldiers to Satan, imagined in Maxwell's mind as the decep-tive and destructive serpent in the Garden of Eden. Maxwell wrote that he hoped Federals would not "retaliate upon the reptile by getting down into the dust and measuring our teeth with him and give bite for bite and poison for poison." D. W. Alvord, a Boston resident, thought, "if in a war with sav-ages, we should imitate the savage," it would leave an "indelible blot" on the Union's character. One Ohioan who labeled Confederates "our inhuman en-emies" also thought S.R. 97 abandoned the "Christianized or civilized posi-tion" that Federals ought to uphold. He continued: "let our nation never resort to any policy unbecoming the grandeur of the position she is assum-ing." Similarly, Orville N. Wilder, a Federal artilleryman stationed in Wash-ington, thought if the Union embraced retaliation in kind it would have to "lay aside the Golden Rule" and therefore no longer be "the exemplification of the Christian Religion which we as a nation have professed to honor and cherish." Another northerner agreed that Federal officials should reject S.R. 97 and instead trust that Confederates guilty of the barbarism would even-tually face divine punishment: "God will vindicate—in his own way and in his own time the outraged rights of his children."[81]

The most thorough and thoughtful letter Charles Sumner received throughout the retaliation debate came from Francis Lieber, who adamantly opposed the original S.R. 97. He feared the proposed retaliation would lead Federals to "sink thereby to the level of the enemy's shame and dishonor," with disastrous consequences for "the great destiny of our people." Lieber be-lieved S.R. 97 endorsed a kind of extreme retaliation not sanctioned by the laws of war. To make matters worse, the resolution's supporters seemed mo-tivated by little more than a base desire to "indulge in revenge," a passion Lie-ber thought "ought never to enter the sphere [of war]." In a *New York Times* editorial published soon thereafter, Lieber reiterated that Federals must ap-proach formal retaliation with "moral calmness," a sober prudence, not merely seeking to satisfy vengeful desires. By subjecting captured Confeder-ates to "the heartless infamy inflicted on our soldiers," Federal officials would stand guilty of a "callous cruelty." Lieber knew Union prisoners suffered at the hands of their Confederate captors. But Federal officials could best end this evil consequence of war (like every other evil byproduct of war) by winning the war as quickly as possible. "The only remedy for this bitter evil as for all other that beset us now is: Let us send men and men and men to our Shermans and Thomasses that they may strike and strike and strike again." Lieber's moral vision of a war in earnest defined his thinking about how best to handle the retaliation issue. A vigorously prosecuted war, not retaliation in kind, was the surest way to end a captured soldier's suffering.[82]

Controversies over the use of retaliation cut to the heart of Federal leaders' ideas about the nature of a justly waged war. Debates over retaliation revealed their basic assumptions about how a supposedly Christian, civilized people should wage war. The northern citizenry reached no consensus in these debates. Yet most Federal political and military leaders who possessed the power to decide when and in what manner to retaliate agreed with Lieber that the war's sternest feature, while often justified, was still a terrible weapon—one to deploy not to satisfy vengeance, but only when it would effectively compel an enemy to abandoned an uncivilized, illegitimate action in war. A persistent reluctance to resort too quickly, too thoroughly, to retaliation resulted from this basic idea about its tenuous place in a justly waged war. Even so, according to Lieber, retaliation still possibly had a legitimate role in a hard yet humane war, as a tool to hasten the war's end. In the final year of the Union military effort, Federal armies surged deep into the Confederacy and resorted to yet another means of ending their war quickly: by unleashing the hard hand of war against Confederate civilians and their property.

Even in the Midst of an Enemy's Country the Dictates of Humanity Must at Least Be Observed

The Hard yet Humane War against Confederate Civilians

In the war's final months, Union armies marched through the Shenandoah Valley and the Georgia and South Carolina countryside emboldened by the moral vision of war contained in Lieber's code. Most Federal soldiers believed they would achieve victory and peace only by unleashing the hard hand of war in all its terrible might against their enemies. A truly just and humane war demanded nothing less, they assumed. Confederate civilians soon experienced the terrifying peril of life at the receiving end of a vigorously prosecuted war, even one tempered with flashes of restraint.

If the war endured well into 1865 and beyond, Gen. Ulysses S. Grant reckoned his armies should leave the Shenandoah Valley a barren waste. Soldiers such as J. H. Kidd fulfilled Grant's orders. Kidd, colonel of the Sixth Michigan cavalry, arrived in the Valley in late summer 1864. He had survived the Battle of Gettysburg and most of Grant's Overland Campaign before being sent to help defeat Jubal Early's Confederate force and decimate the Valley as a vital source of provisions for the Army of Northern Virginia. Kidd relished the chance to subdue Early's army, which lately threatened Washington, D.C., and wreaked havoc in southern Pennsylvania. But when it came time to destroy Valley mills and fields and crops and livestock, Kidd felt far less zeal while fulfilling his duties. "It was a disagreeable business," he later wrote, "and—we can be frank now—I did not relish it."[1] Others did, he admitted, and even he never really doubted that the destruction was necessary or just. Yet, decades later, as he remembered the sound of burning mills as "a mournful requiem," a tinge of ambivalence remained.

One incident amid the destruction made a lasting impression on Kidd. In the heart of the Valley, southeast of Harrisonburg, stood a mill in the little hamlet of Port Republic. The women and children who lived nearby— "bereft of their natural providers," by now all gone to Confederate armies— survived largely on what the local mill produced. As the Union cavalry rode into Port Republic, the women learned of the mill's impending destruction and pleaded with Federals to spare it. The destruction proceeded as planned.

The fire that consumed the mill quickly raged beyond the Union cavalry's control. Kidd hastily ordered every man to stop the spread of the fire. Despite their efforts, the flames engulfed several homes and burned an image forever into Kidd's memory: "Women with children in their arms, stood in the street and gazed frantically upon the threatened ruin of their homes, while the tears rained down their cheeks." Kidd confessed he saw in the anguished faces of these women a grim reality: In war the most terrible and necessary actions were sometimes the same. "It was too much for me," Kidd admitted, "and at the first moment that duty would permit, I hurried away from the scene."[2]

Kidd believed he waged war justly, but even just wars have their tragedies, as he learned in that little hamlet in the Shenandoah Valley. Kidd waged a vigorous war with the confidence that it remained the most humane option for Union armies. But he also believed that destruction in hard wars must proceed according to certain limits, so he felt dismay at the unintended and unjustified burning of private homes. The best intentions of soldiers committed to just conduct in war could go awry; having unleashed war's destruction and devastation, soldiers such as Kidd sometimes found themselves unable to control it completely. But if no army could entirely overcome this tragedy, what did it really mean to wage a just war? The question accompanied tens of thousands of Union soldiers in the war's final months as they turned the destructive might of their hard war against Confederate civilians.

Henry Hitchcock pondered the same question while encamped outside Atlanta in early November 1864. William T. Sherman had recently taken on Hitchcock as a staff officer after a request from Henry's uncle, Ethan Allen Hitchcock. Henry admired Sherman immediately: "The operations of his mind seem to me more like lightening than anything else I can think of," he wrote to his uncle. On the eve of Sherman's march to Savannah, Henry suspected the campaign would wreak great devastation. But he still hoped Federal soldiers would show self-restraint and adhere to the laws of war. Above all, he desired for God to use the fierce fury of Union armies to "bring to a speedy end this terrible and lamentable war."[3]

Hitchcock, like Kidd, believed anything less than a vigorous prosecution of the war would lead only to greater death, suffering, and destruction: "We must make war, and it must *be* war, it must bring destruction and desolation, it must make the innocent suffer as well as the guilty." To concede defeat and Confederate independence would not really end the fighting, Hitchcock thought, for "that is simply to ensure the same thing hereafter, for separate means *ceaseless war*." War was always a "horrible necessity at best" but Sherman's March across Georgia still abided by a particular moral logic: It made war "so terrible that when peace comes it will *last*." The shortest path from war to peace—the surest safeguard for sustaining future peace—was to wage war with great vigor against soldiers and civilians alike.[4]

One Sabbath morning midway to Savannah, having just witnessed the burning of a local courthouse, as the morning fog gave way to piercing sunlight that cut through the leaves of a quiet woods, Hitchcock reflected on the destructive wake of Union armies. He wondered, "How can any man engage in a war unless he believes its prosecution a sacred duty?" Soldiers who marched into battle carried with them a solemn obligation: to wage war justly and thereby forestall war's easy descent into utter depravity.[5]

Kidd and Hitchcock participated in two of the more infamous campaigns of the Civil War's final months—Philip H. Sheridan's 1864 Shenandoah Valley campaign and William T. Sherman's March through Georgia and South Carolina. Union armies in these campaigns brought to fruition the Lieber code's moral vision of war, both the restraint and destruction it endorsed. Federals who participated in Sheridan's and Sherman's campaigns targeted Confederate civilian *property* to hasten the war's end—not, by and large, civilians themselves. But unwarranted violence and depredation still certainly occurred in the Valley and on Sherman's March. Federals often disagreed about what a hard yet humane war looked like in practice, and some soldiers simply did not always abide by rules of conduct. Even so, both stern retribution and humane restraint defined the behavior of Union soldiers who participated in both campaigns. As a result, an element of discretion and self-discipline generally tempered impulses toward extreme and indiscriminate destruction.[6] Yet even as they remained mindful of constraints on their actions, Federal soldiers subjected Confederate civilians to the terrible fury of hard war in the hopes that they might speedily win victory and peace.

The Shenandoah Valley Campaign of 1864

Ulysses S. Grant arrived in Washington, D.C., in early March 1864 to assume the rank of lieutenant general and control of all Union armies. To many northerners, the fate of the Union war effort seemed to hinge on the year's impending military campaigns. "I fear that if we do not crack the dragon during the ensuing summer," Francis Lieber wrote to Henry Halleck in early March, "we shall never do it."[7] Grant planned coordinated offensive operations throughout the Confederacy. Advances by the two main Union armies constituted the centerpiece of this strategy. In the East, the Army of the Potomac would strike against Robert E. Lee and the Army of Northern Virginia; in the West, the armies under Sherman would move against Joseph Johnston's Army of Tennessee. The fighting in Virginia was grim and relentless as late spring gave way to early summer. Casualties escalated yet Grant did not achieve the decisive victory over Lee that the loyal citizenry desperately desired. Confederates stalled the Union advance at the Battle of the Wilderness by 7 May, which saw particularly harsh and often confused fighting in thick woods set ablaze. Grant fixed his gaze south after the fighting in the Wilderness, and moved his army toward Spotsylvania to force a weakened Lee to fight again or retreat. Lee beat Grant to Spotsylvania Court House, and his army prepared entrenchments effective enough to again repel Grant's repeated attacks. The grind continued ever closer to Richmond but ended again in bloody frustration at Cold Harbor. As he plotted his next move, Grant's mind turned south toward Petersburg. Federals suffered more than 50,000 casualties in the previous four-week stretch of fighting, a once unimaginable toll that shocked the home front. A melancholic Lincoln anticipated his likely defeat in the forthcoming presidential election. The prospect of imminent Union victory seemed dim to the loyal citizenry by late summer. In a matter of months, their revived hopes for a triumphant end to the war had been met with bloody stalemate and bitter defeat. Francis Lieber spoke for many northerners in early August when he concluded that the preceding months were "certainly the gravest period we have yet passed through—it is a dark one."[8] Union armies had not cracked the dragon. It was far from guaranteed they ever would.

In these fearful summer days, a dramatic campaign unfolded in the Shenandoah Valley. The fortunes of both armies fluctuated wildly, and the fighting held the rapt attention of the Union citizenry and high command. For three years, Federals had experienced mostly frustration and failure in the Valley. But Grant did not waver in his determination to rob Lee's army of the Valley's bounty. He turned to Maj. Gen. David Hunter to accomplish this task. Hunter's force advanced up the Valley through Piedmont and then Staunton, leaving behind a trail of destruction—most infamously in Lexington, where Hunter's men burned the Virginia Military Institute and the home of John Letcher, a former Virginia governor who had sought to stir up rebel civilians to guerrilla warfare. Lee sent the corps commanded by Jubal A. Early to confront Hunter. Early arrived first to Lynchburg, and Hunter decided to retreat into West Virginia. In doing so, Hunter left open a route down the Valley for Confederates to take to threaten the northern home front, including Washington, D.C. Early seized the opportunity. His army crossed the Potomac River into Maryland by 6 July, defeated a small Federal force near Frederick, Maryland, and soon advanced on Washington's outer fortifications. The corps Grant hastily sent to reinforce Washington, D.C., proved hearty enough to discourage an attack by Early. Though he withdrew for a time, Early soon struck fear and anger into Federals' hearts again—first with a victory at Second Kernstown, and then when a portion of his cavalry burned Chambersburg, Pennsylvania after it refused to pay $500,000 (or $100,000 in gold) to compensate for the property destroyed by David Hunter. "I am perfectly satisfied with my conduct on this occasion," Early wrote of the burning in his memoir, "and see no reason to regret it."[9]

Early's actions hardened Grant's commitment to devote significant resources to the Valley. The beginning of August marked a watershed in the campaign. Grant placed Philip Sheridan in command in the region and gave him three major objectives: drive Confederates from the Potomac and further up the Valley, destroy the Valley's ability to provide provisions to Lee's army, and damage the Virginia Central Railroad. The decisive period of the campaign came between 19 September and 19 October. Sheridan scored a string of victories and forced Early's army to retreat deep up the Valley. After Federal victories at Third Winchester, Fisher's Hill, and Tom's Brook, Early decided to make a last ditch surprise attack at Cedar Creek on 19 October. Sheridan rallied his men for a successful counterattack and left Early's army in shambles. Sheridan's force had by late August already taken to heart a directive Grant earlier gave to Hunter that "nothing should be left to invite the enemy to return. Take all provisions, forage and stock wanted for the use of your command. Such as cannot be consumed, destroy." However, after Federals drove Early all the way to Staunton, they fixed their gaze on the exposed Valley landscape and continued the destruction in earnest. Grant believed this destruction was integral to the present campaign in the Valley. "Do all the damage to railroads and crops you can," he ordered, "so as to prevent further planting. If the war is to last another year, we want the Shenandoah Valley to remain a barren waste." In bringing destruction to Valley residents, especially ardent rebels, Grant sought to ensure Confederate forces could no longer "subsist among them," much less draw resources to send to Lee's army in eastern Virginia.[10]

However, Grant and Sheridan alike sought to set certain restrictions on how soldiers carried out this destruction. When Sheridan directed his subordinates to destroy "all mills, all grains and forage, you can, drive off or kill all stock," he also insisted to a division commander that Federals should not destroy private homes. Sheridan later threatened "summary punishment" for any "wanton and disgraceful" treatment of civilians by his soldiers. He also directed brigade quartermasters to provide civilians with vouchers detailing the items Federals seized, so that "on proof of loyalty to the United States" they might receive some reimbursement. Grant similarly insisted that the chief goal of Sheridan's destruction should be to leave nothing "to invite the enemy to return." "It is in our interest," Grant said, that the region, "should not be capable of subsisting a hostile army, and at the same time we want to inflict as little hardship upon Union men as possible."[11]

Sheridan agreed that destroying the agricultural bounty of the region would "cut off one of Lee's main-stays in the way of subsistence." He further explained: "I do not hold war to mean simply that lines of men shall engage each other in battle, and material interests be ignored." Many Union soldiers under Sheridan's command also justified their destruction of the Valley as a vigorous measure meant to undermine the Confederate war effort and therefore end the conflict more swiftly. Union forces, one soldier wrote, intentionally "destroyed nearly everything that could be used to subcist an Army." A cavalry staff officer deemed such destruction "necessary," for it stripped the Valley "of the sustenance that rendered it possible to subsist an army there." A New York cavalryman hoped that having "burned everything of account to the enemy," the Confederacy would soon "[fall] fast." By early October, a young Rutherford B. Hayes, soon promoted to brigadier general, judged that the destruction had accomplished its intended goal: "This valley will feed and forage no more Rebel armies. It is completely and awfully devastated." One Pennsylvania infantry captain agreed that the devastation decisively harmed Confederate armies but he predicted that if rebel forces ever advanced into Pennsylvania again they would make everything "they pass over a desert waste."[12] These Federal soldiers all agreed that because farmers in the Valley supplied vital provisions to the Army of Northern Virginia, they could not expect to avoid war's devastation.

Therefore, however earnest Grant and Sherman may have been in seeking to restrain indiscriminate devastation in the Valley, the moral vision of war that they and their soldiers shared also unleashed immense destruction and suffering. An Iowa infantryman thought the devastation near Berryville formed "the most desolate looking picture I ever saw." "The country has been pretty well devastated," he wrote, fences and railroads destroyed, "stock all driven off, orchards stripped of fruit." By late summer, Brig. Gen. George A. Custer reported in detail the recent destruction carried out by the force under his command. In one day, Custer said, his men destroyed nine "large mills" full of flour and wheat along with nearly one hundred nearby barns filled with wheat and hay. Custer's force also seized hundreds of sheep and cattle, yet he pointedly reported, "No dwelling houses were destroyed or interfered with." In early October, Rutherford B. Hayes similarly noted how Federals outside of Harrisonburg identified three mills in a nearby neighborhood and travelled to them "to grind up [their] wheat." At the same time, a cavalry force near Staunton destroyed "Military Stores & Railroad material," along with "culverts . . . bridges, barns [and] Grain." Thomas Campbell, an Ohio infantry private, recounted hearing how some cavalrymen deceitfully promised civilians to save their property if they paid a ransom. As soon as the cavalry rode away with the bounty, along came "the squad appointed to do the burning," which, having finished the destruction, "shared the spoils." "Could human depravity go further," Campbell wondered as he lamented war's tendency "to intensify all the baser passions of humane nature."[13]

As they destroyed, Federals also foraged to supply their own needs. A cavalry force raiding near Staunton enjoyed so much "Butter *fine* apples & plenty of Apple Butter & Honey," that most men "had the best supper he ever had" in the region. One private also noted how Federals stripped two towns in the Valley of "everything eatable," raiding smoke houses, chicken coops, and sheep pens. Another soldier wrote home about enjoying all the "fresh beef and all the fruit and green corn" he could eat after a recent forage expedition. A Massachusetts soldier, having enjoyed hearty meals with plenty of sheep and turkey, thought the foraging necessary: "We should not starve . . . as long as we could find anything in the country."[14]

Foraging brought Federals into frequent contact with civilians in the Valley. Sometimes civilians tried to alleviate their potential suffering by extending temporary hospitality to Union soldiers. When one foraging corporal in a New York regiment came upon a large stone house and began to look for something to eat, the patriarch of the family who lived there invited the New Yorker to join them for dinner. The soldier assumed his hosts were

Unionists until at the end of a long meal when the daughters spoke of their brother, a captured Confederate imprisoned at Camp Chase. In contrast, when an officer heading up a foraging party near Winchester asked a "rich old farmer" for some apples, the farmer "abruptly refused." But when the officer's men descended on the farm, he "made no effort to restrain them from helping themselves." Union soldiers could commit far more heinous crimes against civilians. Pvt. Campbell wrote in his diary of efforts under-way to "ferret out the vile rascal" who raped a woman living not far from their camp. The disgusted private hoped the perpetrator would be executed. "Such villains," he concluded, "bring disgrace on the best & holiest causes." A New York cavalryman similarly worried that excessive pillage and plunder by "lawless and drunken" Federals only "rendered often fruitless" the other-wise "worthy" Union effort.[15]

Although some Federals expressed a degree of regret over the destruc-tion, they still insisted it remained necessary to the war effort. One Federal cavalryman admitted to his mother it was "hard to burn barns," but he did so knowing that "if we didn't destroy the grain the Rebels would get it for their army to live on." A Pennsylvania soldier thought it "seemed a shame," that the Union army "burnt all the barns and mills" as far up the Valley as Staunton, yet he too concluded, "I suppose it was a military necessity to keep the rebels from getting supplies." John B. Burrud told his wife how Federals near his regiment's camp used some of "the best wheat I ever saw" to feed their horses. It "looks a pity," Burrud wrote, "but I had rather see it destroyed then let the Enemy have it." Another private described in his di-ary a scene "enough to make a man blush for his kind": a family with seven small children "literally strip'd of everything," first by Confederates, then by Federals, who together took nearly everything edible the family owned. "War is rough business," the private concluded, "and demands all the ami-ties of life to smooth the rugged edges."[16]

By late September, Sheridan bragged to Halleck of the vast extent and importance of his army's destruction in the Valley. "What we have destroyed and can destroy in this Valley is worth millions of dollars to the rebel Gov-ernment," Sheridan concluded. But how immense was the destruction Sheridan unleashed in the Valley? It is important to remember that Sheri-dan primarily embarked on a military campaign, not a raid, in the late sum-mer of 1864. His chief goal was to defeat Early's army, not to utterly ruin the Confederate countryside. Some historians have convincingly argued the cavalry-led devastation was far more targeted, discriminate, and limited than once assumed. The historian William G. Thomas examined in detail the destruction in Rockingham County, among the most extensive anywhere in the Valley. Thomas discovered that official estimates undertaken by the governor of Virginia reported perhaps one-third of the wheat and less than one-seventh of all corn produced in the country was destroyed. This discrepancy led Thomas to conclude: "Sheridan's forces had inflicted limited and targeted damage that neither destroyed the entire Valley nor subjugated its population." The destruction in the Valley, though great, was neither wholesale nor indiscriminate, and therefore in keeping with the ascendant hard yet humane war spirit.[17]

Yet, as in Missouri and the Memphis area, guerrilla warfare in the Valley posed unique challenges to prosecuting the war in accordance with this moral vision of just war. The battalion of partisan cavalry commanded by John S. Mosby presented chronic problems to Sheridan's force, not least in wreaking havoc on its supply lines. When Federals in the Valley turned their full attention to Mosby's Rangers, they inevitably faced many longstanding questions about how to treat guerilla fighters. In late September, near Front Royal, Federals captured six of Mosby's men. News quickly spread within the Union ranks that in a prior engagement the Confederate rangers had killed a wounded Federal soldier after he surrendered. The six captured Confederates were soon executed, a decision Mosby believed that George Custer had authorized without justification. The executions infuriated Mosby. He pledged to retaliate in kind against an equal number of Custer's men. Robert E. Lee and James A. Seddon both approved of the plan. The retaliation occurred on 6 November, though only three, not six, Federals were executed. Mosby later justified the executions as "not an act of revenge, but a judicial sentence to save not only the lives of my own men, but the lives of the enemy." The retaliation proceeded according to the laws of war in an effort to secure for captured Confederates the humane treatment afforded them by the laws of war, Mosby insisted. One week later, Mosby promised Sheridan that "any prisoners falling into my hands will be treated with the kindness due to their condition, unless some new act of barbarity shall compel me reluctantly to adopt a course of policy repulsive to humanity." Sheridan's exact reply is unknown, but the two seemingly settled on some sort of agreement. No additional executions of captured soldiers occurred.[18]

Regardless of whatever understanding Sheridan and Mosby reached, the death of Lt. John Rodgers Meigs in early October revealed the lengths to which Sheridan would resort to stamp out guerrilla activity. Meigs, Sheridan's twenty-three-year-old chief engineer and son of Quartermaster Gen. Montgomery C. Meigs, was killed under somewhat mysterious circumstances. Initial reports suggested that Meigs encountered a band of Confederate partisans during an evening trip back to Harrisonburg, and that as Meigs began to take them prisoner the rebels shot him while he could not fairly defend himself. Later investigations indicated this was not entirely the case, that the Confederates fairly engaged Meigs, but Sheridan initially responded under the assumption that Meigs was murdered in cold blood. Sheridan immediately ordered Federals to burn all the houses within a five-mile radius of Meigs's murder in retaliation for the "atrocious act"—as harsh and far-reaching a retaliation for presumed guerrilla activity as any that occurred in the Valley in 1864. "Of course the whole thing was murder," George B. Sanford, at the time a cavalry staff officer in the Valley, insisted years later. "This sort of work is not war, and is not so regarded in any civilized community." Sheridan later rescinded his orders when more details of the incident came to light, but the harshness of his immediate response is revealing.[19]

When in late November Sheridan fully turned his attention toward subduing Mosby's Rangers and other guerrilla fighters, he reminded the Federals under his command that the hard hand of war was the only just and effective way to deal with the guerrillas. "Their real object is plunder and highway robbery," Sheridan wrote of the partisans, and so they brought "destruction upon the innocent as well as their guilty supporters by their cowardly acts." The solution to defeating the guerrillas, Sheridan concluded, was to carry forth Grant's original vision for the campaign in the Valley: "Consume and destroy all forage and subsistence, burn all barns and mills and their contents, and drive off all stock in the region." Still, in these same orders Sheridan reiterated that "no dwellings are to be burned and that no personal violence be offered to the citizens." Although Sheridan advocated hard war measures to stamp out guerrilla activity, he also sought to reconcile hard war with certain humane constraints on Federal actions toward noncombatants in the Valley.[20]

The Sheridan-led phase of the 1864 Shenandoah Valley Campaign occurred in the heat of Lincoln's reelection campaign. Not surprisingly, some Democrats highlighted the conduct of Union armies in the Valley as a way to criticize the supposedly radical and excessive destruction of the Republican-led war effort. These election-season criticisms reveal how divisive and politically potent the debates over just conduct in war could be.[21]

Although hard war measures secured military victories for the Union army, Lincoln's Democratic critics hoped these same measures might also spell political defeat for the Republican Party. Many Democratic-leaning newspapers highlighted the destruction in the Valley to condemn the Republican war effort. "The damage has been immense," the *Philadelphia Age* sorrowfully reported. "The people, deprived of food and homes, will have to wander off. Few, not accustomed to the desolations of war, can realize the extent of the destruction made." The *Cincinnati Inquirer* declared that the Valley "is now a waste and desolation . . . its old men murdered or starving to death; its women and children the victims of murder, lust and want of food and shelter." The *Valley Spirit* denounced Grant's orders to leave the region a barren waste as "so desperately wicked, so contrary to the spirit of Christianity, and so revolting to the civilization of this age," a war measure utterly contrary to the true character of "a free, civilized, religious nation." Democratic editors evoked heartbreaking scenes of hardship to denounce Republicans for subjecting wayward white southerners to unjustifiably harsh devastation—all in the service of radical, partisan aims. One Massachusetts artillery officer disparaged the Republican-led war effort as "a damn Humbug any way." He explained: "it is not for principle but Party we are fighting."[22]

As the campaigning in the run-up to the election of 1864 intensified, Democrats redoubled their efforts to convince northerners to reject Lincoln and the Republicans because of their radical embrace of unjust, barbaric, unconstitutional war measures. How Union armies waged war again became a controversial political issue. The official 1864 Democratic Platform denounced the Lincoln-led "vigorous war" as not only unjust in its destruction but also ineffective in achieving what it claimed it alone could achieve: a swift end to the war. Republicans only had "four years of failure" to show for their war effort, which they illegitimately carried on "under the pretense of a military necessity of war-power higher than the Constitution." All that the Lincoln administration and its allies had accomplished was to ensure "public liberty and private right alike trodden down, and the material prosperity of the country essentially impaired." This plank of the Democratic platform (an eventual headache for the party's presidential nominee, former Gen. George B. McClellan) called for a "cessation of hostilities" as quickly as possible. Republican partisans responded by defending the morality and necessity of a vigorously waged war, and usually coupled these defenses with terrifying warnings about what might result if the Union did not endure. One such pamphleteer lamented how the "sibilant tongue of the copperhead has been heard to hiss his base whispers of surrender," which demanded only one response: for the government to intensify its efforts "to prosecute the war with the utmost possible vigor to the most complete suppression of the rebellion." Another defender of the Lincoln administration warned that if the Democrats who called for an end to the present vigorous war were in power, their policies would result in the "destruction of our national existence and an unlimited subdivision of the country." In the end, the Democratic charges of barbaric, unjust warfare ultimately failed to sway the 1864 election. Still, the heated campaign season of 1864 exposed volatile disagreements within northern society over how Union armies might best wage a just and successful war.[23]

Federal soldiers in the Valley followed the 1864 election closely. Most tended to favor Lincoln. Their political convictions generally flowed from even more deeply held opinions about how the war should be waged. Federal soldiers who supported Lincoln's reelection usually did so because they believed it would ensure that the Union war effort remained uncompromisingly vigorous in its prosecution. Lincoln's reelection allowed Federal armies to continue their hard war, the swiftest path to lasting peace. A New York soldier wrote home that his infantry regiment voted almost unanimously "for honest Old Abe." The New Yorker wondered how "the Copperheaded traitors" could really believe "that the soldiers don't know any better than to vote for the cause they are *fighting* against." A soldier in the 119th Pennsylvania infantry hoped Lincoln would be reelected because he thought it would "do more to end the war than anything else for the rebels will see that the north are determined to carry the war on." A Vermont infantryman likewise thought David Farragut's success in taking Mobile and Sherman's capture of Atlanta decisively proved the superiority of a vigorously waged war as the surest path to peace, despite what critics of the Lincoln administration might say. "The 'peace' men," he wrote, "don't have so much chance to find fault" after the recent successes of the hard war. Pvt. Thomas Campbell condemned fellow Federal soldiers for their depredations in the Valley, but he directed equal ire toward McClellan and the Democratic platform—a "wishy washy meaningless string of glittering generalities [that] breathes the spirit of peace at any price," he concluded. Campbell thought McClellan ought to "repudiate the platform and come out squarely for the crushing out of the rebellion by force of arms." This hard war, Campbell said, was after all "the only way [the rebellion] will ever be crush'd."[24]

William T. Sherman's March to the Sea and through South Carolina

As Federal soldiers in the Valley ruminated on Lincoln's reelection fortunes and the need to continue their vigorously waged war, Joseph Johnston and William T. Sherman had for several weeks methodically maneuvered their armies across northern Georgia. Grant directed Sherman in early April to strike at Johnston's Army of Tennessee "and get into the interior of the enemy's country as far as you can, inflicting all the damage you can against their war resources."[25] By early July, Sherman's army had advanced nearly to within striking distance of Atlanta. Confronted with the prospect of an imminent siege of the city, President Jefferson Davis yearned for decisive action by the Army of Tennessee, so he replaced Johnston with John Bell Hood. Hood took the offensive for a time, but he too failed to save Atlanta, which his army abandoned on 1 September.

The fall of Atlanta revived northern morale and Lincoln's reelection prospects. Yet it also raised serious strategic considerations for Sherman. Could he hold the city, protect his vulnerable line to Nashville, and still maintain offensive momentum into Georgia? Sherman decided on an action that shocked and infuriated Confederates: He expelled Atlanta's population from the city. Many at the time protested the expulsion, and since then others have deemed it a cruel decision emblematic of a man who relished total war. Sherman infamously replied to criticisms of his order, "war is war, and not popularity-seeking." He believed his decision was not barbaric but fully justified—even humane—given the circumstances.[26]

In announcing the expulsion and outlining how it would proceed, Sherman set off a short and vitriolic argument with Hood. Sherman defended the evacuation as "a kindness to these families of Atlanta to remove them now at once from scenes that women and children should not be exposed to." Hood's protest only aggravated Sherman:

> In the name of common sense I ask you not to appeal to a just God in such a sacreligious manner . . . If we must be Enemies let us be men, and fight it out as we propose to do, and not deal in such hypocritical

appeals to God and humanity. God will judge us in due time, and he will pronounce whether it be more humane to fight with a town full of women, and their families of a brave People at our back or to remove them in time to places of safety among their own friends and People.

Soon after, Sherman also justified the decision to Atlanta officials. He appealed loosely to military necessity, suggesting that the evacuation was essential to "stop the war that now desolates our once Happy and Favored country." But he also insisted that the realities of the raging war made Atlanta no place for civilians, a conclusion he had similarly reached in Memphis. Greater harm would come to civilians if they stayed: "The use of Atlanta for warlike purposes is inconsistent with its character as a home for families. There will be no manufactures, commerce, or agriculture here for the maintenance of families and Sooner or later want will compel the Inhabitants to go."[27] Sherman also defended the expulsion by appealing to an even more fundamental conviction about the nature of military conflict: "War is cruelty, and you cannot refine it: and those who brought war into our Country deserve all the curses and maledictions a people can pour out." The people of Atlanta and their fellow Confederates were responsible for the war. Having unleashed war's horrors, they had no right to expect to escape them unscathed. "You might as well appeal against the thunder storm as against these terrible hardships of war," Sherman said.

Still, these terrible hardships existed in *war*. They would not persist in peace if Confederates promptly gave up their struggle. A war waged in terrible earnest, as Francis Lieber said, should aim for a swiftly restored and gracious peace. Sherman promised as much to the residents of Atlanta: "When that Peace do come you may call on me for anything—Then will I share with you the last cracker, and watch with you to shield your homes & families against danger from every quarter."[28] In evacuating Atlanta, Sherman believed he was simply putting into practice the logic Lieber enshrined in his code: Short wars are the best for humanity, and subjecting a civilian population to the hardships of war helped end war quickly.

Even as he set about to expel Atlanta's population from the city, Sherman fixed his gaze eastward. He envisioned a dramatic raid across Georgia to the Atlantic coast. Lincoln and Grant were initially skeptical of the plan, in part because they feared that in the wake of Sherman's departure Hood might launch a successful attack on Nashville. The arguments in favor of the march, though, were too compelling. Sherman could destroy the war-making resources safely harbored in the untouched Georgia countryside. In the process, he could expose the Confederacy's inability to protect its people from enemy armies. The occupation of Atlanta was "useless," in Sherman's opinion. But, "the utter destruction of its roads, houses, and people will cripple its military resources," he wrote to Grant. "I can make the march and make Georgia howl."[29]

Before marching toward Savannah, Sherman set forth certain restraints on the conduct of Federal soldiers soon to make Georgia howl. In Special Field Orders 119, Sherman called upon his men "to maintain that discipline, patience, and courage which have characterized you in the past."[30] A day later, in Special Field Orders 120, Sherman elaborated on this general proclamation and set forth clear rules to govern soldier conduct in three particular situations: foraging for food, destroying property, and seizing property. Although Sherman infamously directed his men to "forage liberally" in Special Field Orders 120, he also ordered brigade commanders to carefully organize the foraging parties, which only "discrete officers" were to command. Soldiers not part of these parties should not forage. The liberal foraging, Sherman hoped, would proceed in a strictly controlled manner, limited to a select number of soldiers. He granted foraging parties the right to take a wide array of provisions if needed—meats and vegetables and fruits and corn meal and so forth—but he also forbade them from entering civilian homes without prior authorization. For the destruction of property, Sherman invested corps commanders with the power to authorize the destruction of "mills, houses, cotton-gins," when necessary. While Sherman left corps commanders wide discretion, he did firmly establish one general principle: In places where "the army is unmolested," Federals should destroy as little as possible; in areas infested by guerrillas or where local civilians impeded Federal progress by burning bridges or obstructing roads, corps commanders were to "order and enforce a devastation more or less relentless according to the measure of such hostility." In short, Sherman directed soldiers to mete out destruction in rough accordance to civilians' resistance. He also gave soldiers broad license to seize private property. The cavalry and artillery, as well as foragers, could take horses, mules, and wagons as needed. Sherman offered little more guidance for property seizures, except to say that soldiers should discriminate "between the rich, who are usually hostile, and the poor or industrious, usually neutral or friendly."[31]

An Iowa private who took part in the march thought Sherman's two orders were "humane and considerate," reflective of a desire not "to ruin the country or cause unnecessary suffering among the inhabitants." Sherman himself later insisted his orders "were obeyed as well as any similar orders ever were, by an army operating wholly in an enemy's country." But other Federal soldiers took a more sardonic view of the orders. When one officer caught up to an advance guard, he found the men "lying and sitting along the road, very jolly," their cups and canteens overflowing with sorghum molasses taken from a nearby house. One soldier, "with face upturned and buried all but eyes in a cup of molasses," cried out in jubilation, "Forage liberally!" Foraging parties did not always procure a luxurious bounty of food, but many soldiers commented favorably on the provisions secured from the Georgia countryside. "We are now beginning to realize some of the pleasures attending a raid," a telegraph officer declared, who had just enjoyed "one of the best meals it has been my fortune to partake of since I left home." "We are living on the top shelf," one Ohio soldier reported, "& its good enough too." Another soldier thought, "So far as the gratification of the stomach goes, the troops are pursuing a continuous thanksgiving."[32]

Authorized foragers did not always abide by the rules Sherman issued. Neither did the soldiers (typically deserters) known often as "bummers" who engaged in unauthorized foraging. One Union captain expressed shame in a letter home over the "many cruel things . . . many depredations" committed by bummers. "Tis shameful the way some of the men pillage & plunder," an Ohio private wrote. Sherman also admitted that while he thought foragers generally fulfilled their duties with "skill and success," he granted that at times they committed acts of "pillage, robbery, and violence." Union commanders in Sherman's army often lamented unruly behavior and unwarranted confiscation and destruction by foragers, but they too affirmed the essential role foraging played in the Union war effort. Henry Hitchcock, for one, deplored the sight of soldiers eager to leave on daily foraging expeditions, even though he still believed "it *is* a necessity." In stripping the Georgia countryside of food and other provisions, foragers in theory waged the sharp, short war that Francis Lieber advocated. Hitchcock thought foraging was necessary to demoralize and defeat Confederates: "Nothing *can* end this war but some demonstration of their helplessness, and the miserable inability of [Jefferson Davis] to protect them."[33]

Because foraging parties frequently came into contact with Confederate civilians and their property, division and corps commanders tended to closely monitor their behavior. In the process, they reiterated and clarified Sherman's Special Field Orders 119 and 120. Brig. Gen. John M. Corse directed officers in command of foraging parties to "enforce the strictest discipline and order" by preventing soldiers from entering private homes "except by written authority" from Corse himself. Brig. Gen. Giles A. Smith likewise reminded foragers under his command that "we are not warring upon women and children." This meant that while foragers should take whatever they needed for their "health or subsistence," they could not enter private homes without authorization. Smith warned "any person caught firing a building, or any other property, without orders" would be shot on the spot. Several weeks into the march, Maj. Gen. Peter J. Osterhaus denounced the persistent "irregularities existing in foraging," especially the lax discipline that enabled soldiers not belonging to official foraging parties to "straggle from the ranks and forage for themselves, without any authority whatever."[34] These stragglers typically did most of the pillaging, Osterhaus said, and prevented foraging from proceeding in a just manner.

These division and corps commanders all served under the deeply pious Maj. Gen. Oliver Otis Howard, who chronically fretted over unwarranted foraging by Federals. As soon as the march commenced, Howard demanded "more care must be taken in the selection of foragers," for many, he feared, were "drunk and disorderly." Howard especially wanted to prevent plundering by foraging parties. He recognized "it is so tempting in a hostile country for soldiers to load themselves with plunder that it is done almost before we think of it."[35] Foraging remained an essential part of the March to Savannah—necessary to supplying Federal armies and useful in demoralizing Confederate civilians—yet commanders took care not to allow the hard war measure to spiral beyond all humane restraints.

Sherman's army did more than forage across the Georgia countryside. It also destroyed. As the march commenced, Sherman's corps and division commanders issued to their troops strict and extensive rules that would govern the destruction in Georgia. Brig. Gen. William P. Carlin, who commanded a division in the Fourteenth Corps, reminded his soldiers they could not set fire to any "houses, mills, or any buildings of any kind," unless authorized by a division or corps commander. Oliver O. Howard took these prescriptions even further for the Army of the Tennessee when it came to destroying mills. "The mills along the route of this army must not and will not be damaged or destroyed without positive orders from these headquarters," Howard ordered, mostly to keep the mills functional to feed Union armies.[36] Private soldiers—and even the vast majority of officers of all ranks—could not legitimately decide for themselves what to destroy. These same corps, division, and army commanders realized that not all the soldiers under their command strictly abided by their rules. Just days after the march began, Brig. Gen. Jefferson C. Davis, commander of the Fourteenth Corps, issued another stern rebuke against the "straggling and marauding" taking place within his corps. "Men must be taught that, even in the midst of an enemy's country, the dictates of humanity must at least be observed," Davis said, "and that no good can result to the cause of their country from indiscriminate destruction of property or burning of the homes of women and children." Oliver O. Howard went to even greater lengths to prevent "crimes of arson and robbery." Anyone found "pillaging a house or burning a building without proper authority," he informed his Army, would be shot.[37]

As Union commanders handed down these rules, soldiers commenced their work of destruction. They targeted anything that might aid and prolong the Confederate war effort, including miles and miles of railroads—"the Confederacy will never be able to repair it," one soldier predicted—along with mills, factories, and cotton gins. Public property generally stood a better chance of being destroyed than private property. Although Federals usually spared courthouses, they burned to the ground the one in Sandersville because rebels had used it as a makeshift fort from which to fire on Union soldiers. The towns that dotted the Union army's path to Savannah experienced a harrowing ordeal, in part because they did not know if they soon faced immense or comparatively mild devastation. Louisville fared poorly. The town was so "burned & thoroughly sacked," one Ohio soldier said, that "for once I was thoroughly ashamed that I belonged to the army." But the devastation endured by Georgia towns was not always near-total. The fate of Madison well captures the strange mixture of discretion and destruction Federal soldiers often showed. Madison was the home, a soldier reported, of "at least three genuine Union men," including former Congressman Nathaniel Greene Foster. For this reason, the soldier said, Madison "was well guarded from depredations," mostly "for the sake of the small leaven of righteousness it contained." If Federals proved capable of showing mercy to Unionists when possible, they proved equally eager to punish the defiantly disloyal. A prominent local doctor, a "most notorious rebel," also lived in Madison. Federals ransacked his abandoned office in retribution, taking many books and destroying the ones left behind.[38]

Federals often disagreed over how scrupulously they should respect private property on their way to Savannah. One Iowan insisted his regiment did not pillage homes, though he admitted that they "freely helped ourselves to whatever of eatables found in outbuildings." Sherman's chief engineer regretted the "destruction of private property by unauthorized persons," which was, he said, "the great scandal of our army." An artillery officer from New York concluded that the orders concerning the seizure and destruction of private property were "generally complied with, though probably not always."[39] Homes still occupied tended to face less threat of pillage than unoccupied ones. A New York soldier wrote in his diary of the particular care taken "not to wreck residences" when they still housed civilians. An Ohioan likewise noted the strict orders he received from his brigade commander not to "go into a private house if occupied." As an Illinois volunteer came upon a "large and fine plantation," a little girl who lived there asked if the soldiers were going to "burn all our property." The soldier replied, "only the cotton and cotton gins," although Federals made off with some food as well. A larger plantation owner near Madison likewise found that while passing Union armies "stripped him of everything" they could eat, his "smart" hospitality, one soldier recounted, ultimately saved his home from greater destruction.[40]

Vacated homes usually endured greater pillage or destruction. For the civilians who "fled before us," one Ohio soldier wrote, "of course their property had to suffer." Sometimes the suffering was limited. One soldier repeatedly "got some books to read" from vacant houses to pass the long hours in camp. An Indiana infantryman "rummaged around" a large abandoned home that once functioned as a hotel and found "a chest with a lot of silver coins and a bag filled with ivory poker chips." He decided to keep a few as souvenirs. The home of John W. Jones, a former congressman and prominent surgeon in the Confederate army, received far worse treatment. Federals found his home abandoned and, according to one Wisconsin soldier, "broke every piece of furniture in the house, throwing some of it through the windows, scattered his books and pamphlets about the yard, broke open barrels of sorghum syrup and let it run over the kitchen floors; in short, utterly ruined everything." The soldier thought Jones's house would have avoided the devastation "if he had staid at home." John Emerson Anderson, a Massachusetts soldier, found "grim satisfaction" in entering abandoned homes and reading letters left behind that contained "prayers that God would cause this cruel war to cease." Anderson believed "as soon as this sentiment became universal among our enemies the prayer would be answered right speedily, and then we could go to our homes."[41]

The confiscation and destruction of private property easily could devolve into little more than crude plunder. Yet Federal authorities attempted to punish soldiers guilty of excessive and repeated pillaging. Corps commanders issued strict orders prohibiting plunder and the unauthorized entering of homes, and also backed up their orders by threatening strict punishments for anyone who disobeyed. Maj. Gen. Frank Blair warned a cavalry colonel that the "outrages" committed by men under his command called for "some severe and instant mode of correction." If the colonel could not devise a quick correction, Blair himself would arrest the entire regiment and recommend their dishonorable discharge. Some soldiers prone to plunder faced imprisonment for the duration of the term of their service— although there is no evidence any Federal was executed for plunder as some corps commanders warned. These punishments, threatened and carried out, did not prevent all pillaging. But they signaled that Federal commanders would not tolerate blatant disregard of the rules of just conduct set forth for the march across Georgia.[42]

Union soldiers justified their destruction by arguing that it ensured a swifter end to the war and inflicted a just retribution against disloyal civilians. "We destroy immense quantities which would be of service to the enemy's army," a soldier from Ohio explained. Another wrote that Federal armies targeted "that which if left unharmed would be of use to the enemy in prolonging the war." An Illinois surgeon aptly summarized the governing logic of Sherman's March: "We eat up and destroy everything on the route that would tend to keep a man or beast alive," namely in Confederate armies. Property put directly to use in the Confederate war effort faced the sternest treatment. One Federal soldier justified the burning of a house because it "sheltered a rebel" who fired upon Union troops. This sort of persistent resistance angered an Illinois infantry major: "If citizens raise their hands against us to retard our march or play the guerrilla against us, neither youth nor age, nor sex will be respected. Everything must be destroyed." However, Henry Hitchcock insisted the effort to destroy and thereby weaken Confederate armies still required Federals to ensure "the destruction is not wanton, nor unoffending persons injured." Beyond those restraints, he concluded, "the rest is inevitable and necessary to end the war."[43]

Many Union soldiers also rejoiced that Georgians affected by the march finally reaped the hardships of the war they helped cause. In expressing satisfaction over Confederate civilian suffering, Federals sometimes voiced their approval for a kind of mere punishment unauthorized by the Lieber code. The area Union armies covered in the march, one Illinois soldier grudgingly wrote, had "suffered but little from the ravages of the army." The state finally "felt the woes which they have long helped inflict on others," Henry Hitchcock said. A sergeant in the Second Massachusetts Infantry agreed that the relatively unscathed Georgia countryside finally experienced the "war, terrible war," it had helped unleash against "the Union loving district of Eastern Tennessee, and the peace loving hills of Pennsylvania." Another Federal soldier recalled a woman begging him "not to trouble Georgia because it was last to secede." The soldier remained unconvinced by her claims of innocence: "We can't see it," he concluded. A Pennsylvania artilleryman, reflecting on the destruction in Atlanta, admitted it was a "sad calamity," yet he still believed Georgians deserved the fate: "They brought this war on, and therefore must abide by the consequences."[44]

Three particular episodes during the march further reveal how Federal troops tended to justify hard war measures against civilians either as acts of military necessity or legitimate retribution. When Union forces passed through Milledgeville, the capital of Georgia, they proceeded to destroy public property that Confederates could easily convert "to hostile uses," according to Sherman. A drummer boy for a Minnesota regiment witnessed the destruction of "magazines, arsenals, depots, factories, and storehouses containing property belonging to the Confederate government . . . also some seventeen hundred bales of cotton." Federals acted with great irreverence toward the state capitol, mansion, and state library. Some soldiers eagerly took books from the library, but others, like a major in the 123rd Illinois Infantry, objected to its plunder; he thought it should be left alone "to enlarge and increase for the benefit of the loyal generations that are to people this country long after we shall have fought." Federals insisted that their destruction spared private homes, but one Confederate surgeon lamented that the city's residents were "plundered and robbed of their provisions & clothing & many families to day have nothing to eat." Still, a soldier in an Illinois infantry regiment ultimately argued that the destruction in Milledgeville was justified because it sought "the ruin of all property that could be used by the rebel army."[45]

Nearly ninety miles east of Milledgeville, Union forces arrived in Millen and discovered a prisoner of war camp that held around 1,300 Federals. The camp was little more than a makeshift "hideous prison-pen," even by Civil War–era standards. One soldier described it as "three hundred feet square, inclosed by a stockade, without any covering whatsoever," exposing Federals "to heavy dews, biting frosts, and pelting rains." The camp was a "hellhole . . . so filthy and forsaken," an Iowan wrote. Another soldier could only rejoice he was not "taken to one of these hells at the time I was wounded at Chancellorsville." Rumor soon spread among Union troops that as many as 750 soldiers had died there, and that some even had been killed just prior to the Union army's arrival.[46] In response, Federals burned "everything here that a match would ignite," in the words of one soldier. The destruction in Millen was a "magnificent spectacle," another Federal reported with satisfaction. Union troops protected at least one local widow's plantation from destruction because for four months she had nursed back to health a Union soldier from the prison. One officer spoke for many Federals who passed through Millen when he warned, "God certainly will visit the authors of all this crime with a terrible judgment."[47]

Not far from Millen was the plantation of a Mr. Stubbs, apparently a vicious hunter of runaway slaves and Union prisoners of war. Knowledge of Stubbs's reputation had spread among at least some Union troops by the time they arrived at his plantation. One Federal thought that Stubbs's heinous hunting of slaves and prisoners of war was an "excellent reason" for the vast destruction of his property, which the soldier described in detail: "The house, cotton-gin, press, corn-ricks, stables, every thing that could burn was in flames, and in the door-yard lay the dead bodies of several bloodhounds, which had been used to track and pull down negroes and our escaped prisoners." Henry Hitchcock affirmed that most Union soldiers who passed directly by Stubbs's plantation knew his reputation and approved the near-total destruction of the man's home and property. "He kept hounds to hunt our men with," an Iowa soldier wrote in his diary, which to him sufficiently justified the harsh retribution.[48]

Thousands of fugitive slaves flocked to and followed Sherman's army through Georgia in anticipation of freedom. One Michigan infantryman noted that while passing by a plantation near Milledgeville "every able bodied negro was taken with the army . . . and the side of the road was lined with them." Federal soldiers' attitudes toward these fugitives varied widely. One Wisconsin soldier scorned them as "a great hindrance, if not to say a nuisance." In contrast, an Ohio captain lamented that the "silly prejudice of color is as deeply rooted among northern as among southern men," leaving the Federal soldiers with "no idea of treating the oppressed race with justice." Ultimately, for Federals who participated in Sherman's March the pre-eminent just-war concern was not how to treat fugitive slaves but how to unleash the hard hand of war against Confederate civilians.[49]

In little more than a month after leaving Atlanta, Sherman's army had cut across Georgia and captured Savannah. The end of the march prompted Federals to reflect on the nature and necessity of the destruction they had caused in the state. Many Union soldiers believed they had dealt a consequential defeat to the Confederacy. "I think the backbone of rebellion is pretty well cracked by this time," one Pennsylvania cavalry officer wrote. An Illinois soldier proudly agreed: "The march has been the greatest blow to the Confederacy that has yet been struck." Another soldier who wrote home to describe the march could not help but think of what Georgians now had to endure: "I tell you we didn't leave them plenty. Starvation, gaunt and hunger stares them in the face. God pity them."[50] Feelings of pity, though, did not outweigh the certainty that the march accorded with the spirit of the Union army's hard yet humane war effort. Henry Hitchcock admitted it was "a terrible thing to consume and destroy the sustenance of thousands of people, and most sad and distressing in itself to see and hear the terror and grief of these women and children." But he also ultimately concluded that only by these "means the war can be ended." "War is terrible," Brig. Gen. Judson Kilpatrick wrote, "and the people of Georgia are now being made to feel this in all its force." Still, the march proceeded "as a means to an end, and not as an essential act of war." Sherman's soldiers justified their march as a quintessential example of a war vigorously prosecuted and therefore ultimately humane in endeavoring to end war as quickly as possible. As one Indiana soldier put it after the march, "The only way to stop the war is to fight it out."[51]

When Sherman arrived outside of Savannah in the waning days of December 1864, he sent word to Confederate Lt. Gen. William J. Hardee that if he promptly surrendered the city the Federals would "grant liberal terms to the inhabitants." Sherman's promise of mild treatment came also with an ominous threat. If the Confederate did not surrender, and thereby forced Federals to assault or lay siege to the city, Sherman would resort to "the harshest measures, and shall make little effort to restrain my Army, burning to avenge a great National wrong they attach to Savannah." Three days later, Hardee evacuated the city and left it effectively defenseless. The next day, the mayor of Savannah formally surrendered to Sherman and pleaded for merciful "protection of the lives and private property of the citizens and of our women and children."[52]

Sherman worked to uphold his pledge to occupy the city in a humane and restrained manner. He directed his chief commissary to cooperate with the municipal government to distribute provisions to "destitute families" as needed. Only the chief quartermaster was authorized to seize public property, not regular soldiers or officers. Sherman also proclaimed that "where there is no conflict every encouragement should be given to well-disposed and peaceful inhabitants to resume their usual pursuits." Families should feel safe and undisturbed in their homes; churches, schools, and "places of amusement" should continue their normal activities; commercial activity should resume, all under the close watch of occupying Federals. But this mild occupation had its limits. For example, Sherman threatened stern punishment for any newspaper that printed "libelous publications, mischievous matter, premature news, exaggerated statements, or any comments whatever upon the acts of the constituted authorities."[53]

As Federals prepared to leave Savannah to march north, they nursed "an insatiable desire to wreak vengeance upon South Carolina," Sherman informed Halleck. "I almost tremble at her fate, but feel that she deserves all that seems in store for her." Francis Lieber confessed to Charles Sumner he feared once Sherman's army entered South Carolina it would act "in a ruthless manner."[54] On the eve and outset of the march through the Palmetto state, many Union soldiers called for a particularly harsh treatment of what they deemed the cradle and sustainer of the rebellion. Soldiers justified this treatment as South Carolina's just reward for causing the war.

Union soldiers frequently affirmed a fundamental difference between South Carolina and Georgia, North Carolina, or any other Confederate state— certainly in terms of the destruction and devastation it deserved. "We have laid a heavy hand on Georgia," an Indiana surgeon wrote, "but that is light compared to what S.C. will catch." Union soldiers "had it in" for South Carolina, an Illinois infantryman explained, "and they took it out in their own way." By comparison, Federals generally avoided treating North Carolina civilians and their property in the same distinctly harsh manner. "We are now in North Carolina," an Ohioan wrote home, "& we will burn nothing save what is rebel government property." A fellow soldier from Ohio agreed that there was "a marked change in the conduct of the troops" once they passed from South to North Carolina—"less vandalism," he explained. Having passed through North Carolina, another soldier concluded that the state received "a little more compassion" than South Carolina but, he added, Federals still burned enough in the state "to keep the memory alive, for where we passed through nothing edible remained."[55]

South Carolina deserved sterner treatment because it seceded first and was "the viper's nest of this rebellion," as Francis Lieber said soon after Sherman left Savannah. Upon entering South Carolina, an Illinois infantryman issued in his diary a "dire warning to South Carolina," the place "where treason was conceived, where this dreadful war was launched": "You have been in the forefront—you have brought us here—you are responsible—you must pay the penalty." A "terrible retribution" awaited South Carolina, one soldier similarly warned, "the great heart of treason, from which fires the strength of the rebellion." Another confessed he felt a "terrible gladness" in seeing the "cowardly traitor state" that "dragged her Southern sisters into the caldron of secession" finally receiving the punishment it deserved. "It does me good," an Ohio soldier admitted, "to see the instigators of secession suffer." The "Mother State of Secession," another soldier proclaimed, now "severely yet justly" reaped the discord and war it had sowed. A chaplain who saw many "fine plantation residences" burned just north of Orangeburg concluded: "Thus the instigators and abettors of Rebellion get their reward." When Federals destroyed property known to belong to an "active secessionist," a New York soldier explained, they "excused their actions by saying that they wished such people to suffer for their responsibility in bringing upon our country the Civil War."[56]

Federals affirmed that the destruction in South Carolina was not only just retribution but also necessary to ending the war more quickly. One soldier predicted the devastation in South Carolina would bring "the overthrow of this Rebellion." An Iowa private contended that the Union army's destruction in South Carolina was not about "making war on women and old men, but on men with guns, able to fight." This devastation of the home front hastened the defeat of Confederate armies, which the Iowan believed justified it. Sherman assured a New Yorker shortly before leaving Savannah that he would pass through South Carolina "not as they say with a heart bent on desolation and destruction, but to vindicate the just power of the Government." Sherman promised he would gladly "try to temper the harsh acts of war," because, ultimately, he sought "to accomplish Peace and honor at as small a cost to life and property as possible."[57]

Sherman and his corps and division commanders reiterated that the same rules that governed the march through Georgia still applied in South Carolina. Soon after arriving in the state, Maj. Gen. Alpheus S. Williams, commander of the Twentieth Corps, ordered all officers under his command to endeavor to end all "practices disgraceful to our arms and shocking to humanity," namely, the "indiscriminate pillage of houses." Williams called for stricter control over foraging parties, sterner punishments against unauthorized foragers, and rigid daily roll calls to prevent straggling. Maj. Gen. John A. Logan, commander of the Fifteenth Corps, also labeled the pillaging of private homes "disgraceful in the extreme," and reminded his men they could not enter occupied homes without authorization. Oliver O. Howard likewise reiterated to the Army of the Tennessee his zero tolerance for "wanton and indiscriminate destruction." Still, as a soldier in the 105th Ohio Infantry noted while watching "two splendid plantations" burn, Federals had long "wished 'to be let loose' in S.C. & now the wish is realized." Wanton and indiscriminate destruction remained unauthorized, yet destroying public and private property was still an essential part of the Union army's war in earnest against South Carolina. "We, as an army," the Ohioan proudly concluded, "are marking our course with fire."[58]

Foraging continued. So too did the destruction of public property—what Oliver O. Howard called, "property made use of for furthering the interests of the war," such as railroads and railroad stations, powder mills, armories and other stashes of "small arms and ammunition." Federals also on occasion destroyed private homes; as Sherman explained, "we don't burn occupied houses, but if people vacate their own houses I don't think they should expect us to protect them." Not long after Sherman penned these words, one soldier wrote in his diary of the destruction of a particularly "elegant large fine" plantation home, which occurred mostly because there was "no one at home except the negroes." An Illinois soldier agreed that "this kind of campaigning" was essential to defeating Confederates but he worried it might become "just as vicious to our army in its discipline." Towns such as Winnsboro soon encountered the destructive force of an army that marked its course with fire and zealously sought to punish rebel instigators of war. One New York soldier called the sight in the town "deplorable." Federals destroyed all the buildings "holding supplies" useful to the Confederate war effort, but also "many of the private houses were badly dealt with."[59] Although Union commanders sought to restrain excessive and indiscriminate destruction, war in earnest had come to South Carolina.

If the South Carolina countryside felt the hard hand of war, Columbia endured the most infamous destruction of the Union army's entire march through the state. Soon after the city fell on 17 February, fires erupted as Federal soldiers destroyed and plundered, many emboldened by a hearty helping of liquor. While careful recent study has debunked the myth that

Sherman intentionally started these fires, the fact remains that gusty winds quickly swept the blaze across Columbia and Federals did little to prevent the destruction of much of the city.[60]

Many Union soldiers who witnessed the destruction in Columbia could not help but comment on its arresting magnitude. "I never saw such a sight," one Federal wrote in his diary as he came upon the "city almost in ruins." Another soldier simply concluded, "It was a night of terrors and distress the like of which I had never before witnessed and hope I may never witness the like again." A New York artillery officer agreed that the burning city appeared "both terrible and grand," for despite the "scene of pillaging, the suffering and terror of the citizens," there remained a "magnificent splendor" in the image of Columbia destroyed.[61]

Although some Federals disavowed the scope and scale of the destruction in Columbia, others entered the city ready to make it feel the hard hand of war. "The boys were full of hatred for the center of rebelldom," an Iowa infantryman concluded. Arriving in Columbia, another soldier wrote, awakened "bad feelings" like no other place. The "temper and feeling of the men in the ranks," the soldier continued, left little doubt that "a terrible day of retribution had at last come to this beleaguered and doomed city."[62]

Not surprisingly, reports of unwarranted plunder and destruction soon appeared. A soldier in the 11th Iowa Infantry noted that as the destruction of the city began, "the boys were just going in for trophies." Another soldier confessed, "Oh, you [ought] to of seen us go for things. The store doors and everything just flew," and soon his regiment enjoyed an abundance of tobacco and whiskey, even though, the soldier said, "It was the awfulest time I ever seen." One Federal pessimistically concluded "nothing but violence has pervaded" the city, and "the United States uniform has received no lustre." An Illinois soldier agreed that Federals could justly destroy Columbia, but he denounced the behavior of some troops engaged in the destruction: "The boys loaded themselves with what they wanted. Whiskey and wine flowed like water, and the whole division is now drunk. This gobbling of things so, disgusts me much. I think the city should be burned, but would like to see it done decently." These sorts of comments from Federal soldiers are more than merely proof that excessive destruction and illegitimate plunder occurred in Columbia. They also confirm that some soldiers viewed such behavior as a gross violation of just conduct in war—a violation, as the Illinoisan put it, of destroying the city "decently."[63]

The Federals who witnessed the burning of Columbia could not help but often look upon suffering civilians and the hardships they now faced as a tragic culmination to the rebellion, a "scene of appalling distress," as one private wrote. A sergeant in the 11th Iowa Infantry thought it was "a sad sight to see the citizens standing in groups on the streets, holding little bundles of their most valued effects and not knowing what to do." A New Yorker recounted how civilians stood in the charred streets of Columbia "stupefied by the terror of last night and their present destitution . . . they had neither provisions nor clothing, nor did they know where to go to procure it." Another Federal wrote in his diary of the "terrible" sight of "old men, women and children unknown to indigence, or suffering, thrown, at once, upon the almost hopeless charities of a destroyed city." The soldier had no idea who would care for them all, but he did appeal to God "to save their unnecessary suffering."[64]

Federals made some effort to alleviate civilian suffering after the destruction of Columbia, namely to help feed the city's newly destitute. Oliver O. Howard, at Sherman's prompting, gave the mayor of Columbia 500 cattle, along with salt and other provisions from the Union army, to help provide for the impoverished citizens of the city. Howard also urged Columbia's mayor to advise citizens "to leave Columbia for the country as far as possible." One family who lost their home and decided to take Howard's advice headed north with Union armies and soon found themselves traveling with a soldier in the 55th Illinois infantry who sought to make "everything as comfortable for them as it was possible for me to do." The soldier explained in his diary: "I feel that it is doing as I would wish to be done by."[65]

This sympathy had its limits, and never outweighed Federals' certainty that Columbia and its citizens had received a "just retribution," as a New York soldier put it. One Missouri private, after recounting scenes of "the screaming of women and children turned into the streets destitute of homes or food," ultimately concluded, "such is the fortunes of war and nothing else better be expected." An Ohioan agreed the burning of Columbia "is what the Confederacy gets" for its rebellion. A private in the Fourth Iowa Infantry similarly thought Confederates now received what they deserved: Columbia "was the spot where they had sown the wind, and now at last had come the whirlwind." Another Federal soldier, after recounting scenes of burned buildings and plundered private property, observed: "God only knows how much of this is in accordance with his will, and how guiltless are our commanders for this abandonment of rule and order, and the sacking of this beautiful, but rebellious city. To *our* mind, the punishment is but commensurate with the crime. The Capital, where treason was cradled, and reared a mighty raving monster, is a blackened ruin."[66]

Scenes of blackened ruins in Columbia, across South Carolina and Georgia, and throughout the Shenandoah Valley confirmed that the Union's hard war effort had come to fruition in the final months of the conflict. Civilians living in areas where Federal armies traveled frequently found themselves subjected to war's hardships and horrors. Yet these campaigns in the Valley and across Georgia and South Carolina witnessed not only far-reaching destruction but also persistent restraints on the devastation unleashed by Federal armies. Hard war and humane war measures remained conjoined in the final phase of the Union military effort, as they had in the opening months of the conflict in Missouri and occupied Memphis and New Orleans. Soldiers under Sherman's and Sheridan's command did not always abide by official restraints—unwarranted abuses and depredations persisted—but most usually did, and Union army rules governing just conduct continued to define the spirit and limits of its hard war against the Confederacy. Sheridan, Sherman, and the soldiers they commanded ultimately considered the devastation they unleashed moral and humane—for the vigorous war, though often terrible in its prosecution, offered the swiftest path to victory and peace.

Conclusion

Was the American Civil War a Just War?

Did the Union succeed in waging a truly just war against the Confederacy? Does a historian really have any business answering such a question, or is it best left to ethicists, philosophers, and theologians? I have not tried in this book to pronounce some kind of final verdict on the justice and morality of the actions of Civil War Americans. But neither do I think historians should quickly dismiss the question, "Was the American Civil War a just war?" If nothing else, the question beckons serious consideration of the nature of the war as a military conflict—why the fighting took on the distinct character that it did. It is a question that ultimately confronts historians with the challenge of untangling one of the Civil War's great paradoxes: Why did the war possess a peculiar mixture of destructiveness and restraint? How could the same war unleash the costliest carnage in American history and yet also inspire earnest, innovative efforts to define just conduct in war and restrain the conflict's devastation?

The only way to make sense of this paradox is to resist quick condemnation of Civil War Americans and instead cultivate the empathy needed to understand the moral thinking that shaped how the Union waged war against the Confederacy. How did the loyal Union citizenry define a justly waged war? What, in their minds, were its key qualities? What sort of violence did it authorize and prohibit? Did Federals abide by their own notions of just warfare? When they did not, what were their reasons, if any? In answering these questions, I have tried to provide a better framework for understanding the inspiration, nature, and limits of the Civil War's violence and destruction—a necessary first step in answering a more fundamental question, "Was the American Civil War a just war?"

A particular vision of *jus in bello*, just conduct in war, certainly shaped the actions of Union armies. An array of legal, religious, and political ideas informed this Union just-war thinking, but the most important one was the belief that the truly moral way to wage war was to end it victoriously as quickly as possible (while still abiding by certain inviolable constraints). Still, the Civil War confronted Union armies with a vexing moral quandary. How could they possibly reconcile the hard war measures they deemed necessary for defeating the Confederacy with the humane restraints they considered incumbent upon themselves as a civilized people? The prevailing Union moral vision of war contended not only that just wars possessed both hard war measures and humane restraints. It also said, more boldly, that hard wars *were* humane wars. The moral quandary inherent in hard yet humane warfare did not alarm Federals who believed that all the carnage unleashed by Union armies ultimately served the humanitarian goal of ending war quickly.

Federals ultimately faced a far more difficult task than simply reconciling in theory hard and humane warfare. They also had to translate ideas about just warfare into actual military policies. At the outset of the Civil War, Union commanders in guerrilla-ravaged Missouri and occupied New Orleans and Memphis first worked to join hard war measures and humane restraints into detailed rules of conduct. Eventually, Federal officials entrusted Francis Lieber with adapting this particular vision of just warfare into a coherent, comprehensive code of conduct for all Union armies. Lieber's code sought to vindicate vigorous wars as truly moral wars. Even though most Union soldiers and officers possessed little knowledge of the laws of war, Lieber's code cohered with their assumptions about the nature of just warfare. Not surprisingly, then, Union soldiers largely acted in accordance with the letter and spirit of Lieber's code. In doing so, they curtailed the carnage and casualties in their war against the Confederacy. At the same time, however, they also committed the immense destruction authorized by their vision of just warfare. This paradoxical blend of violence and restraint was particularly evident in the war's final year in the Union's formal use of retaliation and its treatment of southern civilians. In both instances, Federals largely accepted certain constraints on their actions but still assumed that a vigorously waged war was truly just, Christian, and civilized.

The Union's effort to wage a just war is a story of millions of people, soldiers and civilians alike, confronting the moral dilemmas of warfare. It is a story ultimately not merely of ideas, but, in Lieber's words, of "moral beings, responsible to one another and to God." Take, for example, Ulysses S. Grant and Francis Lieber, two men who have figured prominently in this book and who tried to fulfill their obligation, as best they understood it, to wage war justly. Neither Grant nor even Lieber might immediately come to mind as individuals emblematic of a just war effort. Grant still sometimes faces censure as a forefather of modern total war, a military leader who cruelly maximized the war's death and destruction. As for Lieber, whatever restraints he might have set forth in his code, he still also ominously declared, "To save the country is paramount to all other considerations."[1] Both men are easy to caricature. But doing so risks missing the vision of just warfare that profoundly shaped Grant's and Lieber's thinking about how best to defeat the Confederacy. Both Grant and Lieber invite careful consideration of how the Union tried to resolve a first order moral crisis: How could Federals defeat the Confederacy and restore peace as quickly as possible while not utterly abandoning their moral obligations in war?

Grant certainly believed the most humane course of action during war was to do whatever was necessary to end the war as quickly as possible. "I have never felt any sort of fondness for war and I have never advocated it except as a means of peace," Grant later explained. Even as the bloodshed stubbornly continued and the war dragged on, Grant never lost faith in the humanity and effectiveness of a vigorously prosecuted war. In fact, he only redoubled his commitment to waging the war in this spirit. Grant later remembered the ghastly carnage at the battle of Shiloh in April 1862 as a watershed moment that convinced him to give up "all idea of saving the Union except by complete conquest." But even this "complete conquest," as Grant defined it, had to balance competing moral demands: "I regarded it as humane to both sides to protect the persons of those found at their homes, but to consume everything that could be used to support or supply armies." The foraging and destruction carried out by Federals was immense, yet Grant insisted, "promiscuous pillaging, however, was discouraged and punished." What mattered most was what the vigorously waged war achieved: "This policy I believe," Grant concluded, "exercised a material influence in hastening the end."[2]

This same logic influenced Grant's behavior in two of the more defining moments of his career as a Union military leader: his unwavering insistence on the unconditional surrender of defeated Confederate forces and his relative magnanimity in victory, particularly at Appomattox in April 1865. "No terms except complete and unconditional surrender can be accepted," Grant tersely told Confederate Gen. Simon Bolivar Buckner when in February 1862 he captured Fort Donelson along the Cumberland River. Just shy of a year and a half later, after the long sought fall of Vicksburg, Grant insisted again on unconditional surrender from the conquered Confederates. In Grant's mind, only such an uncompromising policy, especially when yoked with unleashing the hard hand of war against Confederate civilians, offered a sure and swift path to peace. But a civilized war demanded not only restraint in battle but also graciousness in victory. When the fate of Gen.

Robert E. Lee's Army of Northern Virginia was sealed at Appomattox Court House, Grant again demanded unconditional surrender, but not a humiliating or vindictive one. Soldiers in Lee's army were to give up their arms, accept paroles, and return home. But they soon received much-needed rations from Grant, who also allowed the Confederates to keep their horses. Grant reasoned that the defeated men could not survive the coming year without them: "The whole country had been so raided by the two armies that it was doubtful whether they would be able to put in a crop to carry themselves and their families through the next winter without the aid of the horses they were riding." To Grant, this was the most fitting conclusion to a hard yet humane war.[3]

Lieber likewise urgently pleaded for a "sharp, short" war. He did not abandon this plea even as the Union's "sharp" war did not prove as "short" as he had hoped. But his pleading continued, which he offered not simply as an expert on the laws of war but also as a father of three soldiers. Lieber lost one son and saw another maimed by the war—all before he drafted his code. "The more vigorously wars are pursued, the better it is for humanity. Sharp wars are brief."[4] These words are not reckless bombast from a warmonger posing as an intellectual authority. They are closer to the anguished cries of a father who had tasted the war's heartbreak. It may seem strange for a man to find anything humane in a war uncompromising in its prosecution. But Lieber's moral vision presumed that only this sort of war could truly limit the total suffering and destruction that all wars inevitably unleash. Lieber came to believe that only a vigorously waged war could save more fathers and sons from the pain and turmoil the Lieber family had experienced.

Lieber, like Grant, was also always an ardent champion of the Union. He praised it as an exceptional, morally upright beacon of freedom and opportunity in the world. In fact, Lieber's understanding of the meaning and mission of the Union shaped his sense of why waging a just war mattered. He assumed that if America was to remain a model of enlightened civilization, Union armies had to act in an enlightened civilized manner. At the war's outset, Lieber expressed his confidence in the Union's moral exceptionalism in poetic verse. The white on the American flag, he wrote, symbolized the Union's "purity and solemn truth, / Unsullied justice, sacred right." The Union stood for liberty and rule of law against authoritarian tyranny, Lieber continued, and its citizens ought to ensure it continued to do so: "Let never Emp'ror rule this land, / Nor fitful Crowd, nor senseless Pride. / *Our* Master is our self-made Law; / To *him* we bow, and none beside." As Lieber later proclaimed in a political pamphlet in support of Lincoln in the heat of the 1864 presidential campaign, the Union upheld "all the rights of the free citizen; where skill and industry would surely find their reward." If the Union truly embodied the "unsullied justice, sacred right" of freedom in the world, it helps explain why to Lieber the stakes were so high for waging war justly. Only by waging a just war could the Union remain an unsullied example to the world of free, enlightened, Christian civilization. When Lieber proclaimed in his code that to "save the country is paramount to all other considerations," he undoubtedly had a very literal meaning in mind: Federals needed to earnestly endeavor to restore a unified nation. Yet there was for Lieber an even grander sense in which waging war justly was, in a way, "saving the country": A just war vindicated the Union's highest claims about itself, its supposed mission and uniqueness in world history. The only Union worth saving was a Union saved by a justly waged war, one waged in accordance with the highest ideals of free and civilized people.[5]

Grant, Lieber, and their fellow Civil War Americans lived at the onset of a modern world in which, tragically, against the hopes of many, war would endure. Confronted by their Civil War, Federals embraced a distinct vision of *jus en bello* that they hoped would guide them in waging civilized warfare. At the heart of this moral vision of war was the belief that the most humane and just course of action open to Federal armies was to do *nearly* whatever was necessary to win their war against the Confederacy as quickly as possible. A just war deftly balanced far-reaching destruction and civilized constraints, all in the hopes of humanely ending war quickly without resorting to indiscriminate, wholesale slaughter. Federals hoped their war would do more than simply subdue the rebellion that threatened their cherished Union; they believed it could also temper the tragedies of modern warfare by ultimately causing less carnage and anguish than any other type of war. The death and destruction wrought by Union armies far surpassed what anyone could have imagined in the fearful spring of 1861. It is not surprising that the four terrible years that followed witnessed awful catastrophes and unexpected ecstasies. Far more remarkable is that even as Federals fought to preserve their Union, they continued to earnestly consider their moral obligations as a warring people responsible to God.

Notes

Abbreviations

FLP   Papers of Francis Lieber
HL   The Huntington Library, San Marino, California
JHU   Milton S. Eisenhower Library, The Johns Hopkins University,
          Baltimore, Maryland
LC   Manuscript Division, Library of Congress
MHM   Missouri History Museum Archives, St. Louis, Missouri
OR   U.S. War Department, *The War of the Rebellion: A Compilation of the
          Official Records of the Union and Confederate Armies*, 127 vols., index and
          atlas (Washington, D.C.: GPO, 1880–1901)
USAMHI   U.S. Army Military History Institute, Carlisle Barracks, Pennsylvania

Introduction

1. Lennard, " 'Give Yourself No Trouble about Me,' " 26.

2. The most important works on the life and thought of Francis Lieber and his code include Freidel, *Francis Lieber*; Hartigan, *Lieber's Code and the Law of War*; Witt, *Lincoln's Code*; Mancini, "Francis Lieber, Slavery, and the 'Genesis' of the Laws of War"; Carnahan, "Lincoln, Lieber and the Laws of War"; Childress, "Francis Lieber's Interpretation of the Laws of War."

3. "Instructions for the Government of Armies of the United States in the Field," article 15. The full text General Orders No. 100 appears in *OR*, ser. 3, vol. 3, 148–64.

4. Hacker, "A Census-Based Count of the Civil War Dead." Hacker's article suggests the often-cited figure of 620,000 deaths is far too low and was likely closer to 752,000.

5. More notable and influential works from this camp include, Faust, *This Republic of Suffering*; Royster, *The Destructive War*; Fellman, *Inside War*; McPherson, "From Limited to Total War"; Dawson, "The First of the Modern Wars?"; Janda, "Shutting the Gates of Mercy." For a perceptive critique of this perspective, see Hsieh, "Total War and the American Civil War Reconsidered."

6. For an extended argument that the loyal citizenry's civil religion was responsible for a dearth of just-war thinking within the wartime Union, see Stout, *Upon the Altar of the Nation.*

7. The most persuasive works from this camp are Grimsley, *The Hard Hand of War*; Neely, *The Civil War and the Limits of Destruction.*

8. Mark Grimsley notes the "deep sense of moral justice" that undergirded the Federal military policy of "directed severity," though he does not thoroughly plumb the content of this "moral justice." Grimsley and Mark Neely both suggest cultural and racial similarities between Federals and Confederates as sources of restraint. As Grimsley put it, "the claims of morality are stronger when one can recognize the enemy's human face." Neely argued that the "central restraining force on the destructive abilities of Civil War soldiers was their visceral perceptions of racial identity." White Federals and Confederates, despite all their mutual animosity, saw each other as members of the same civilized white race and therefore did not wage war against each other with the same unrestrained ferocity shown toward nonwhite Mexicans or Native Americans. Grimsley, *The Hard Hand of War*, 222–24; Neely, *The Civil War and the Limits of Destruction*, 219. Neely rightly points to "racial beliefs" as a key reason white Federals abided by the restraints of "civilized" warfare against white Confederates. But these racial beliefs do not explain the specific substance and rationale of Federal just-war policies. That is, while racial beliefs convinced many Federals they *ought* to wage a restrained, civilized war against the Confederacy, these same racial beliefs did not instruct Federals *how exactly* to do so.

9. "Instructions for the Government of Armies of the United States in the Field," article 29; Lieber, "Twenty-Seven Definitions and Elementary Positions Concerning the Law and Usages of War," FLP, box 2, fol. 15, JHU; Sylvester, " 'Gone for a Soldier,' " 221.

10. Hitchcock, *Marching with Sherman*, 62.

11. For an introduction to the laws of war tradition, see Neff, *War and the Law of Nations*; Howard, Andreopoulos, and Shulman, *The Laws of War*.

12. Halleck, *International Law*, 327; Marszalek, *Commander of All Lincoln's Armies*.

13. Francis Lieber to Charles Sumner and George Hillard, 16 March 1844, FLP, box 41, HL.

14. *Daily Missouri Republican*, 18, 19, and 20 December 1861; *Daily Missouri Republican*, 12 January 1862; Hartigan, *Lieber's Code and the Law of War*; Witt, *Lincoln's Code*, 181.

15. Bellows, *How We Are to Fulfill Our Lord's Commandment*, 10; Bacon, *Conciliation*, 6; Livermore, *Perseverance in the War*, 14.

16. L. Abbott to Charles Sumner, 25 January 1865, Papers of Charles Sumner, HL; Douglass, "The Slaveholders' Rebellion," in Foner, *The Life and Writings of Frederick Douglass*, 3:242; *New York Herald*, 16 April 1864.

17. *Congressional Globe*, 38th Cong., 2nd sess., pt. 1:382, 279.

18. Grimsley, *The Hard Hand of War*, 2, 222–25; Abernethy, "Incidents of an Iowa Soldier's Life," 427; W. C. Johnson Journal, 5 February 1865, LC.

19. John Suter to Wife, 25 November 1864, John Suter Papers, The Harrisburg Civil War Roundtable Collection, box 32, USAMHI; *Congressional Globe*, 38th Cong., 2nd sess., pt. 1:391.

20. Mark Grimsley defines the "common element" of "hard war" measures as "the erosion of the enemy's will to resist by deliberately or concomitantly subjecting the civilian population to the pressures of war." Grimsley, *The Hard Hand of War*, 4–5.

21. See for example, Fellman, *Inside War*, vi; McPherson, "From Limited to Total War, 1861–1865," 72; Grimsley, *The Hard Hand of War*, 35–39; Phillips, "Lincoln's Grasp of War."

22. Lieber, "Twenty-Seven Definitions and Elementary Positions Concerning the Law and Usages of War," FLP, box 2, fol.15, JHU.

Chapter One

1. For depictions of Civil War Missouri as an early crucible of total war or hard war tactics, see Fellman, *Inside War*; Goodrich, *Black Flag*; Mackey, *The Uncivil War*.

2. Mark Grimsley suggests that the Union military effort in Missouri never exhibited a "conciliatory" spirit and opted instead always for hard war alternatives. I agree with Grimsley, but add that that equally important is the fact that these hard war measures in Missouri were also, from the beginning, accompanied by efforts to humanely constrain Union military actions. See Grimsley, *The Hard Hand of War*, 35–39. Mark Neely similarly argues in passing, "the principal direct effect of the Missouri experience . . . was to cause the Northern high command to commission, codify, and publish rules to limit the destructiveness of war." Neely, *The Civil War and the Limits of Destruction*, 206.

3. Henry G. Ankeny to Lina and Sis, 25 August 1861, Correspondence of Henry Giesey Ankeny, HL; James Overton Broadhead to Edwin Stanton, 4 June 1861, James Overton Broadhead Papers, box 4, MHM. For two representative examples of Union forces facing guerrilla-ravaged railroads, see Grant, *Memoirs and Selected Letters*, 970; *OR*, ser. 1, vol. 3, 40–41.

4. *Daily Missouri Democrat*, 18 and 23 July 1861.

5. Grant, *Memoirs and Selected Letters*, 973.

6. *OR*, ser. 1, vol. 3, 370, 372.

7. *The U.S. American Volunteer*, 21 May 1861, MHM.

8. *OR*, ser. 2, vol. 1, 185; Galusha Anderson, *The Story of a Border City during the Civil War*, 120–46.

9. *OR*, ser. 1, vol. 3, 9–10.

10. L. W. Burris to Hamilton Rowen Gamble, 8 August 1861, Hamilton Rowen Gamble Papers, box 9, MHM.

11. Grant, *Memoirs and Selected Letters*, 165–66.

12. *OR*, ser. 1, vol. 3, 407.

13. For a sympathetic treatment of Pope, see Schutz and Trenerry, *Abandoned by Lincoln*.

14. *Daily Missouri Democrat*, 5 August 1861; James Overton Broadhead Papers, box 1, 31 July 1861, MHM; Gert Goebel, *Laenger als ein Menschenleben in Missouri*, trans. M. Heinrichsmeyer, chap. 31, MHM.

15. *OR*, ser. 1, vol. 3, 404; *OR*, ser. 2, vol. 1, 191–92.

16. *OR*, ser. 2, vol. 1, 195–96. For further discussion of the formation and implementation of Pope's orders, see Schutz and Trenerry, *Abandoned by Lincoln*, 65–68.

17. *OR*, ser. 1, vol. 3, 423–24. *Military News of the Missouri Volunteers*, 29 June 1861, MHM. Daniel Sutherland calls Pope's orders "the first move to crush guerrilla resistance." Sutherland, *A Savage Conflict*, 20–21.

18. *OR*, ser. 1, vol. 3, 434–35.

19. Ibid., 135, 212. Pope believed General Orders No. 3 would be effective only if sternly enforced. He warned Gen. Stephen A. Hurlbut on 9 August 1861: "Don't fail to act promptly and vigorously according to orders. Go to the county where the marauders fired on the train. Force the people under penalty to tell where those men came from . . . Don't fail in severity or in strict compliance with orders or upon yourself will rest a serious responsibility." *OR*, ser. 2, vol. 1, 202–3.

20. *OR*, ser. 2, vol. 1, 214–15.

21. Ibid., 215–16.

22. *Daily Missouri Democrat*, 26 August 1861.

23. James Edwin Love to Molly Wilson, 23 July 1861, James Edwin Love Papers, MHM.

24. *OR*, ser. 2, vol. 1, 220–21.

25. Sutherland, *A Savage Conflict*, 25.

26. *OR*, ser. 1, vol. 3, 466–68.

27. Ethan Allen Hitchcock to Henry Hitchcock, 1 November 1861, Hitchcock Family Papers, box 2, MHM; Strong, *The Diary of George Templeton Strong*, 3:177.

28. Basler, *The Collected Works of Abraham Lincoln*, 4:506–607, 517–18, 531–33.

29. William Greenleaf Eliot, "Loyalty and Religion," William Greenleaf Eliot Papers, box 1, fol. 4, MHM.

30. Eliot, "Loyalty and Religion," MHM; Joseph G. Best to Cousin, 9 February 1862, Leslie Anders Collection, USAMHI; *Camp Sweeney Spy*, 4 July 1861, MHM.

31. Barton Bates to Edward Bates, 8 September 1861, Bates Family Papers, box 9, MHM.

32. George W. Lowe to his wife, 19 October 1861, Papers of George W. Lowe, HL; *Daily Missouri Republican*, 3 October 1861.

33. James Edwin Love to Molly Wilson, 10 October 1861, James Edwin Love Papers, MHM; Quoted in Fellman, *Inside War*, 155.

34. *OR*, ser. 1, vol. 3, 539–40.

35. Ibid., 381. John M. Schofield (in a further testament to the particularly troublesome situation in northeast Missouri) denounced the "practice of plundering and robbing peaceable citizens and of wantonly destroying private property [that] has become so prevalent in some portion of this command." Guilty soldiers would face immediate arrest, Schofield warned. Officers who failed to arrest them would be punished as complicit in the crime committed. *OR*, ser. 1, vol. 3, 478.

36. *Daily Missouri Republican*, 28 November 1861.

37. *OR*, ser. 1, vol. 8, 405–7.

38. *Harper's Weekly*, 28 December 1861, 818.

39. *OR*, ser. 1, vol. 8, 407; Boman, *Lincoln and Citizens' Rights in Civil War Missouri*, 49.

40. *Daily Missouri Republican*, 18 December 1861. The four parts of the editorial were published on December 18, 19, 20, 1861 and January 12, 1862.

41. *Daily Missouri Republican*, 19 and 20 December 1861 and 12 January 1861.

42. William M. Anderson, *The Story of a Border City*, 253. For Provost Marshal Leighton's assessment of the loyalties of leading St. Louis residents, see *OR* ser. 2, vol. 1, 140–41.

43. *OR*, ser. 1, vol. 8, 431–32; W. Wayne Smith, "An Experiment in Counterinsurgency."

44. William H. Ball to Brother Smith, 17 March 1862, William H. Ball Collection, USAMHI; Banaski, *Missouri in 1861*, 277; *OR* ser. 1, vol. 8, 439; Galusha Anderson, *The Story of a Border City*, 236–37; *OR*, ser. 1, vol. 8, 439.

45. Galusha Anderson, *The Story of a Border City*, 243–34; *OR*, ser. 1, vol. 8, 452, 490.

46. *OR*, ser. 1, vol. 8, 464, 404, 464, 475–76.

47. Ibid., 448–49.

48. *OR*, ser. 1, vol. 1, 155; Neely, *Fate of Liberty*, 41, 50, 43–44. Reports of these trials are found in *OR*, ser. 2, vol. 1, 282–504. See also Boman, *Lincoln and Citizens' Rights in Civil War Missouri*, 70–88.

49. Simpson and Berlin, *Sherman's Civil War*, 177–83.

50. William Greenleaf Eliot, "A Discourse Delivered before the Members of the Old Guard of St. Louis," William Greenleaf Eliot Papers, box 1, fol. 9, MHM; *Daily Missouri Republican*, 12 June 1862; *OR*, ser. 2, vol. 1, 174, 270.

51. *OR*, ser. 1, vol. 8, 344–45, 346–47; *OR*, ser. 1, vol. 13, 53–54.

52. Quoted in Fellman, *Inside War*, 157; *OR*, ser. 1, vol. 8, 641–42.

53. *OR*, ser. 1, vol. 13, 402–3; *OR*, ser. 1, vol. 8, 607. John Dunlap Stevenson to his wife, 7 March 1862, John Dunlap Stevenson Papers, MHM; Fellman, *Inside War*, 149. On 6 June, E. B. Brown issued orders almost identical to Pope's for the Southwest Division in Missouri. *OR*, ser. 1, vol. 8, 420.

54. *OR*, ser. 1, vol. 13, 506; John M. Schofield to Edwin Stanton, 24 July 1862, John M. Schofield Papers, container 45, LC; *OR*, ser. 1, vol. 13, 508, 513; Connelly, *John M. Schofield and the Politics of Generalship*, 51; Parrish, *Turbulent Partnership*, 92; Sutherland, *A Savage Conflict*, 64; Sude, "Federal Military Policy and Strategy in Missouri and Arkansas," 71–87.

55. *OR*, ser. 1, vol. 13, 516–17, 522–23.

56. *Daily Missouri Republican*, 27 July 1862.

57. *OR*, ser. 1, vol. 13, 509, 518, 434–35.

58. *Frank Leslie's Illustrated Newspaper*, 6 December 1862, 164; *OR*, ser. 1, vol. 13, 201.

59. Witt, *Lincoln's Code*, 170–73, 187. Francis Lieber went on to arrange for his son to recuperate in St. Louis in the home of Henry Hitchcock. Francis Lieber to Henry Hitchcock, 11 March 1861, Hitchcock Family Papers, box 3, MHM.

60. Confederate major general Sterling Price and Henry Halleck exchanged a pointed set of letters on the actions of recently commissioned Confederate partisans. *OR*, ser. 2, vol. 1, 255–56; 258–59.

61. Witt, *Lincoln's Code*, 194.

62. *OR*, ser. 3, vol. 2, pt. 1, 302–3; Childress, "Francis Lieber's Interpretation of the Laws of War," 53–54.

63. Ibid., 303.

64. Ibid., 309.

Chapter Two

1. *Harper's Weekly*, 5 July 1862; Parton, *General Butler in New Orleans*, 346–52; Butler, *Autobiography and Personal Reminiscences*, 437–44; Capers, *Occupied City*, 69–71; Hearn, *When the Devil Came Down to Dixie*, 134–40.

2. *Frank Leslie's Illustrated Newspaper*, 14 June 1862; Butler, *Autobiography and Personal Reminiscences*, 440, 442–43; *OR*, ser. 2, vol. 3, 140; Solomon, *The Civil War Diary of Clara Solomon*, 399.

3. For an introduction to the Union occupations of New Orleans and Memphis, see Capers, *Occupied City*; Capers, *Biography of a River Town*; Blassingame, *Black New Orleans*; Nystrom, *New Orleans After the Civil War*.

4. Ash, *When the Yankees Came*, ix–x. Ash concludes that this development signaled the evolution of the war "from a limited war into a revolution." For two more recent occupation studies that in various ways emphasize the disillusioning effect that serving as an occupying force had on Federal soldiers, see Browning, " 'I Am Not So Patriotic as I Was Once' "; Lang, "The Garrison War."

5. Butler remained in command in New Orleans from May to mid-December 1862. Sherman led the Federal force in Memphis from late July to late November 1862.

6. Steven V. Ash also notes the fundamental restraint, despite all the horrors perpetrated during the Civil War, that still marked the early Union occupations: "Though they came to hate the Southern people and sought to subjugate and punish them . . . they did not often pursue such tactics to their logical extreme." Ash, *When the Yankees Came*, 61.

7. Rowland and Croxall, *The Journal of Julia LeGrand*, 39; *OR*, ser. 1, vol. 6, 720.

8. *OR*, ser. 1, vol. 6, 720; "Letters of General Thomas Williams, 1862," 317.

9. De Forest, *A Volunteer's Adventures*, 19.

10. *OR*, ser. 1, vol. 6, 717–20.

11. Benjamin F. Butler to Edwin Stanton, 8 May 1862, Benjamin F. Butler Papers, LC; *New Orleans Commercial Bulletin*, 5 May 1862; *New Orleans Daily Crescent*, 3 May 1862; Butler, *Private and Official Correspondence of Gen. Benjamin F. Butler*, 1:455.

12. De Forest, *A Volunteer's Adventures*, 21.

13. *OR*, ser. 1, vol. 6, 720–22; *Private and Official Correspondence of Gen. Benjamin F. Butler*, 1:448–9. The "wife of a southern planter" further informed Butler that they had burned their remaining supply of cotton to ensure Union armies could not confiscate it.

14. *OR*, ser. 1, vol. 6, 722–25; *Harper's Weekly*, 14 June 1862.

15. *OR*, ser. 1, vol. 6, 722–25; *OR*, ser. 1, vol. 15, 447.

16. Benjamin F. Butler to Edwin Stanton, 16 May 1862, Butler Papers, LC. I am not suggesting that for the poorer classes of New Orleans hunger always outweighed loyalty to the Confederacy. Still, journalist Thomas Butler Gunn recorded in late December 1862 that Butler "was far from unpopular among the poorer classes in New Orleans, whom he had set to work and relieved from the misery brought upon them by secession." Thomas Butler Gunn Diaries, 22 December 1862, MHM.

17. *OR*, ser. 1, vol. 15, 421–22. *New Orleans Bee*, one of the newspapers suppressed for supposedly encouraging the destruction of cotton, had by late June "reappeared with an apology and explanation." Butler allowed the newspaper to resume publication. *Harper's Weekly*, 14 and 28 June 1862.

18. Palmer, *Thanksgiving Sermon*, 7; Reed, *Life of A. P. Dostie*, 55; *OR*, ser. 1, vol. 15, 426. For an extended discussion of wartime conflicts between clergy and Union and Confederate armies, see Rable, *God's Almost Chosen Peoples*, 317–34.

19. Solomon, *The Civil War Diary of Clara Solomon*, 354. For a convincing analysis of the reactions of New Orleans women to Butler's General Orders No. 28, see Jacqueline G. Campbell, " 'The Unmeaning Twaddle about Order 28,' " 11–30.

20. Porter, *Incidents and Anecdotes of the Civil War*, 72–73; Newton Williams Perkins to Brother, 29 May 1862, box 2, Montgomery Family Papers, LC; John B. Burrud to Ocean Newton Burrud, 28 December 1862, John B. Burrud Papers, HL; Corsan, *Two Months in the Confederate States*, 16.

21. *OR*, ser. 1, vol. 15, 426.

22. *OR*, ser. 1, vol. 10, pt. 2, 531; Parton, *General Butler in New Orleans*, 341; Benjamin F. Butler to Edwin Stanton, 16 May 1862, Butler Papers, LC.

23. Butler, *Private and Official Correspondence of Gen. Benjamin F. Butler*, 2:35–36. Jacqueline G. Campbell, " 'The Unmeaning Twaddle about Order 28,' " 16.

24. *Frank Leslie's Illustrated Weekly*, 12 July 1862; *Harper's Weekly*, 12 July 1862; Butler, *Private and Official Correspondence of Gen. Benjamin F. Butler*, 1:486–89.

25. Parton, *General Butler in New Orleans*, 295–96; *OR*, ser. 1, vol. 6, 732–34; Butler, *Private and Official Correspondence of Gen. Benjamin F. Butler*, 1:499–501; *OR*, ser. 1, vol. 15, 467.

26. Butler, *Autobiography and Personal Reminiscences*, 394; Rowland and Croxall, *The Journal of Julia LeGrand*, 46; *OR*, ser. 1, vol. 15, 462.

27. Chase, *Diary and Correspondence of Salmon P. Chase*, 310.

28. *Harper's Weekly*, 31 May 1862, 14 June 1862.

29. *OR*, ser. 2, vol. 4, 134–35, 650, 350; Butler, *Autobiography and Personal Reminiscences*, 449. In one of the strangest twists in Civil War history, the paths of Butler and William Mumford's widow crossed again after the war ended. Butler had supposedly promised to assist Mary Mumford if ever needed. In 1869, while living in Wytheville, Virginia, she pleaded with Butler for help retiring outstanding debt. Butler complied, helped her secure a place to live in Washington, D.C., and used his influence to secure a job for her at the Department of Internal Revenue. When Mary lost that job for

political reasons, Butler found her another one with the postal service. Butler even saw Mumford's sons on occasion. There are a substantial number of letters between Butler and Mary Mumford in Benjamin F. Butler Papers, LC, from mid-August 1866 to mid-April 1881.

30. *OR*, ser. 2, vol. 4, 19–20, 105–6; Butler, *Private and Official Correspondence of Gen. Benjamin F. Butler*, 2:24–25; *OR*, ser. 2, vol. 4, 105; Phillips, "A Southern Woman's Story of Her Imprisonments," box 1, Phillip Phillips Family Papers, LC.

31. *Harper's Weekly*, 5 July 1862.

32. John W. DeForest to Lillie Devereux Blake, 7 August 1862, Lillie Devereux Blake Papers, MHM.

33. *OR*, ser. 1, vol. 6, 717; John W. DeForest to Lillie Umsted, 12 October 1862, Lillie Devereux Blake Papers, MHM; De Forest, *A Volunteer's Adventures*, 50; *OR*, ser. 1, vol. 15, 445, 478.

34. *OR*, ser. 1, vol. 15, 538–41; Butler, *Private and Official Correspondence of Gen. Benjamin F. Butler* 2:366. In early December, Butler imposed another set of fines against the same residents. *OR*, ser. 1, vol. 15, 607.

35. *Harper's Weekly*, 16 August 1862; Porter, *Incidents and Anecdotes of the Civil War*, 73.

36. Butler, *Private and Official Correspondence of Gen. Benjamin F. Butler*, 1:463–64; Benjamin F. Butler to George C. Coppel, 11 May 1862, Butler Papers, LC. As a legal question, Butler believed the British subjects plainly disregarded their neutrality and thereby deserved to be treated as belligerents loyal to the Confederacy.

37. Benjamin F. Butler to Edwin Stanton, 16 May 1862, Butler Papers, LC; Butler, *Private and Official Correspondence of Gen. Benjamin F. Butler*, 469.

38. *OR*, ser. 3, vol. 2, 117–19, 122.

39. Ibid., 132–35, 503–5.

40. *OR*, ser. 1, vol. 15, 483–84.

41. Ibid., 497–98.

42. Ibid., 571; Butler, *Private and Official Correspondence of Gen. Benjamin F. Butler*, 298–99.

43. Benjamin F. Butler to Edwin Stanton, 1 October 1862, Butler Papers, LC.

44. *Harper's Weekly*, 16 Aug. 1862.

45. Newton Williams Perkins to his brother, 21 May 1862, Montgomery Family Papers, LC.

46. Historians have tended to characterize Sherman's time in Memphis as indicative merely of the Union army's shift from conciliatory war policies. See, for example, Marszalek, *Sherman*, 189; Fellman, *Citizen Sherman*, 136–39; Capers, *Biography of a River Town*, 157–58.

47. Sherman, *Memoirs of General William T. Sherman*, 285; Letter from J. Watts Judson, 19 June 1862, Judson-Fairbanks Papers, HL.

48. *OR*, ser. 1, vol. 17, pt. 2, 117–18, 112–13; Marszalek, *Sherman*, 190.

49. Simpson and Berlin, *Sherman's Civil War*, 258–59; *OR*, ser. 1, vol. 17, pt. 2, 294–96.

50. *OR*, ser. 1, vol. 17, pt. 2, 140–41.

51. Simpson and Berlin, *Sherman's Civil War*, 269–72.

52. *OR*, ser. 3, vol. 2, 382; *OR*, ser. 1, vol. 17, pt. 2, 186.

53. *OR*, ser. 1, vol. 17, pt. 2, 122, 150. The women of Memphis, Sherman wrote, all "are secesh. Of course they keep their tongues, but they look the Devil to every one of our cloth." Simpson and Berlin, *Sherman's Civil War*, 281.

54. Simpson and Berlin, *Sherman's Civil War*, 262.

55. *OR*, ser. 1, vol. 17, pt. 2, 156–57; Simpson and Berlin, *Sherman's Civil War*, 286. Sherman, following Grant, affirmed that vacated proprietors might eventually return, reassert their loyalty to the Union, and reclaim the rents lately collected from tenants by the Federals.

56. *OR*, ser. 1, vol. 17, pt. 2, 219–20; Simpson and Berlin, *Sherman's Civil War*, 262; *OR*, ser. 1, vol. 17, pt. 2, 173; Hallum, *The Diary of an Old Lawyer*, 187–88; Simpson and Berlin, *Sherman's Civil War*, 298–300.

57. Simpson and Berlin, *Sherman's Civil War*, 279, 283–84, 307–8.

58. *OR*, ser. 1, vol. 17, pt. 2, 235–36, 244, 273.

59. Simpson and Berlin, *Sherman's Civil War*, 316–17; *OR*, ser. 1, vol. 17, pt. 2, 287. On another occasion, when weighing an appropriate response to the attacks from the banks of the Mississippi, Sherman became all the more convinced "adherents of their cause must suffer for these cowardly acts," and even briefly considered expelling "ten secession families for every boat fired on." *OR*, ser. 1, vol. 17, pt. 2, 280.

60. Simpson and Berlin, *Sherman's Civil War*, 263, 266, 263–64.

61. Ibid., 263–64, 297; Thorndike, *The Sherman Letters*, 169.

62. Berlin et al., *Freedom*, ser. 1, vol. 1, 192.

63. Ibid., 201. For more on Phelps and his conflict with Butler, see Oakes, *Freedom National*, 219–23.

64. DeForest, *A Volunteer's Adventures*, 22–23, 31.

65. Berlin et al., *Freedom*, ser. 1, vol. 1, 202–3, 209–10.

66. Berlin et al., *Freedom*, ser. 1, vol. 1, 211–13.

67. *OR*, ser. 1, vol. 15, 443–44.

68. Ibid., 439–40.

69. Ibid., 440, 485–86, 516.

70. Ibid., 534–35; Butler, *Private and Official Correspondence of Gen. Benjamin F. Butler*, 2:126–27.

71. *OR*, ser. 1, vol. 15, 536. By late August, however, Butler had decided to incorporate into his armies the existing "Native Guard" regiments of free African Americans. "I must have more troops," he wrote his wife, "and I see no way of getting them save by arming the black brigade." Butler, *Private and Official Correspondence of Gen. Benjamin F. Butler*, 2:186.

72. *OR*, ser. 1, vol. 17, pt. 2, 15.

73. Ibid., 113.

74. Ibid., 158–59; Simpson and Berlin, *Sherman's Civil War*, 260, 285.

75. Simpson and Berlin, *Sherman's Civil War*, 285.

76. William T. Sherman to John Sherman, 1 October 1862, Papers of William T. Sherman, reel 6, LC.

Chapter Three

1. "Instructions for the Government of Armies of the United States in the Field," article 29.

2. Abraham Lincoln was not involved in the drafting of General Orders No. 100. He entrusted this task wholly to Francis Lieber, Henry W. Halleck, and the committee formed to write the code. The document was not in any meaningful sense "Lincoln's Code," contrary to what John Fabian Witt has suggested. Witt, *Lincoln's Code*, 212–19, 226–27, 229–32, 237.

3. *OR*, ser. 3, vol. 2, 951.

4. For one insightful example see Childress, "Francis Lieber's Interpretation of the Laws of War."

5. Recent scholarship on Lieber wrongly emphasizes slavery-related issues and emancipation as Lieber's primary motivation for drafting the code. See Witt, *Lincoln's Code*, 197–229, 240–49; Mancini, "Francis Lieber, Slavery, and the 'Genesis' of the Laws of War."

6. In Mark Grimsley's influential study of the evolution of Union military policy from "conciliation" to "hard war," he labels the period of the code's appearance (from July 1862 through 1863) as a transitional era of "pragmatism" between conciliation and hard war. In contrast, I seek to show that this middle period of war was not a somewhat muddled moment of transition but instead a moment of clarity in which the soon-dominant hard yet humane war policy received its clearest and most influential articulation in the Lieber code. See Grimsley, *Hard Hand of War*, 2–4.

7. Lieber, *Miscellaneous Writings*, 1:149–71; Lieber, "A Reminiscence," 553–58.

8. Joseph Story quoted in Freidel, *Francis Lieber*, 141; Freidel, *Francis Lieber*, 80–81; Witt, *Lincoln's Code*, 176; O'Brien, "The Stranger in the South," in Mack and Lesesne, *Francis Lieber and the Culture of the Mind*, 34.

9. Lieber, "Law and Usages of War," 29 October 1861, FLP, box 2, fol. 16, JHU; Lieber, *Manual of Political Ethics*, 2: 632–33.

10. Francis Lieber to Samuel B. Ruggles, 23 April 1847, FLP, box 39, HL; Sumner, *The True Grandeur of Nations*, 4–5; Perry, *The Life and Letters of Francis Lieber*, 198; Francis Lieber to George Hillard, 18 April 1854, FLP, box 31, HL; Francis Lieber to Charles Sumner and George Hillard, 16 March 1844, FLP, box 41, HL.

11. Francis Lieber to Edward Bates, 23 July 1861, FLP, box 23, HL; Francis Lieber, "A Song on Our Country and Her Flag," FLP, container 1, LC; Freidel, *Francis Lieber*, 299–319.

12. Lieber, "Law and Usages of War," 29 October 1861, FLP, box 2, fol. 16, JHU; Lieber, "Twenty-Seven Definitions and Elementary Positions Concerning the Law and Usages of War," FLP, box 2, fol. 15, JHU.

13. Francis Lieber, "Twenty-Seven Definitions and Elementary Positions Concerning the Law and Usages of War," FLP, box 2, fol. 15, JHU.

14. Francis Lieber to George Hillard, 11 May 1861, FLP, box 31, HL; Francis Lieber to Oscar Lieber, 2 November 1860, FLP, box 37, HL.

15. Francis Lieber to Guido Norman Lieber, 4 March 1862, FLP, box 32, HL; Francis Lieber to Henry Halleck, 9 August 1862, FLP, box 27, HL.

16. Freidel, *Francis Lieber,* 325.

17. Francis Lieber to Guido Norman Lieber, 25 March 1862, FLP, box 32, HL; Foner, *The Life and Writings of Frederick Douglass,* 3:252; Grimsley, *Hard Hand of War,* 67–95.

18. Siddali, *From Property to Person,* 120–44; Oakes, *Freedom National,* 226–40; Grimsley, *Hard Hand of War,* 68–75.

19. Francis Lieber to Henry Halleck, 9 August 1862, FLP, box 27, HL.

20. Ransom Allen Perkins to "Dear Friends," 21 January 1863, Civil War Letters of Ransom Allen Perkins, HL; Francis Lieber to Henry Halleck, 9 March 1863, FLP, box 27, HL; McPherson, *Battle Cry of Freedom,* 538–45; Oakes, *Freedom National,* 301–39.

21. Bacon, *Conciliation,* 18; Bellows, *The War to End Only When the Rebellion Ceases,* 15; S. M. Campbell, *The Light in the Clouds,* 13; Bacon, *Conciliation,* 18; Thompson, *The Psalter and the Sword,* 12; Post, *A Thanksgiving Sermon,* 12.

22. Albert Barnes, *The Conditions of Peace,* 12–13; Armitage, *The Past, Present, and Future of the United States,* 13; Shedd, *The Union and the War,* 15; Bacon, *Conciliation,* 6.

23. Beecher, *Freedom and War,* 389–90; Thompson, *The Psalter and the Sword,* 3; Bacon, *Conciliation,* 5–6; Breed, *Faith and Patience,* 21; Leavitt, *God the Protector and Hope of the Nation,* 6, 13.

24. Armitage, *The Past, Present, and Future of the United States,* 15; Shedd, *The Union and the War,* 39; Thompson, *The Psalter and the Sword,* 21.

25. S. M. Campbell, *The Light in the Clouds,* 14.

26. *New York Times,* 17 December 1862; Quoted in Rable, *Fredericksburg! Fredericksburg!,* 325. Quoted in Freidel, *Francis Lieber,* 344.

27. Francis Lieber to Charles Sumner, 19 May 1863, FLP, box 43, HL.

28. In highlighting these three issues, I argue against recent trends in scholarship on Lieber that emphasize emancipation as the chief inspiration of the code, an argument made most forcefully by John Fabian Witt in *Lincoln's Code.* Before Witt, Matthew Mancini drew attention to a letter from Lieber to Benjamin Lossing dated January 1866. In this letter, solicited by Lossing (then at work on his massive *Pictorial History of the Civil War in the United States of America*), Lieber offers a starkly different account of the genesis of the code. Here Lieber does not mention the issues he

raised in 1863 with Sumner, but instead credits emancipation as the chief inspiration for the code. Mancini concludes slavery (especially the self-emancipation of slaves) was the "principal" consideration behind Lieber's code. Mancini's argument breaks down in his explanation for why the postwar letter should be trusted as more accurate than the one written weeks after the code's issuance. Mancini suggests Lieber played down slavery to Sumner because he feared raising the volatile issue might ruin their recently restored friendship. But Lieber and Sumner agreed completely on all the essential points concerning slavery and the laws of war. It is likelier that Lieber emphasized slavery retrospectively as a "genesis" of the code because by 1866 it would have been well apparent that the momentous and internationally lauded consequence of the American Civil War was the abolition of slavery. The always-ambitious Lieber naturally would have sought to secure for his signal work a central place in the historic story of American emancipation. Lieber had no reason not to recount in honest detail the true genesis of the code to Sumner; there are plausible reasons why he would not have been equally honest to Lossing, misleadingly emphasizing slavery instead. See Mancini, "Francis Lieber, Slavery, and the 'Genesis' of the Laws of War."

29. Neff, *Justice in Blue and Gray*, 15–29.

30. The blockade of Confederate ports raised the same legal and diplomatic concerns. Lieber concluded, "We do not acknowledge the Carolinians as an independent nation, by blockading Charleston anymore than we declare the 'Confederacy' a sovereign government by treating their captured soldier as prisoners of war." Francis Lieber to Edward Bates, 9 November 1862, FLP, box 23, HL.

31. "The Disposal of Prisoners: Would the Exchange of Prisoners Amount to a Partial Acknowledgement of the Insurgents as Belligerents, According to International Law?" *New York Times*, 19 August 1861; Freidel, *Francis Lieber*, 320; Hartigan, *Lieber's Code and the Law of War*, 9.

32. Francis Lieber to Charles Sumner, 19 August 1861, FLP, box 42, HL.

33. George Hillard to Francis Lieber, 15 September 1862, FLP, box 14, HL; Witt, *Lincoln's Code*, 191–92.

34. Francis Lieber to Henry Halleck, 23 July 1862, FLP, box 27, HL; Henry Halleck to Francis Lieber, 30 July 1862, FLP, box 9, HL; Francis Lieber to Henry Halleck, 1 August 1862, FLP, box 27, HL; Henry Halleck to Francis Lieber, 20 August 1862, FLP, box 9, HL; George Hillard to Francis Lieber, 15 September 1862, FLP, box 14, HL; Evert Augustus Duyckinck to Francis Lieber, 22 September 1862, FLP, box 6, HL.

35. *OR*, ser. 3, vol. 2, 304, 307–8; Hartigan, *Lieber's Code and the Law of War*, 11. Lieber did not refer explicitly to Mosby and Quantrill as emblematic examples of legitimate partisans and lawless guerrillas as I have done.

36. Francis Lieber to Charles Sumner, 20 August 1861, FLP, box 42, HL; McPherson, *Battle Cry of Freedom*, 536–38.

37. Francis Lieber to Henry Halleck, 25 November 1862, FLP, box 27, HL; Lieber to Sumner quoted in Mancini, "Francis Lieber, Slavery, and the 'Genesis' of the Laws of War," 339; Freidel, *Francis Lieber*, 321.

38. Francis Lieber to Henry Halleck, 13 November 1862, FLP, box 27, HL; Witt, *Lincoln's Code*, 230.

39. Francis Lieber to Henry Halleck, 20 February 1863, FLP, box 37, HL.

40. Childress, "Francis Lieber's Interpretation of the Laws of War," 38–40.

41. Henry Halleck to Francis Lieber, 25 May 1863, FLP, box 9, HL.

42. "Instructions for the Government of Armies of the United States in the Field," article 29.

43. Ibid., article 14.

44. Ibid., article 14.

45. Ibid., articles 15, 20.

46. Ibid., article 68. For an insightful introduction to Lieber's thinking in relation to Vattel and Clausewitz, see Witt, *Lincoln's Code*, 182–86.

47. Instructions for the Government of Armies of the United States in the Field," article 30. In James Turner Johnson's words, Lieber added to Clausewitz "a renewed emphasis on the limits defined in the customary usages of war." Johnson, "Lieber and the Theory of War," 66.

48. "Instructions for the Government of Armies of the United States in the Field," articles 5, 16, and 29.

49. Ibid., articles 105–10, 152; Hartigan, *Lieber's Code and the Law of War*, 18–19.

50. "Instructions for the Government of Armies of the United States in the Field," article 128. Lieber's sixteen-article section on the parole was issued to Union armies nearly two months in advance of the full code as General Order No. 49. *OR*, ser. 2, vol. 5, 306–7.

51. "Instructions for the Government of Armies of the United States in the Field," article 82.

52. Ibid., articles 111–14.

53. Francis Lieber to Charles Sumner, December 19, 1861, FLP, box 42, HL; Francis Lieber, "A Memoir on the Military Use of Coloured Persons, free or slave, that come to our armies for support or protection," in Francis Lieber to Henry Halleck, August 9, 1862, FLP, box 27, HL; "Instructions for the Government of Armies of the United States in the Field," articles 42–43.

54. John Fabian Witt has argued unconvincingly that Lieber intended for his code to "[remake] the American law of war tradition for the age of Emancipation," an argument undermined by Lieber's own letter to Sumner. More perplexing is Witt's suggestion that slavery and emancipation were dominant concerns of the code's articles, which often leads him to misread particular articles. For example, Witt incorrectly interprets article 82—an article on guerrilla warfare, falling within a section devoted to that issue, and drawn explicitly from Lieber's *Guerrilla Parties Considered*—as in fact about "uprisings of freedpeople behind Confederate lines." Witt, *Lincoln's Code*, 240.

55. "Instructions for the Government of Armies of the United States in the Field," articles 49–50, 56, 75, 76, 80, 72, 60–63.

56. Ibid., article 57.

57. Ibid., articles 27–28, 59; Childress, "Francis Lieber's Interpretation of the Laws of War," 66–68.

58. "Instructions for the Government of Armies of the United States in the Field," articles 22–25.

59. Ibid., articles 43–44. Henry Halleck had in early March 1863 advised Maj. Gen. William S. Rosencrans, and by extension all Union commanders in the West, to show precisely this same sort of discretion in treating civilians differently according to their loyalties. *OR*, ser. 1, vol. 23, pt. 2, 107–9.

60. "Instructions for the Government of Armies of the United States in the Field," articles 23, 37.

61. Theodore Dwight Woolsey to Francis Lieber, 21 May 1863, FLP, box 66, HL; Alexander Dallas Bache to Francis Lieber, 25 February 1863, FLP, box 1, HL; William Wirt Howe to Francis Lieber, [September 1863?], FLP, box 11, HL; For a sample of northern newspapers' reports about the Code, see *Daily Cleveland Herald*, 18 May 1863; *Boston Daily Advertiser*, 18 May 1863; *Milwaukee Daily Sentinel*, 19 May 1863; *Baltimore Sun*, 21 May 1863; *New York Times*, 24 May 1863; *Washington Daily National Intelligencer*, 5 June 1863; George Hillard to Francis Lieber, 12 June 1863, FLP, box 14, HL.

62. Francis Lieber to Karl Josef Mittermaier, 24 June 1863, FLP, box 38, HL.

63. *OR*, ser. 2, vol. 6, 41. Some Confederate newspapers reported on the code and briefly summarized its content, but did not offer critical editorial commentary on the code. See *The Charleston Mercury*, 30 May 1863 and *The New Orleans Daily Picayune*, 5 June 1863, 2. These two reports were verbatim copies of a 24 May 1863 story published by the *New York Times*.

64. Francis Lieber to Henry Halleck, 20 May 1863, FLP, box 27, HL; Francis Lieber to Charles Sumner, 19 May 1863, FLP, box 43, HL; Francis Lieber to S. Austin Allibone, 9 November 1863, FLP, box 22, HL; Ethan Allen Hitchcock to Francis Lieber, 22 October 1863, FLP, box 11, HL.

65. Geoffrey Best quoted in Mancini, "Francis Lieber," 328.

Chapter Four

1. "Instructions for the Government of Armies of the United States in the Field," articles 27–28.

2. Most scholarship on retaliation focuses primarily on atrocities against African American troops and reactions by Federal authorities, often with the goal of demonstrating how racial attitudes inhibited efforts to compel Confederates to recognize African Americans as legitimate soldiers. See for example, Urwin, *Black Flag over Dixie*; Burkhardt, *Confederate Rage, Yankee Wrath*. A far less illuminating strand of scholarship simply catalogs, with little analytical rigor, occasions when Federals or

Confederates resorted to retaliation, obscuring both rationales and instances of restraint. See Speer, *War of Vengeance*.

3. *The Liberator*, 13 May 1864.

4. *Ibid.*

5. For a similar effort to explain why Federals were wary of resorting to retaliation in kind, see Neely, *The Civil War and the Limits of Destruction*, 170–97.

6. Aaron Sheehan-Dean has likewise argued the "practice of retaliation emerged as a method of curtailing violence." Sheehan-Dean, *"Lex Talionis* in the U.S. Civil War," 183.

7. Edwards Pierrepont to Charles Sumner, 26 February 1865, Papers of Charles Sumner, Houghton Library, Harvard University, microfilm edition, series 1, reel 32; *The Liberator*, 13 May 1864; *Congressional Globe*, 38th Cong., 2nd sess., pt. 1:381; Basler, *The Collected Works of Abraham Lincoln*, 7:345; *New York Herald*, 11 December 1864.

8. *Harper's Weekly*, 7 January 1865; *Army and Navy Journal*, 30 July 1864.

9. *Congressional Globe*, 38th Cong., 2nd sess., pt. 1:404; *Boston Daily Advertiser*, 4 August 1863.

10. *New York Times*, 27 December 1864; Frederick Douglass, *Autobiographies*, 787.

11. *Congressional Globe*, 38th Cong., 2nd sess., pt. 1:364; L. Abbott to Charles Sumner, 25 January 1865, Papers of Charles Sumner, ser. 1, reel 32; *Congressional Globe*, 38th Cong., 2nd sess., pt. 1:391.

12. *OR*, ser. 2, vol. 6, 73; *Harper's Weekly*, 11 July 1863; Francis Lieber to Lafayette Sabine Foster, 2 February 1865, FLP, box 26, HL.

13. "Instructions for the Government of Armies of the United States in the Field," articles 27 and 28; Francis Lieber to Henry Halleck, 19 April 1864, FLP, box 9, HL.

14. Francis Lieber to Henry Halleck, 2 June 1863, FLP, box 9, HL.

15. Burkhardt, *Confederate Rage, Yankee Wrath*, 2.

16. Glatthaar, *Forged in Battle*; Berlin, Reidy, and Rowland, *Freedom's Soldiers*.

17. Quoted in Neff, *Justice in Blue and Gray*, 72; James G. Hollandsworth concludes that eleven white officers were likely executed in accordance with this Confederate threat. Hollandsworth, "The Execution of White Officers from Black Units by Confederate Forces During the Civil War," in Urwin, *Black Flag over Dixie*, 52–64.

18. Basler, *The Collected Works of Abraham Lincoln*, 6:357.

19. Francis Lieber to Joseph Holt, 15 July 1863, FLP, box 11, HL; *Harper's Weekly*, 15 August 1863.

20. *OR*, ser. 1, vol. 24, pt. 3, 426; Francis Lieber to Henry Halleck, 7 January 1863, FLP, box 27, HL.

21. For a meticulous account of the atrocities at Fort Pillow, see Albert Castel, "The Fort Pillow Massacre: An Examination of the Evidence," in Urwin, *Black Flag over Dixie*, 89–103.

22. Basler, *The Collected Works of Abraham Lincoln*, 7:302–3.

23. *Frank Leslie's Illustrated Newspaper*, 7 May 1864; *Christian Advocate and Journal*, June 1864; *New York Times*, 16 April 1864; *Chicago Tribune*, 16 April 1864; *New York Herald*, 16 April 1864; *Harper's Weekly*, 30 April 1864.

24. *Harper's Weekly*, 30 April 1864; *Chicago Tribune*, 30 April 1864; *New York Times*, 2 May 1864.

25. For more on the Committee's investigation and report, see Tap, *Over Lincoln's Shoulder*, 193–203.

26. U.S. Congress, *Fort Pillow Massacre*, 38th Cong., 1st sess., 1864, H. Rept. 65, 2; Derek W. Frisby, "Remember Fort Pillow!: Politics, Atrocity Propaganda, and the Evolution of Hard War," in Urwin, *Black Flag over Dixie*, 118.

27. Welles, *Diary of Gideon Welles*, 2:24.

28. Edward Bates to Lincoln, 4 May 1864; Edwin Stanton to Lincoln, 5 May 1864, reel 73, both in Abraham Lincoln Papers, LC.

29. Montgomery Blair to Lincoln, 6 May 1864; Edward Bates to Lincoln, 4 May 1864; William Seward to Lincoln, 4 May 1864, reel 73, all in Abraham Lincoln Papers, LC.

30. Basler, *The Collected Works of Abraham Lincoln*, 7:345–46.

31. Michael Sanders has argued that the May 1864 ration reduction, "signaled nothing less than the advent of a new and far more determined effort to develop and implement a policy of successive rounds of retaliation, deliberately designed to lower conditions in the camps and increase immeasurably the suffering of prisoners." Sanders, *While in the Hands of the Enemy*, 237.

32. *OR*, ser. 2, vol. 6, 446, 486.

33. Ibid., 512, 513–14, 530.

34. *New York Times*, 17 and 22 April 1864; *Christian Advocate and Journal*, May 1864; *Harper's Weekly*, 9 January 1864.

35. *Chicago Tribune*, 19 November 1863; *New York Herald*, 11 November 1863; *New York Times*, 31 October 1863. For similar reactions see *Harper's Weekly*, 9 January 1864 and *New York Times*, 6 November 1863.

36. *OR*, ser. 2, vol. 6, 515.

37. Ibid., 537–38, 552. Days later, Ould provided Meredith a detailed account of conditions in camps in Richmond to corroborate his claims. See *OR*, ser. 2, vol. 6, 544–47.

38. A New York cavalryman later told Hitchcock that he agreed with this rationale, explaining, "An unyielding adherence to a line of conduct that will compel an observance of the rules of honorable warfare is an absolute necessity." *OR*, ser. 2, vol. 6, 630.

39. *New York Times*, 2 December 1863. Hitchcock's letter is also reprinted in full in *OR*, ser. 2, vol. 6, 594–600. For a report from Meredith on his effort to exchange 12,000 prisoners, see *OR*, ser. 2, vol. 6, 555–56.

40. *OR*, ser. 2, vol. 6, 686, 648.

41. Quoted in Tap, *Over Lincoln's Shoulder*, 201; *OR*, ser. 2, vol. 7, 110–11.

42. *OR*, ser. 2, vol. 7, 110–11.

43. U.S. Congress. Joint Committee on the Conduct of the War, *Fort Pillow Massacre Report*, 1–3; Tap, *Over Lincoln's Shoulder*, 203.

44. *Harper's Weekly*, 18 June 1864.

45. *OR*, ser. 2, vol. 7, 73, 150–51.

46. *OR*, ser. 2, vol. 5, 480, 556–57.

47. Ibid., 691.

48. Ibid., 703–4, 716.

49. *OR*, ser. 2, vol. 6, 108–9, 114; *New York Times*, 26 July 1863. For examples of the northern press reporting on Sawyer and Flinn, see *Harper's Weekly*, 5 September 1863, 3 October 1863, and 17 October 1863.

50. Lippincott, "Lee-Sawyer Exchange."

51. *OR*, ser. 2, vol. 6, 69, 118, 350–51. Lippincott, "Lee-Sawyer Exchange"; Neal, "Rebels, Ropes, and Reprieves."

52. *OR*, ser. 2, vol. 6, 927, 975–76, 990–91. *New York Times*, 13 March 1864; *Harper's Weekly*, 19 March 1864.

53. *OR*, ser. 2, vol. 7, 185, 216–17.

54. *OR*, ser. 1, vol. 35, pt. 2, 134.

55. Ibid., 105–7.

56. *New York Times*, 23 June 1864. *OR*, ser. 2, vol. 7, 371; *OR*, ser. 1, vol. 35, pt. 2, 141. In its 16 July 1864 edition, *Harper's Weekly* reprinted the names every officer held in Charleston.

57. *OR*, ser. 1, vol. 35, pt. 2, 143, 150, 164. The fifty officers that Hoffman sent to Foster included two major generals, three brigadier generals, fifteen colonels, thirteen lieutenant colonels, and seventeen majors. The complete list of prisoners sent—including rank, regiment, and date and location of capture, can be found in *OR*, ser. 1, vol. 35, pt. 2, 147–48.

58. *OR*, ser. 1, vol. 35, pt. 2, 161–62.

59. Ibid., 170, 174–75, 212–13; *Brooklyn Daily Eagle*, 18 August 1864; *Chicago Tribune*, 11 August 1864; *Harper's Weekly*, 20 August 1864.

60. *OR*, ser. 2, vol. 7, 502.

61. Ibid., 568, 598.

62. Ibid., 625.

63. Ibid., 768, 773, 789, 894, 900, 817, 783.

64. Ibid., 826–27; *New York Herald*, 17 September 1864.

65. *OR*, ser. 2, vol. 7, 819; Fulkerson, "The Prison Experience of a Confederate Soldier Who Was under Fire"; Francis Barnes, "Imprisoned under Fire."

66. *OR*, ser. 2, vol. 7, 874–75.

67. Ibid., 981–82, 1007, 1058, 1073.

68. Murray, *The Immortal Six Hundred*, 268.

69. *New York Times*, 8 August 1864; *Boston Daily Advertiser*, 25 October 1864.

70. The paragraphs that follow are indebted to Mark Neely's illuminating discussion of the Senate's 1865 retaliation debate in Neely, *The Civil War and the Limits of Destruction*, 170–97.

71. *Congressional Globe*, 38th Cong., 2nd sess., pt. 1:73, 267–69, 363–64.

72. Admittedly, some Senators may have had ulterior or multiple motives for participating in the debate. Mark Neely has argued that Radicals in Congress revived the prisoner of war issue in this moment of the war in the hopes of turning public opinion against rumored peace negotiations with Confederates. Neely, *The Civil War and the Limits of Destruction*, 188–90.

73. *Congressional Globe*, 38th Cong., 2nd sess., pt. 1:363–65.

74. Ibid., 1:381–82, 453, 389–91, 386–88.

75. Ibid., 1:474. Lieber's editorial was published 26 December 1864.

76. *Congressional Globe*, 38th Cong., 2nd sess., pt. 1:410.

77. The amended resolution received almost unanimous support among Senate Democrats, as well as opposition from a core group of Radical Republicans. Ultimately, some of the strongest supporters of the original resolution—Benjamin Wade, Morton Wilkinson, and Jacob Howard—voted against the final version.

78. *Monthly Religious Magazine*, March 1865; *Boston Daily Advertiser*, 27 January 1865; *Chicago Tribune*, 22 December 1864, 1 February 1865.

79. *New York Times*, 27 December 1864; *Harper's Weekly*, 7 January 1865.

80. Neely, *The Civil War and the Limits of Destruction*, 182–85.

81. John Maxwell to Charles Sumner, 27 January 1865; D. W. Alvord to Charles Sumner, 29 January 1865; L. Abbott to Charles Sumner, 25 January 1865; Orville Wilder to Charles Sumner, 27 February 1865; William Dix to Charles Sumner, 28 February 1865, all in The Papers of Charles Sumner, ser. 1, reel 32.

82. Francis Lieber to Charles Sumner, 22 January 1865, The Papers of Charles Sumner, ser. 1, reel 32; *New York Times*, 26 December 1864.

Chapter Five

1. Kidd, *A Cavalryman with Custer*, 290–92.

2. Ibid.

3. Henry Hitchcock to Ethan Allen Hitchcock, 9 November 1864, Hitchcock Family Papers, MHM; Hitchcock, *Marching with Sherman*, 62.

4. Hitchcock, *Marching with Sherman*, 77, 93.

5. Ibid., 99.

6. Although some historians have suggested Sheridan's "burning" of the Valley and Sherman's March to the Sea eerily foreshadowed modern total warfare in the nature of its violence, others have more convincingly documented how both campaigns were not indiscriminate in their destruction. See William G. Thomas, "Nothing Ought to Astonish Us," in Gallagher, *The Shenandoah Valley Campaign of 1864*; Neely, *The Civil*

War and the Limits of Destruction, 110–19; Grimsley, *The Hard Hand of War*, 190; Marszalek, *Sherman's March to the Sea*, 14; Glatthaar, *The March to the Sea and Beyond*.

7. Francis Lieber to Henry Halleck, 8 March 1864, FLP, box 28, HL; Hattaway and Jones, *How the North Won*, 515–16; Grimsley, *The Hard Hand of War*, 162–70.

8. Francis Lieber to Martin Russell Thayer, 8 August 1864, FLP, box 50, HL; Hattaway and Jones, *How the North Won*, 552–615; McPherson, *Battle Cry of Freedom*, 725–35.

9. Early, *A Memoir of the Last Year of the War for Independence*, 70; Gallagher, *The Shenandoah Valley Campaign of 1864*, x–xii, 6–8, 42; McPherson, *Battle Cry of Freedom*, 737–39, 756–57; Hattaway and Jones, *How the North Won*, 575, 585–87, 615; Grimsley, *The Hard Hand of War*, 166–67, 178–81.

10. *OR*, ser.1, vol. 43, pt. 1, 698; *OR*, ser. 1, vol. 43, pt. 2, 202; *OR*, ser. 1, vol. 43, pt. 1, 58; Hattaway and Jones, *How the North Won*, 615–20; Gallagher, *The Shenandoah Valley Campaign of 1864*, xiv, 9, 14–16.

11. *OR*, ser. 1, vol. 43, pt. 2, 202; *OR*, ser. 1, vol. 43, pt. 2, 50, 58; *OR*, ser. 1, vol. 43, pt. 1, 698; Sheridan, *Personal Memoirs*, 478.

12. Sheridan, *Personal Memoirs*, 485; Britton and Reed, *To My Beloved Wife and Boy at Home*, 293; Wittenberg, *With Sheridan in the Final Campaign Against Lee*, 9; "With the First New York Dragoons," Letters of Jared L. Ainsworth, The Harrisburg Civil War Roundtable Collection, box 1, USAMHI; Williams, *Diary and Letters of Rutherford Birchard Hayes*, 2:523; John Suter to Wife, 1 November 1864, John Suter Papers, The Harrisburg Civil War Roundtable Collection, box 32, USAMHI.

13. Holcomb, *Southern Sons, Northern Soldiers*, 157; *OR* ser. 1, vol. 43, pt. 2, 220; Williams, *Diary and Letters of Rutherford Birchard Hayes*, 2: 519; Britton and Reed, *To My Beloved Wife and Boy at Home*, 293; Diary of Thomas Campbell, 30 September 1864, Civil War Document Collection, box 20, USAMHI.

14. Britton and Reed, *To My Beloved Wife and Boy at Home*, 293; Diary of Thomas Campbell, 16 August 1864, Civil War Document Collection, box 20, USAMHI; Kiper, *Dear Catharine, Dear Taylor*, 257; Collier and Collier, *Yours for the Union*, 361.

15. Bayard Taylor to Sister, 20 August 1864, Taylor Family Correspondence, HL; Britton and Reed, *To My Beloved Wife and Boy at Home*, 310; Diary of Thomas Campbell, 7 September 1864, Civil War Document Collection, box 20, USAMHI; "With the First New York Dragoons," Letters of Jared L. Ainsworth, The Harrisburg Civil War Roundtable Collection, box 1, USAMHI.

16. Morgan W. Lindsley to Mother, 18 October 1864, Lewis Leigh Collection, box 5, USAMHI; William M. Martindell to Father, 12 October 1864, Civil War Document Collection, box 76, USAMHI; John B. Burrud to Wife, 20 August 1864, John B. Burrud Papers, box 3, HL; Diary of Thomas Campbell, 15 August 1864, Civil War Document Collection, box 20, USAMHI; Diary of Thomas Campbell, 26 September 1864, Civil War Document Collection, box 20, USAMHI.

17. *OR*, ser. 1, vol. 43, pt. 2, 250; Thomas, "Nothing Ought to Astonish Us," in Gallagher, *The Shenandoah Valley Campaign of 1864*, 240–41. Thomas compares the

estimated losses with agricultural production levels recorded in the 1860 census; *OR*, ser. 1, vol. 43, pt. 1, 40–57. For additional estimates from Sheridan on the extent of the destruction committed by his army, see *OR*, ser. 1, vol. 43, pt. 1, 28–33, 43–57.

18. Quoted in Wert, *Mosby's Rangers*, 246, 250.

19. *OR*, ser. 1, vol. 43, pt. 1, 30; Hagemann, *Fighting Rebels and Redskins*, 302–3; Rutherford B. Hayes disapproved of Sheridan's initial retaliation, which, he said, did not accord with "my views or feelings." Williams, *Diary and Letters of Rutherford Birchard Hayes*, 2:522.

20. *OR*, ser. 1, vol. 43, pt. 2, 679.

21. The paragraphs that follow rely on Andre Fleche, "Uncivilized War: The Shenandoah Valley Campaign, the Northern Democratic Press, and the Election of 1864," in Gallagher, *The Shenandoah Valley Campaign of 1864*.

22. Quoted in Fleche, "Uncivilized War," 210; Collier and Collier, *Yours for the Union*, 359.

23. "1864 Democratic Party Platform," in Mackey, *A Documentary History of the American Civil War Era*, 2:130; Freidel, *Union Pamphlets of the Civil War*, 2:1030, 1144.

24. Bayard Taylor to Elizabeth H. Taylor, 22 October 1864, Taylor Family Correspondence, HL; William Martindell to Father, 12 October 1864, Civil War Document Collection, box 76, USAMHI; George H. Mellish to Mother, 4 September 1864, Papers of George H. Mellish, HL; Diary of Thomas Campbell, 1 and 12 September 1864, Civil War Document Collection, box 20, USAMHI.

25. *OR*, ser. 1, vol. 32, pt. 3, 246.

26. Mark Grimsley argues Sherman "did not regard the [expulsion] as barbaric or cruel, and its execution was carried out with as much regard for the civilians as circumstances allowed . . . the expulsion was hardly devoid of humanity." Grimsley, *The Hard Hand of War*, 187–89.

27. Simpson and Berlin, *Sherman's Civil War*, 704–7.

28. Ibid., 707–9.

29. Ibid., 731.

30. *OR*, ser. 1, vol. 39, pt. 3, 701.

31. Ibid., 713–14.

32. Arbuckle, *Civil War Experiences of a Foot-Soldier*, 107; Sherman, *Memoirs*, 651; Hitchcock, *Marching with Sherman*, 69; Brockman, "The John Van Duser Diary," 221; Diary of Lovell Newton Parker, 27 November 1864, HL; Nichols, *The Story of the Great March*, 66.

33. Wimer Bedford Diary, LC; Diary of Thomas Campbell, 29 September 1864, Civil War Document Collection, box 20, USAMHI; Sherman, *Memoirs*, 658–60; Hitchcock, *Marching with Sherman*, 82.

34. *OR*, ser. 1, vol. 44, 481–82, 480, 594. For a similar set of earlier rules from Maj. Gen. Frank Blair, commander of the XVII corps, see *OR*, ser. 1, vol. 44, 500.

35. *OR*, ser. 1, vol. 44, 493, 579, 508–9.

36. Ibid., 483, 537. Brig. Gen. Alpheus S. Williams, commander of the XX Corps, issued similar orders. *OR*, ser. 1, vol. 44, 503.

37. *OR*, ser. 1, vol. 44, 489–90, 521.

38. Friedrich P. Kappelmann to Parents, 28 December 1864, Civil War Times Illustrated Collection, box 17, USAMHI; Hitchcock, *Marching with Sherman*, 99; Diary of Lovell Newton Parker, 29 November 1864, HL; Byrne, *Uncommon Soldiers*, 208.

39. Arbuckle, *Civil War Experiences of a Foot-Soldier*, 107; Diary of O. M. Poe, 15 November 1864, The Papers of O. M. Poe, box 1, LC; Thomas Ward Osborn, *The Fiery Trial*, 54.

40. Bauer, *Soldier*, 180; Diary of Lovell Newton Parker, 20 November 1864, HL; Diary of James E. Morrow, 28 November 1864, Civil War Times Illustrated Collection, box 15, USAMHI; Robert Hale Strong, *A Yankee Private's Civil War*, 110–13.

41. Joyner, "With Sherman in Georgia—A Letter from the Coast," 440; Diary of Lovell Newton Parker, 29 November and 18 December 1864, HL; Winther, *With Sherman to the Sea*, 135; Byrne, *Uncommon Soldiers*, 206; John Emerson Anderson Memoir, LC.

42. *OR*, ser. 1, vol. 44, 504–5; Glatthaar, *The March to the Sea and Beyond*, 150. For similar conclusions from Union officers, see *OR*, ser. 1, vol. 44, 201, 226, 508–9.

43. Diary of Lovell Newton Parker, 20 November 1864, HL; John Emerson Anderson Memoir, LC; "Civil War Letters of Major James Roberts Zearing," 190–91; Brockman, "The John Van Duser Diary," 227; Connolly, *Three Years in the Army of the Cumberland*, 314; Hitchcock, *Marching with Sherman*, 67.

44. Geer, *The Civil War Diary of Allen Morgan Geer*, 176; Hitchcock, *Marching with Sherman*, 77; John Emerson Anderson Memoirs, LC; Diary of James E. Morrow, 18 November 1864, Civil War Times Illustrated Collection, box 15, USAMHI; David Nichol to Mother, 26 October 1864, The Harrisburg Civil War Roundtable Collection, box 28, USAMHI.

45. Sherman, *Memoirs*, 666; Bircher, *A Drummer-Boy's Diary*, 143; Connolly, *Three Years in the Army of the Cumberland*, 318; Bratton, "Letter of a Confederate Surgeon," 232; James A. Congleton Diary, 23 November 1864, LC.

46. Nichols, *The Story of the Great March*, 84; Downing, *Downing's Civil War Diary*, 234; Bauer, *Soldier*, 193; Sylvester Daniels of the 11th Iowa Volunteer Infantry records hearing these rumors. Diary of Sylvester Daniels, 3 December 1864, Theophilus M. Magaw Papers, HL.

47. Downing, *Downing's Civil War Diary*, 234; Geer, *Civil War Diary*, 180; Diary of O. M. Poe, 2 December 1864, Papers of O. M. Poe, box 1, LC; Diary of James E. Morrow, 3 December 1864, Civil War Times Illustrated Collection, box 15, USAMHI; Nichols, *The Story of the Great March*, 84.

48. Nichols, *The Story of the Great March*, 83–84; Hitchcock, *Marching with Sherman*, 143; Diary of Sylvester Daniels, 5 December 1864, Theophilus M. Magaw Papers, HL.

49. Delos W. Lake to Mother and Brother, 16 December 1864, Delos W. Lake Correspondence, HL; Quoted in Glatthaar, *The March to the Sea and Beyond*, 53–56.

50. Diary of George Shuman, 17 December 1865, The Harrisburg Civil War Round-table Collection, box 11-A, USAMHI; Capron, "The War Diary," 397; Delos Van Deusen to Wife, 28 December 1864, Delos Van Deusen Correspondence, HL.

51. Hitchcock, *Marching with Sherman*, 124–25; *OR*, ser. 1, vol. 44, 706–7; Sherman, *Memoirs*, 697; Sylvester, " 'Gone for a Soldier,' " 221.

52. Simpson and Berlin, *Sherman's Civil War*, 769; *OR*, ser. 1, vol. 44, 772.

53. *OR*, ser. 1, vol. 44, 801–2, 812–13.

54. *OR*, ser. 1, vol. 39, 799; Francis Lieber to Charles Sumner, 7 February 1865, The Papers of Charles Sumner, Houghton Library, Harvard University, microfilm edition, reel 79.

55. Athern, "An Indiana Doctor Marches with Sherman," 420; Connolly, *Three Years in the Army of the Cumberland*, 384; Wilfred W. Black, "Marching Through South Carolina," 193; Lovel Newton Parker Diary, 6 March 1865, HL; Fridrich P. Kappelman to Parents, 26 March 1865, Civil War Times Illustrated Collection, box 25, USAMHI.

56. Francis Lieber to Henry Halleck, 18 February 1864, The Papers of Francis Lieber, box 10, HL; James A. Congleton Diary, 4 January 1865, LC; John J. Safely to Mary Frances McEwen, 22 December 1864, McEwen Family Papers, MHM; Nichols, *The Story of the Great March*, 131–32; Lovel Newton Parker Diary, 8 February 1865, HL; W. C. Johnson Journal, 8 February 1864, LC; Ensign H. King Diary, 15 February 1865, Civil War Document Collection, box 65, USAMHI; Bauer, *Soldier*, 207.

57. William N. Benedict to Mother, 18 January 1865, The Harrisburg Civil War Roundtable Collection, box 2, USAMHI; Arbuckle, *Civil War Experiences of a Foot-Soldier*, 124; Simpson and Berlin, *Sherman's Civil War*, 803; Marszalek, *Sherman*, 14.

58. *OR*, ser. 1, vol., 47, pt. 2, 184–85, 331, 360; Lovel Newton Parker Diary, 7 February 1865, HL.

59. Howard, *Autobiography*, 2:125–26; *OR*, ser. 1, vol., 47, part 2, 351; W. C. Johnson Journal, 22 February 1864, LC; Bohrnstedt, *Soldiering with Sherman*, 161–62; Bauer, *Soldier*, 214.

60. For further detail on the burning of Columbia and the contentious question of who started the fires, see Jacqueline Glass Campbell, *When Sherman Marched North from the Sea*, 58–74; Royster, *The Destructive War*, 3–33; Glatthaar, *The March to the Sea and Beyond*, 143–45.

61. Diary of John W. Bates, 18 February 1865, Civil War Document Collection, box 6, USAMHI; Arbuckle, *Civil War Experiences of a Foot-Soldier*, 133; Thomas Ward Osborn, *The Fiery Trial*, 127, 131.

62. Monnett, " 'The Awfulest Time I Ever Seen,' " 286; Arbuckle, *Civil War Experiences of a Foot-Soldier*, 128.

63. Diary of Sylvester Daniels, 17 February 1865, Theophilus M. Magaw Papers, HL; Monnett, " 'The Awfulest Time I Ever Seen,' " 285; Diary of O. M. Poe, 19 February

1865, Papers of O. M. Poe, box 1, LC; Wills, *Army Life of an Illinois Soldier*, 350. Oliver O. Howard quickly sought to establish clear rules and punishments to prevent destruction and pillage inside Columbia. *OR*, ser. 1, vol. 47, pt. 2, 475–76.

64. Arbuckle, *Civil War Experiences of a Foot-Soldier*, 135; Downing, *Downing's Civil War Diary*, 255; Thomas Ward Osborn, *The Fiery Trial*, 134; Diary of Ensign H. King, 18 February 1865, Civil War Document Collection, box 65, USAMHI.

65. *OR*, ser. 1, vol. 47, pt. 2, 485; Howard, *Autobiography*, 124–25; Capron, "The War Diary," 399.

66. Thomas Ward Osborn, *The Fiery Trial*, 132; Solomon B. Childress Journal, 17 February 1865, MHM; William Garret to Sister, 29 March 1865, The Harrisburg Civil War Roundtable Collection, box 4, USAMHI; Arbuckle, *Civil War Experiences of a Foot-Soldier*, 135; Diary of Ensign H. King, 18 February 1865, Civil War Document Collection, box 65, USAMHI.

Conclusion

1. "Instructions for the Government of Armies of the United States in the Field," article 5.

2. Grant, *Memoirs and Selected Letters*, 246–47. Mark Grimsley has convincingly questioned the accuracy of Grant's postwar recollection that the Battle of Shiloh, more than any other single event, convinced him of the necessity of abandoning a "conciliatory" military policy. Grimsley, *The Hard Hand of War*, 93.

3. Simon, *Papers of Ulysses S. Grant*, 4:218; Grant, *Memoirs and Selected Letters*, 740.

4. "Instructions for the Government of Armies of the United States in the Field," article 29.

5. Francis Lieber, "A Song on Our Country and Her Flag," FLP, container 1, LC; Francis Lieber, "Lincoln or McClellan," in Freidel, *Union Pamphlets*, 2:1131; "Instructions for the Government of Armies of the United States in the Field," article 5.

Bibliography

Primary Sources

ARCHIVAL MATERIAL

Houghton Library, Harvard University, Cambridge, Massachusetts
    Papers of Charles Sumner [microfilm edition]
The Huntington Library, San Marino, California
    Papers of Lewis N. T. Allen
    Correspondence and Diary of George W. Andrews
    Correspondence of Henry Glesey Ankeny
    Civil War Letters of Charles Atkin
    Papers of Frank Dwight Baldwin
    Papers of Samuel L. M. Barlow
    Papers of Hiram Barney
    Beecher Family Papers
    Henry Breidenthal Diary
    Letters of Alfred C. Brundage
    Papers of John B. Burrud
    Papers of Leonard T. Caplinger
    Letters of Joseph M. Chambers
    Papers of Joseph W. Collingwood
    Correspondence of Henry I. Colyer
    Papers of R. Curtis Edgerton
    Papers of Edmund English
    Papers of James Monro Forbes
    Correspondence of Samuel F. Gay
    Papers of John A. Gilmore
    Papers of James Edward Glazier
    Papers of Goff-Williams
    Papers of Levi S. Graybill
    Papers of Lemuel H. Hazzard
    Civil War Diaries of Harvey Henderson
    Papers of Daniel Horn
    Papers of Calvin Gibbs Hutchinson
    Papers of Judson-Fairbanks
    Papers of William Devereux Kendall
    Papers of Delos W. Lake

Papers of Francis Lieber
Papers of George W. Lowe
Papers of Theophilus M. Magaw
Letters of Harvey A. Marckres
Papers of James M. McClintock
Papers of Moses Ayers McCoid
Papers of George H. Mellish
Miller Family Correspondence
Letters of Friedrich Ockershauser
Papers of Luther Osborn
Papers of Lovel Newton Parker
Papers of George D. Patten
Civil War Letters of Ransom Allen Perkins
Papers of George S. Phillips
Papers of William James Potter
Papers of Samuel Roper
Papers of Saxton Family
Papers of Edward E. Schweitzer
Correspondence of Charles Steedman
Papers of George Tate
Taylor Family Correspondence
Diary of William S. Trask
Correspondence of Delos Van Deusen
Library of Congress, Manuscript Division, Washington, D.C.
John Emerson Anderson Memoir
Daniel Carter Beard Papers
Wimer Bedford Papers
Blair Family Papers
William H. Bradbury Papers
Charles Buford Papers
Benjamin F. Butler Papers
James A. Congleton Diary
Josiah Dexter Cotton Papers
Sylvanus Crossly Diary
George Stanton Denison Papers
Andrew Jackson Donelson Papers
Hamilton Fish Papers
Henry W. Halleck Papers
James J. Hartley Papers
Nathaniel Hayden Family Papers
William G. Hills Diary
Ethan Allen Hitchcock Papers

Hiram P. Howe Papers
Andrew Johnson Papers
Reverdy Johnson Papers
W. C. Johnson Journal
Harriette C. Keatinge Papers
Joseph Warren Keifer Papers
Peter B. Kellenberger Letters
John A. Lair Correspondence
Francis Lieber Papers
Abraham Lincoln Papers
John Alexander Logan Family Papers
Low-Mills Family Papers
William Gibbs McAdoo Papers
Rufus Mead Papers
Marshall Mortimer Miller Papers
Montgomery Family Papers
Philip Phillips Family Papers
O. M. Poe Papers
David D. Porter Family Papers
John M. Schofield Papers
William T. Sherman Papers
Hazard Stevens Papers
Samuel Treat Correspondence
Benjamin F. Wade Papers
Daniel Webster Whittle Papers
Nathaniel Wright Family Papers
The Milton S. Eisenhower Library, Special Collections,
    The Johns Hopkins University
Francis Lieber Papers
Missouri History Museum Archives, St. Louis, Missouri
Bates Family Papers
Lillie Devereux Blake Papers
Blow Family Papers
James Overton Broadhead Papers
Burlingame Family Papers
Solomon B. Childress Journal
Peter F. Clark Papers
Henry Lowndes Davis Papers
Dorsey Family Papers
Lucien Eaton Papers
William Greenleaf Eliot Papers
Louis Philip Fusz Diary

Hamilton Rowen Gamble Papers
Charles Gibson Papers
Gert Goebel, *Laenger als ein Menschenleben in Missouri*
Thomas Butler Gunn Diaries
Thomas S. Hawley Papers
Hitchcock Family Papers
Richard M. Hubbell Papers
William Carr Lane Papers
George Eliot Leighton Papers
James Edwin Love Papers
Ludlow-Field-Maury Family Papers
Ellen Waddle McCoy Papers
McEwen Family Papers
Monroe Joshua Miller Papers
Kelion Franklin Peddicord Papers
Pettus Family Papers
William Charles Pfeffer Diary
William T. Sherman Papers
John Dunlap Stevenson Papers
Isaac H. Sturgeon Papers
Tiffany Family Papers
Alfred Warner Letters
Robert White Papers
U.S. Army Military History Institute, Carlisle Barracks, Pennsylvania
Leslie Anders Collection
Bailey-Stroud Papers
William H. Ball Collection
Bowman Family Papers
Henry Burrell Papers
Robert H. Carnahan Papers
Civil War Document Collection
Ira A. Abbott
Samuel E. Adams
G. E. Andrews
James Armstrong
Albert H. Artman
Allen Baker
John W. Bates
G. F. Blanchard
Charles S. Bullard
Thomas Campbell
Charles Chapin

Alexander N. Coffin
Charles Shumway Culver
Arnold P. Dains
William Dunlap
Abner Eisenhower
Henry W. Gay
Alpheus Harding
F. Hermann Hesse
Dennis L. Kemp
Ensign H. King
Fred R. Laubach
William M. Martindell
John J. McKee
James David Michaels
Ambrose B. Morgan
James W. Mulligan
John A. Rowe
Franz Schwenzer
George W. Scothorn
James Sherwood
John A. Shirley
Henry E. Skaggs
Amos Stevens
David C. Thorn
Samuel West
Civil War Times Illustrated Collection
James Abraham
Newton Adams
Lyman Daniel Ames
George Bargus
Albert A. Clapp
William Corin
Francis Dawes
Paul Dorweiler
Fergus Elliott
Marcus O. Frost
Henry Henney
Friedrich P. Kappelmann
Thomas Lynch
James E. Morrow
Joseph Parkinson
Thomas E. Pierce

　　Anthony Ross
　　Edward E. Schweitzer
　　Silas D. Wesson
George W. Gordon Papers
Harrisburg Civil War Roundtable Collection
　　Jared L. Ainsworth
　　Schuyler S. Ballou
　　William N. Benedict
　　John Brislin
　　Robert B. Cornwell
　　John Eicker
　　William Garrett
　　William Wallace Geety
　　Jacob W. Haas
　　John and Samuel Hamer
　　M. Keys Harrison
　　Henry Keiser
　　Dunning K. Lockwood
　　Charles J. Marble
　　George P. Metcalf
　　Charles J. Mills
　　David Nichol
　　David Seibert
　　George Shuman
　　John Suter
　　William Tritt
Lewis Leigh Collection
　　Jacob Dunn
　　John D. Fehnley
　　Samuel B. Fisher
　　David Gurner
　　Robert Guyton
　　Sondus W. Haskell
　　William Klice
　　Morgan W. Lindsley
　　D. Maupay
　　James McChesney
　　James D. Miller
　　George M. Morrison
　　Edwin B. Payne
　　David S. Scott
　　Ora H. Seymour

Charles H. Walker
Laurens W. Wolcott
Marvin Family Collection
McPheeters Family Papers
John S. Miles
Park Family Papers

NEWSPAPERS

Army and Navy Journal
Army and Navy Register
Baltimore Sun
Boston Daily Advertiser
Boston Evening Transcript
Boston Post
Brooklyn Daily Eagle
The Charleston Mercury
Chicago Times
Chicago Tribune
Christian Advocate and Journal
Cincinnati Commercial
Cincinnati Daily Gazette
Daily Cleveland Herald
Daily Missouri Democrat
Daily Missouri Republican

Frank Leslie's Illustrated Newspaper
Harper's Weekly
The Liberator
Memphis Bulletin
Memphis Daily Appeal
Milwaukee Daily Sentinel
Monthly Religious Magazine
New Orleans Commercial Bulletin
New Orleans Daily Crescent
New Orleans Daily Picayune
New York Herald
New York Times
New York Tribune
New York World
*Washington Daily National
    Intelligencer*

GOVERNMENT DOCUMENTS

Congressional Globe
Instructions for the Government of Armies of the United States in the Field. Washington:
    War Department, 1863.
U.S. Congress. Joint Committee on the Conduct of the War. *Fort Pillow Massacre
    Report.* 38th Congress, 1st session, 1865.
U.S. War Department. *War of the Rebellion: A Compilation of the Official Records of
    the Union and Confederate Armies.* 128 vols. Washington: Government Printing
    Office, 1880–1901.

PUBLISHED PRIMARY SOURCES

Abernethy, Alonzo. "Incidents of an Iowa Soldier's Life, or Four Years in Dixie."
    Annals of Iowa 12, no. 6 (October 1920): 401–28.
Anderson, Galusha. *The Story of a Border City during the Civil War.* Boston: Little,
    Brown, and Company, 1908.
Anderson, William M., ed. *We Are Sherman's Men: The Civil War Letters of Henry
    Orendorff.* Macomb: Western Illinois University, 1986.

Angle, Paul M., ed. *Three Years in the Army of the Cumberland: The Letters and Diary of Major James A. Connolly*. Bloomington: Indiana University Press, 1959.

Arbuckle, John C. *Civil War Experiences of a Foot-Soldier Who Marched with Sherman*. Columbus, Ohio: n.p., 1930.

Armitage, Thomas. *The Past, Present, and Future of the United States*. New York: Holman, 1862.

Ashkenazi, Elliott, ed. *The Civil War Diary of Clara Solomon: Growing Up in New Orleans, 1861–1862*. Baton Rouge: Louisiana State University Press, 1995.

Athern, Robert G., ed. "An Indiana Doctor Marches with Sherman: The Diary of James Comfort Patten." *Indiana Magazine of History* 49, no. 4 (December 1953): 405–22.

Bacon, Leonard. *Conciliation: A Discourse at a Sunday Evening Service, New Haven, July 20, 1862*. New Haven: Peck, White, & Peck, 1862.

Banaski, Michael E., ed. *Missouri in 1861: The Civil War Letters of Franc B. Wilkie, Newspaper Correspondent*. Iowa City, Iowa: Camp Pope Bookshop, 2001.

Barnes, Albert. *The Conditions of Peace. A Thanksgiving Discourse Delivered in the First Presbyterian Church, Philadelphia, November 27, 1862*. Philadelphia, Pa.: William B. Evans, 1863.

Barnes, Francis C. "Imprisoned under Fire." *Southern Historical Society Papers* 25 (January–December 1897).

Bascom, Elizabeth Ethel Parker, ed. *"Dear Lizzie": Letters Written by James "Jimmy" Garvin Crawford to his Sweet Heart Martha Elizabeth "Lizzie" Wilson while He Was in the Federal Army during the War between the States, 1862–1865*. Bascom, 1978.

Basler, Roy P., ed. *The Collected Works of Abraham Lincoln*. 9 vols. New Brunswick, N.J.: Rutgers University Press, 1953–55.

Bauer, K. Jack, ed. *Soldier: The Civil War Diary of Rice C. Bull, 123rd New York Volunteer Infantry*. San Rafael, Cal.: Presidio Press, 1977.

Beecher, Henry Ward. *Freedom and War: Discourses on Topics Suggested by the Times*. Boston: Ticknor and Fields, 1863.

Bellows, Henry W. *How We Are to Fulfill Our Lord's Commandment, "Love your Enemies," in a Time of War*. New York: Baker & Godwin, 1861.

———. *The War to End Only When the Rebellion Ceases*. New York: Anson D. F. Randolph, 1863.

Berlin, Ira, et al., eds. *Freedom: A Documentary History of Emancipation, 1861–1867*. Ser. 1, Vol. 1, *The Destruction of Slavery*. Cambridge, U.K.: Cambridge University Press, 1985.

Bircher, William. *A Drummer-Boy's Diary: Comprising Four Years of Service with the Second Regiment Minnesota Veteran Volunteers, 1861 to 1865*. St. Paul, Minn.: St. Paul Book and Stationary Company, 1889.

Black, Wilfred W., ed. "Marching Through South Carolina: Another Civil War Letter of Lieutenant George M. Wise." *Ohio Historical Quarterly* 66 (January 1956): 187–95.

————, ed. "Marching with Sherman through Georgia and the Carolinas Civil War Diary of Jesse L. Dozer, Part II." *The Georgia Historical Quarterly* 52, no. 4 (December, 1968): 451–79.

Boardman, Henry A. *The Sovereignty of God, the Sure and Only Stay of the Christian Patriot in Our National Troubles. A Sermon Preached in the Tenth Presbyterian Church, Philadelphia, Sept. 14 and in the West Spruce Street Church, September 25, 1862.* Philadelphia, Pa.: William S. & Alfred Martien, 1862.

Bohrnstedt, Jennifer Cain, ed. *Soldiering with Sherman: Civil War Letters of George F. Cram.* DeKalb: Northern Illinois University Press, 2000.

Bratton, J. R. "Letter of a Confederate Surgeon on Sherman's Occupation of Milledgeville." *The Georgia Historical Quarterly* 32, no. 3 (September 1948): 231–32.

Breed, William P. *Faith and Patience.* Philadelphia, Pa.: John Alexander, n.d.

Britton, Anne Hartwell and Thomas J. Reed, eds. *To My Beloved Wife and Boy at Home: The Letters and Diaries of Orderly Sergeant John F.L. Hartwell.* Madison, N.J.: Fairleigh Dickinson University Press, 1997.

Brockman, Charles J., ed. "The John Van Duser Diary of Sherman's March from Atlanta to Hilton Head." *The Georgia Historical Quarterly* 53, no. 2 (June 1969): 220–40.

Burton, E. P. *Diary of E. P. Burton, Surgeon 7th Reg. Ill. 3rd Brig. 2nd Div. 16A.C.* Des Moines, Iowa: The Historical Records Survey, 1939.

Butler, Benjamin F. *Autobiography and Personal Reminiscences of Major-General Benjamin F. Butler.* Boston: A. M. Thayer, 1892.

————. *Private and Official Correspondence of Gen. Benjamin F. Butler during the Period of the City War.* Norwood, Mass.: The Plimpton Press, 1917.

Byrne, Frank L., ed. *Uncommon Soldiers: Harvey Reid and the 22nd Wisconsin March with Sherman.* Knoxville: The University of Tennessee Press, 2001.

Campbell, S. M. *The Light in the Clouds. A Thanksgiving Discourse, Delivered before the United Congregations of the Reformed Dutch, First Presbyterian and Westminster Churches, of Utica, N.Y. November 27, 1862, in the Reformed Dutch Church.* Utica, N.Y.: Curtiss & White, 1862.

Capron, Thaddeus H. "The War Diary of Thaddeus H. Capron, 1861–1865." *Journal of the Illinois State Historical Society* 12, no. 3 (October 1919): 330–406.

Carmony, Donald F., ed. "Jacob W. Bartmess Civil War Letters." *Indiana Magazine of History* 52, no. 2 (June 1956): 157–86.

Chase, Salmon P. *Diary and Correspondence of Salmon P. Chase.* Washington, D.C.: American Historical Association, 1903.

"Civil War Letters of Major James Roberts Zearing, M.D., 1861–1865," in *Publication Number Twenty-Eight of the Illinois State Historical Library: Transactions of the Illinois State Historical Society for the Year 1921.* Springfield, Ill.: Phillips Bros Print, 1922.

Collier, John S. and Bonnie B. Collier, eds. *Yours for the Union: The Civil War Letters of John W. Chase, First Massachusetts Light Artillery.* New York: Fordham University Press, 2004.

Connolly, James Austin. *Three Years in the Army of the Cumberland: The Letters and Diary of Major James A. Connolly*. Bloomington: Indiana University Press, 1996.

Conyngham, David P. *Sherman's March through the South*. New York: Sheldon and Company, 1865.

Corsan, W. C. *Two Months in the Confederate States: An Englishman's Travels through the South*. Baton Rouge: Louisiana State University Press, 1996.

Cozzens, Peter and Robert I. Girardi, eds., *The Military Memoirs of General John Pope*. Chapel Hill: University of North Carolina Press, 1998.

Croffut, W. A., ed. *Fifty Years in Camp and Field: Diary of Major-General Ethan Allen Hitchcock*. New York: G. P. Putnam's Sons, 1909.

De Forest, John William. *A Volunteer's Adventures: A Union Captain's Record of the Civil War*. New Haven, Conn.: Yale University Press, 1946.

De Laubenfels, David J. "With Sherman through Georgia: A Journal." *The Georgia Historical Quarterly* 41, no. 3 (September 1957): 288–300.

Douglass, Frederick. *Autobiographies*. New York: Library of America, 1994.

Downing, Alexander G. *Downing's Civil War Diary*. Des Moines: The Historical Department of Iowa, 1916.

Early, Jubal A. *A Memoir of the Last Year of the War for Independence*. Lynchburg, Va.: Charles W. Button, 1867.

Eaton, Clement, ed. "Diary of an Officer in Sherman's Army Marching through the Carolinas." *The Journal of Southern History* 9, no. 2 (May 1943): 238–54.

Ellison, Janet Correll, ed. *On to Atlanta: The Civil War Diaries of John Hill Ferguson, Illinois Tenth Regiment of Volunteers*. Lincoln: University of Nebraska Press, 2001.

Ferrell, Robert H., ed. *Harry S. Truman and the Bomb: A Documentary History*. Worland, Wyo.: High Plains Publishing Company, 1996.

Foner, Philip S., ed. *The Life and Writings of Frederick Douglass, Volume III: The Civil War, 1861–1865*. New York: International Publishers, 1952.

Freidel, Frank, ed. *Union Pamphlets of the Civil War*. Cambridge, Mass.: Harvard University Press, 1967.

Friedman, Leon. *The Law of War: A Documentary History*. New York: Random House, 1972.

Fulkerson, Abram. "The Prison Experience of a Confederate Soldier Who Was under Fire, on Morris Island, from Confederate Batteries." *Southern Historical Society Papers* 22 (January-December 1894).

Geer, Allen Morgan. *The Civil War Diary of Allen Morgan Geer: Twentieth Regiment, Illinois Volunteers*. New York: Cosmos Press, 1977.

Giunta, Mary A., ed. *A Civil War Soldier of Christ and Country: The Selected Correspondence of John Ridgers Meigs, 1859–1864*. Urbana: University of Illinois Press, 2006.

Grant, Ulysses S. *Ulysses S. Grant: Memoirs and Selected Letters*. New York: Library of America, 1990.

Hagemann, E. R. *Fighting Rebels and Redskins: Experiences in Army Life of Colonel George B. Sanford, 1861–1892*. Norman: University of Oklahoma Press, 1969.

Halleck, Henry. *International Law; or, Rules Regulating the Intercourse of States in Peace and War*. New York: D. Van Nostrand, 1861.

Hallum, John. *The Diary of an Old Lawyer, or Scenes behind the Curtain*. Nashville. Tenn.: Southwestern Publishing House, 1895.

Harwell, Richard, and Philip N. Racine, eds. *The Fiery Trial: A Union Officer's Account of Sherman's Last Campaigns*. Knoxville: The University of Tennessee Press, 1986.

Hay, John. *Letters of John Hay and Extracts from Diary*. Washington: n.p., 1908.

Hazen, W. B. *A Narrative of Military Service*. Boston: Ticknor and Company, 1885.

Hedley, F. Y. *Marching Through Georgia*. Chicago: Donohue, Hennenberry & Co., 1890.

Hill, Sarah Jane Full. *Mrs. Hill's Journal—Civil War Reminiscences*. Chicago: R. R. Donnelley & Sons Company, 1980.

Hitchcock, Henry. *Marching with Sherman: Passages from the Letters and Campaign Diaries of Henry Hitchcock, Major and Assistant Adjutant General of Volunteers, November 1864–May 1865* (New Haven, Conn.: Yale University Press, 1927).

Holcomb, Julie, ed. *Southern Sons, Northern Soldiers: The Civil War Letters of the Remley Brothers, 22nd Iowa Infantry*. Dekalb: Northern Illinois University Press, 2004.

Hotchkiss, Jedediah. *Make Me a Map of the Valley: The Civil War Journal of Stonewall Jackson's Topographer*. Dallas, Tex.: Southern Methodist University Press, 1973.

Howard, Oliver Otis. *Autobiography of Oliver Otis Howard*. New York: Baker and Taylor, 1907.

Howe, Mark Anthony de Wolfe., ed. *Marching with Sherman: Passages from the Letters and Campaign Diaries of Henry Hitchcock, Major and Assistant Adjutant General of Volunteers, November 1864–May 1865*. New Haven, Conn.: Yale University Press, 1927.

Joyner, F. B. "With Sherman in Georgia—A Letter from the Coast." *The Georgia Historical Quarterly* 42, no. 4 (December, 1958): 440–41.

Kallgren, Beverly Hayes and James L. Crouthamel, eds. *"Dear Friend Anna": The Civil War Letters of a Common Soldier from Maine*. Orono: University of Maine Press, 1992.

Kidd, J. H. *A Cavalryman with Custer: Custer's Michigan Cavalry Brigade in the Civil War*. New York: Bantam Books, 1991.

Kiper, Richard L., ed. *Dear Catharine, Dear Taylor: The Civil War Letters of a Union Soldier and His Wife*. Lawrence: University Press of Kansas, 2002.

Leavitt, W. S. *God the Protector and Hope of the Nation. A Sermon, Preached on Thanksgiving Day, November 27, 1862, by Rev. W. S. Leavitt, Pastor of the First Presbyterian Church, Hudson, N.Y.* Hudson, N.Y.: Bryan &Webb, 1862.

Lennard, George. "'Give Yourself No Trouble about Me': The Shiloh Letters of George W. Lennard." Edited by Paul Hubbard and Christine Lews. *Indiana Magazine of History* 76, no. 1 (March 1980): 21–53.

"Letters of General Thomas Williams, 1862." *The American Historical Review* 14, no. 2 (January 1909): 304–28.

Lieber, Francis. *Manual of Political Ethics*. Boston: Charles Little and James Brown, 1839.

———. *The Miscellaneous Writings of Francis Lieber*. Philadelphia, Pa.: Lippincott, 1881.

———. "A Reminiscence." *Southern Literary Messenger* 2, no. 10 (August 1836): 553–58.

Livermore, L. J. *Perseverance in the War, the Interest and Duty of the Nation: A Sermon, Preached in the Church of the First Parish, Lexington, Sunday, September 11, 1864*. Boston: T. R. Marvin, 1864.

Mackey, Thomas C. *A Documentary History of the American Civil War Era*. Knoxville: The University of Tennessee Press, 2013.

Monnett, Howard Norman, ed. "'The Awfulest Time I Ever Seen': A Letter from Sherman's Army." *Civil War History* 8, no. 3 (September 1962): 283–89.

Morrison, Marion. *A History of the Ninth Regiment, Illinois Volunteer Infantry*. Monmouth, Ill.: J. S. Clark, 1864.

Nichols, George War. *The Story of the Great March*. New York: Harper & Brothers, 1865.

Norton, Sara, and Mark Anthony de Wolfe Howe, eds. *Letters of Charles Eliot Norton*. Boston: Houghton Mifflin, 1913.

Osborn, George C., ed. "Sherman's March through Georgia: Letters from Charles Ewing to His Father Thomas Ewing." *The Georgia Historical Quarterly* 42, no. 3 (September 1958): 323–27.

Osborn, Thomas Ward. *The Fiery Trial: A Union Officer's Account of Sherman's Last Campaigns*. Knoxville, University of Tennessee Press, 1986.

Palmer, Benjamin Morgan. *Thanksgiving Sermon, Delivered at the Presbyterian Church, New Orleans*. New York: George F. Nesbitt, 1861.

Perry, Thomas Sergeant, ed. *The Life and Letters of Francis Lieber*. Boston: James R. Osgood, 1882.

Porter, David Dixon. *Incidents and Anecdotes of the Civil War*. New York: D. Appleton, 1885.

Post, M. M. *A Thanksgiving Sermon, Delivered at Logansport, Ind., November 27, 1862*. Logansport, Ind.: Dague & Rayhouser, 1862.

Reminiscences of the Civil War from Diaries of Members of the 103d Illinois Volunteer Infantry. Chicago: J. F. Learning, 1914.

Root, Elihu. *Addresses on International Subjects*. Cambridge, Mass.: Harvard University Press, 1916.

Roth, Margaret Brobst, ed. *Well, Mary: Civil War Letters of a Wisconsin Volunteer*. Madison: The University of Wisconsin Press, 1960.

Rowland, Kate Mason and Morris L. Croxall, eds. *The Journal of Julia LeGrand: New Orleans, 1862–1863*. Richmond: Everett Waddey, 1911.

Shedd, William G. T. *The Union and the War. A Sermon, Preached November 27, 1862*. New York: Charles Scribner, 1863.

Sheridan, Philip H. *Personal Memoirs of P. H. Sheridan*. New York: Charles L. Webster, 1883.

Sherman, William T. *Memoirs of General William T. Sherman*. New York: Library of America, 1990.

Simon, John Y., ed. *The Papers of Ulysses S. Grant*. Carbondale and Edwardsville: Southern Illinois University Press, 1967–2009.

Simpson, Brooks D. and Jean V. Berlin, eds. *Sherman's Civil War: Selected Correspondence of William T. Sherman, 1860–1865*. Chapel Hill: University of North Carolina Press, 1999.

Solomon, Clara. *The Civil War Diary of Clara Solomon: Growing Up in New Orleans, 1861–1862*. Baton Rouge: Louisiana State University Press, 1995.

Strong, George Templeton. *The Diary of George Templeton Strong*. New York: The MacMillan Company, 1952.

Strong, Robert Hale. *A Yankee Private's Civil War*. Chicago: Henry Regnery Company, 1961.

Sumner, Charles. *The True Grandeur of Nations: An Oration Delivered before the Authorities of the City of Boston*. Boston: William D. Ticknor, 1845.

Sylvester, Lorna Lutes, ed. " 'Gone for a Soldier': The Civil War Letters of Charles Harding Cox." *Indiana Magazine of History* 68, no. 3 (September 1972): 181–239.

Thompson, Joseph P. *The Psalter and the Sword, A Sermon Preached in the Broadway Tabernacle Church, On Thanksgiving Day, November 27, 1862*. New York: W. L. S. Harrison, 1863.

Thorndike, Rachel Sherman, ed. *The Sherman Letters: Correspondence between General and Senator Sherman from 1837 to 1891*. New York: Charles Scribner's Sons, 1894.

Welles, Gideon. *The Diary of Gideon Welles*. Boston: Houghton Mifflin, 1911.

Williams, Charles Richard, ed. *Diary and Letters of Rutherford Birchard Hayes*. Columbus: F. J. Heer Printing Company, 1922.

Wills, Charles W. *Army Life of an Illinois Soldier: Including a Day-by-Day Record of Sherman's March to the Sea*. Carbondale: Southern Illinois University Press, 1996.

Winther, Oscar Osburn, ed. *With Sherman to the Sea: The Civil War Letters, Diaries, & Reminiscences of Theodore F. Upson*. Bloomington: Indiana University Press, 1958.

Wittenberg, Eric J., ed. *With Sheridan in the Final Campaign against Lee, by Lt. Col. Frederick C. Newhall, Sixth Pennsylvania Cavalry*. Baton Rouge: Louisiana State University Press, 2002.

Secondary Sources

BOOKS

Adamson, Hans Christian. *Rebellion in Missouri: Nathaniel Lyon and His Army of the West*. Philadelphia, Pa.: Chilton Company, 1961.

Alotta, Robert Ignatius. *Military Executions of the Union Army, 1861–1866*. Philadelphia, Pa.: Temple University, 1984.

Arenson, Adam. *The Great Heart of the Republic: St. Louis and the Cultural Civil War*. Cambridge, Mass.: Harvard University Press, 2011.

Ash, Steven V. *When the Yankees Came: Conflict and Chaos in the Occupied South, 1861–1865*. Chapel Hill: University of North Carolina Press, 1995.

Astor, Aaron. *Rebels on the Border: Civil War, Emancipation, and the Reconstruction of Kentucky and Missouri*. Baton Rouge: Louisiana State University Press, 2012.

Benedict, Michael Les. *A Compromise of Principle: Congressional Republicans and Reconstruction 1863–1869*. New York: W. W. Norton, 1974.

Berlin, Ira, Joseph P. Reidy, and Leslie S. Rowland, eds. *Freedom's Soldiers: The Black Military Experience in the Civil War*. Cambridge, U.K.: Cambridge University Press, 1998.

Berry, Mary Frances. *Military Necessity and Civil Rights Policy: Black Citizenship and the Constitution, 1861–1868*. Port Washington, N.Y.: Kennikat Press, 1977.

Best, Geoffrey. *Humanity in Warfare*. New York: Columbia University Press, 1980.

Black, Jeremy. *Rethinking Military History*. London: Routledge, 2004.

Blassingame, John W. *Black New Orleans, 1860–1880*. Chicago: University of Chicago Press, 1973.

Boman, Dennis K. *Lincoln and Citizens' Rights in Civil War Missouri: Balancing Freedom and Security*. Baton Rouge: Louisiana State University Press, 2011.

Bragg, Jefferson Davis. *Louisiana in the Confederacy*. Baton Rouge: Louisiana State University Press, 1941.

Brasher, Glenn David. *The Peninsula Campaign and the Necessity of Emancipation*. Chapel Hill: The University of North Carolina Press, 2012.

Browning, Judkin. *Shifting Loyalties: The Union Occupation of Eastern North Carolina*. Chapel Hill: University of North Carolina Press, 2011.

Bruce, Robert V. *Lincoln and the Tools of War*. Urbana: University of Illinois Press, 1989.

Burkhardt, George S. *Confederate Rage, Yankee Wrath: No Quarter in the Civil War*. Carbondale: Southern Illinois University Press, 2007.

Burnham, Philip. *So Far from Dixie: Confederates in Yankee Prisons*. Lanham, Md.: Taylor Trade, 2003.

Campbell, Jacqueline Glass. *When Sherman Marched North from the Sea: Resistance on the Confederate Home Front*. Chapel Hill: University of North Carolina Press, 2003.

Capers, Gerald M. *The Biography of a River Town: Memphis, Its Heroic Age.* Chapel Hill: University of North Carolina Press, 1939.

———. *Occupied City: New Orleans Under the Federals, 1862–1865.* Lexington: University of Kentucky Press, 1965.

Carnahan, Burrus M. *Act of Justice: Lincoln's Emancipation Proclamation and the Laws of War.* Lexington: University Press of Kentucky, 2007.

———. *Lincoln on Trial: Southern Civilians and the Law of War.* Louisville: University Press of Kentucky, 2010.

Cimprich, John. *Fort Pillow, a Civil War Massacre, and Public Memory.* Baton Rouge: Louisiana State University Press, 2005.

Clausewitz, Carl von. *On War.* Princeton, N.J.: Princeton University Press, 1976.

Connelly, Donald B. *John M. Schofield and the Politics of Generalship.* Chapel Hill: University of North Carolina Press, 2006.

Curran, Thomas F. *Soldiers of Peace: Civil War Pacifism and the Post War Radical Peace Movement.* New York: Fordham University Press, 2003.

Davis, James D. *History of Memphis: The History of the City of Memphis, Being a Compilation of the Most Important Documents and Historical Events.* Memphis, Tenn.: Hite, Crumpton, & Kelly, 1873.

Dawson, Joseph G. *Army Generals and Reconstruction: Louisiana, 1862–1877.* Baton Rouge: Louisiana State University Press, 1982.

Dawson, Joseph G. "The First of the Modern Wars?" In *The American Civil War: Explorations and Reconsiderations,* edited by Susan-Mary Grant and Brian Holden Reid, 121–41. New York: Longman, 2000.

Faust, Drew Gilpin. *This Republic of Suffering: Death and the American Civil War.* New York: Knopf, 2008.

Fellman, Michael. *Citizen Sherman: A Life of William Tecumseh Sherman.* New York: Random House, 1995.

———. *Inside War: The Guerrilla Conflict in Missouri during the American Civil War.* New York: Oxford University Press, 1989.

Forster, Stig, and Jorg Nagler. *On the Road to Total War: The American Civil War and the German Wars of Unification, 1861–1871.* Cambridge, U.K.: Cambridge University Press, 1997.

Freidel, Frank. *Francis Lieber: Nineteenth-Century Liberal.* Baton Rouge: Louisiana State University Press, 1947.

Gallagher, Gary W., ed. *The Antietam Campaign.* Chapel Hill: University of North Carolina Press, 1999.

———, ed. *The Shenandoah Valley Campaign of 1864.* Chapel Hill: University of North Carolina Press, 2006.

Garrison, Webb. *Civil War Hostage: Hostage-Taking in the Civil War.* Shippensburg, Pa.: White Mane, 2000.

Gerteis, Louis S. *Civil War St. Louis.* Lawrence: University of Kansas Press, 2001.

Gillespie, Alexander. *A History of the Laws of War.* Oxford: Hart Publishing, 2011.

Gillispie, James M. *Andersonvilles of the North: The Myths and Realities of Northern Treatment of Civil War Confederate Prisoners.* Denton: University of North Texas Press, 2008.

Glatthaar, Joseph. *Forged in Battle: The Civil War Alliance of Black Soldiers and White Officers.* New York: Free Press, 1990.

———. *The March to the Sea and Beyond.* New York: New York University Press, 1985.

Goldfield, David. *America Aflame: How the Civil War Created a Nation.* New York: Bloomsbury, 2011.

Goodrich, Thomas. *Black Flag: Guerrilla Warfare on the Western Border, 1861–1865.* Bloomington: Indiana University Press, 1995.

Goss, Thomas J. *The War Within the Union High Command: Politics and Generalship during the Civil War.* Lawrence: University Press of Kansas, 2003.

Grant, Susan-Mary and Brian Holden Reid, eds., *Themes of the American Civil War: The War Between the States.* London: Routledge, 2009.

Griffith, Paddy. *Battle Tactics of the Civil War.* New Haven, Conn.: Yale University Press, 1987.

Grimsley, Mark, ed. *Civilians in the Path of War.* Lincoln: University of Nebraska, 2002.

———. *The Hard Hand of War: Union Military Policy toward Southern Civilians, 1861–1865.* Cambridge, U.K.: Cambridge University Press, 1995.

Guelzo, Allen C. *Fateful Lightening: A New History of the Civil War and Reconstruction.* New York: Oxford University Press, 2012.

———. *Lincoln's Emancipation Proclamation: The End of Slavery in America.* New York: Simon & Schuster, 2004.

Hagerman, Edward. *The American Civil War and the Origins of Modern Warfare: Ideas, Organization, and Field Command.* Bloomington: Indiana University Press, 1988.

Hamilton, Daniel W. *The Limits of Sovereignty: Property Confiscation in the Union and the Confederacy during the Civil War.* Chicago: University of Chicago Press, 2007.

Harris, William C. *Lincoln and the Border State: Preserving the Union.* Lawrence: University Press of Kansas, 2011.

Hartigan, Richard Shelly. *Lieber's Code and the Law of War.* Chicago: Precedent, 1983
———, ed. *Military Rules, Regulations and the Code of War: Francis Lieber and the Certification of Conflict.* New Brunswick, N.J.: Transaction Publishers, 2011.

Hattaway, Herman. *Shades of Blue and Gray: An Introductory Military History of the Civil War.* Columbia: University of Missouri Press, 1997.

Hattaway, Herman and Archer Jones. *How the North Won.* Urbana: University of Illinois Press, 1983.

Hearn, Chester G. *When the Devil Came Down to Dixie: Ben Butler in New Orleans.* Baton Rouge: Louisiana State University Press, 1997.

Heatwole, John L. *The Burning: Sheridan in the Shenandoah Valley.* Charlottesville, Va.: Rockbridge Publishing, 1998.

Hess, Earl J. *The Civil War in the West: Victory and Defeat from the Appalachians to the Mississippi.* Chapel Hill: University of North Carolina Press, 2012.

Hesseltine, William Best. *Civil War Prisons: A Study in War Psychology.* Columbus: The Ohio State University Press, 1930.

Hirshon, Stanley P. *The White Tecumseh: A Biography of General William T. Sherman.* New York: John Wiley & Sons, 1997.

Holt, Earl K. *William Greenleaf Eliot: Conservative Radical.* Belleville, Ill.: Village Publishers, 2011.

Horigan, Michael. *Elmira: Death Camp of the North.* Mechanicsburg, Pa.: Stackpole Books, 2002

Howard, Michael, George J. Andreopoulos, and Mark R. Shulman eds. *The Laws of War: Constraints on Warfare in the Western World.* New Haven, Conn.: Yale University Press, 1994.

Johnson, James Turner. *Just War Tradition and the Restraint of War: A Moral and Historical Inquiry.* Princeton, N.J.: Princeton University Press, 1981.

Johnson, James Turner. "Lieber and the Theory of War." In *Francis Lieber and the Culture of the Mind,* 61–68. Columbia, SC: University of South Carolina Press, 2005.

Josephy, Alvin M., Jr. *The Civil War in the American West.* New York: Alfred A. Knopf, 1991.

Kalyvas, Stathis N. *The Logic of Violence in Civil War.* New York: Cambridge University Press, 2006.

Kennett, Lee B. *Sherman: A Soldiers Life.* New York: HarperCollins, 2009.

Klement, Frank L. *The Limits of Dissent: Clement Vallandigham and the Civil War.* New York: Fordham University Press, 1998.

Leonard, Elizabeth D. *Lincoln's Forgotten Ally: Judge Advocate General Joseph Holt of Kentucky.* Chapel Hill: University of North Carolina Press, 2011.

Lufkin, Edwin B. *History of the Thirteenth Main Regiment.* Brighton, Maine: H. A. Shorey, 1898.

Mack, Charles R. and Henry H. Lesesne, eds. *Francis Lieber and the Culture of the Mind.* Columbia: University of South Carolina Press, 2005.

McPherson, James M. "From Limited to Total War, 1861–1865." In *Drawn with the Sword: Reflections on the American Civil War,* 66–86. New York: Oxford University Press, 1996.

Mackey, Robert R. *The Uncivil War: Irregular Warfare in the Upper South, 1861–1865.* Norman: University of Oklahoma Press, 2004.

Manning, Chandra. *What This Cruel War Was Over.* New York: Vintage, 2007.

Marszalek, John F. *Commander of All Lincoln's Armies: A Life of General Henry Halleck.* Cambridge, Mass.: Harvard University Press, 2004.

———. *Sherman: A Soldier's Passion for Order.* New York: Free Press, 1993.

———. *Sherman's March to the Sea*. Abilene, Tex.: McWhiney Foundation Press, 2005.

Masur, Louis P. *Lincoln's Hundred Days: The Emancipation Proclamation and the War for the Union*. Cambridge, Mass.: Harvard University Press, 2012.

McGinty, Brian. *The Body of John Merryman: Abraham Lincoln and the Suspension of Habeas Corpus*. Cambridge, Mass.: Harvard University Press, 2011.

McKenzie, Robert. *Lincolnites and Rebels: A Divided Town in Civil War America*. New York: Oxford University Press, 2006.

McPherson, James. *Battle Cry of Freedom: The Civil War Era*. New York: Oxford University Press, 1988.

———. *Drawn with the Sword: Reflections on the American Civil War*. New York: Oxford University Press, 1996.

———. *Tried by War: Abraham Lincoln as Commander in Chief*. New York: Penguin, 2008.

———. *War on the Waters: The Union and Confederate Navies*. Chapel Hill: University of North Carolina Press, 2012.

Mitchell, Reid. *Civil War Soldiers*. New York: Viking, 1988.

Murray, John Ogden. *The Immortal Six Hundred: A Story of Cruelty to Confederate Prisoners of War*. Winchester, Va.: Eddy Press, 1905.

Nash, Howard P. *Stormy Petrel: The Life and Times of General Benjamin F. Butler, 1818–1893*. Rutherford, N.J.: Fairleigh Dickinson University Press, 1969.

Neely, Mark E. *The Civil War and the Limits of Destruction*. Cambridge, Mass.: Harvard University Press, 2007.

———. *The Fate of Liberty: Abraham Lincoln and Civil Liberties*. New York: Oxford University Press, 1991.

———. *Lincoln and the Triumph of the Nation: Constitutional Conflict in the American Civil War*. Chapel Hill: University of North Carolina Press, 2012.

———. *Retaliation: The Problem of Atrocity in the American Civil War*. Gettysburg, Pa.: Gettysburg College, 2002.

Neff, Stephen C. *Justice in Blue and Gray: A Legal History of the Civil War*. Cambridge, Mass.: Harvard University Press, 2010.

———. *War and the Law of Nations: A General History*. Cambridge, U.K.: Cambridge University Press, 2005.

Nelson, Scott Reynolds. "An American War of Incarceration: Guerrilla Warfare, Occupation, and Imprisonment in the American South, 1863–65." In *Inventing Collateral Damage: Civilian Casualties, War, and Empire*, edited by Stephen J. Rockel and Rich Halpern, 115–25. Toronto: Between the Lines, 2009.

Nelson, Scott Reynolds and Carol Sheriff. *A People at War: Civilians and Soldiers in America's Civil War, 1854–1877*. New York: Oxford University Press, 2008.

Nosworthy, Brent. *The Bloody Crucible of Courage: Fighting Methods and Combat Experience of the Civil War*. New York: Carroll & Graf, 2003.

Nystrom, Justin A. *New Orleans after the Civil War: Race, Politics, and a New Birth of Freedom*. Baltimore, Md.: Johns Hopkins University Press, 2010.

Oakes, James. *Freedom National: The Destruction of Slavery in the United States, 1861–1865*. New York: W. W. Norton, 2013.

Paludan, Phillip Shaw. *Victims: A True Story of the Civil War*. Knoxville: The University of Tennessee Press, 1981.

Paret, Peter, ed. *Makers of Modern Strategy: From Machiavelli to the Nuclear Age*. Princeton, N.J.: Princeton University Press, 1986.

Parrish, William E. *Turbulent Partnership: Missouri and the Union, 1861–1865*. Columbia: University of Missouri Press, 1963.

Parton, James. *General Butler in New Orleans. History of the Administration of the Department of the Gulf in the Year 1862*. New York: Mason Brothers, 1864.

Pickenpaugh, Roger. *Camp Chase and the Evolution of Union Prison Policy*. Tuscaloosa, Ala.: University of Alabama Press, 2007.

———. *Captives in Gray: The Civil War Prisons of the Union*. Tuscaloosa: University of Alabama Press, 2009.

Pierce, Lyman B. *History of the Second Iowa Cavalry*. Burlington, Iowa: Hawk-Eye Steam Book: 1865.

Pierson, Michael D. *The Mutiny at Fort Jackson: The Untold Story of the Fall of New Orleans*. Chapel Hill: University of North Carolina Press, 2008.

Rable, George, *Fredericksburg! Fredericksburg!* Chapel Hill: The University of North Carolina Press, 2002.

———. *God's Almost Chosen Peoples*. Chapel Hill: University of North Carolina Press, 2010.

Reardon, Carol. *With a Sword in One Hand and Jomini in the Other: The Problem of Military Thought in the Civil War North*. Chapel Hill: University of North Carolina Press, 2012.

Reed, Emily Hazen. *Life of A. P. Dostie; or, The Conflict in New Orleans*. New York: Wm. P. Tomlinson, 1868.

Rolfs, David. *No Peace for the Wicked: Northern Protestant Soldiers and the American Civil War*. Knoxville: University of Tennessee Press, 2009.

Royster, Charles. *The Destructive War: William Tecumseh Sherman, Stonewall Jackson, and the Americans*. New York: Knopf, 1991.

Sanders, Charles W. *While in the Hands of the Enemy: Military Prisons of the Civil War*. Baton Rouge: Louisiana State University Press, 2005.

Schantz, Mark. *Awaiting the Heavenly Country: The Civil War and America's Culture of Death*. Ithaca, N.Y.: Cornell University Press, 2008.

Schutz, Wallace J. and Walter N. Trenerry. *Abandoned by Lincoln: A Military Biography of General John Pope*. Urbana: University of Illinois Press, 1900.

Scott, Sean. *A Visitation of God: Northern Civilians Interpret the Civil War*. New York: Oxford University Press, 2010.

Sheehan-Dean, Aaron. "*Lex Talionis* in the U.S. Civil War: Retaliation and the Limits of Atrocity." In *The Civil War as a Global Conflict: Transnational Meanings of the American Civil War*, edited by David T. Gleeson and Simon Lewis, 172–89. Columbia: The University of South Carolina Press, 2014.

Siddali, Silvana R. *From Property to Person: Slavery and the Confiscation Acts, 1861–1862*. Baton Rouge: Louisiana State University Press, 2005.

Solis, Gary D. *The Law of Armed Conflict: International Humanitarian Law in War*. Cambridge, U.K.: Cambridge University Press, 2010.

Slocum, Charles Elihu. *The Life and Services of Major-General Henry Warner Slocum*. Toledo, Ohio: The Slocum Publishing Company, 1913.

Smith, Ronald D. *Thomas Ewing Jr. Frontier Lawyer and Civil War General*. Columbia: University of Missouri Press, 2008.

Speer, Lonnie R. *War of Vengeance: Acts of Retaliation against Civil War POWs*. Mechanicsburg, Pa.: Stackpole Books, 2002.

Stout, Harry. *Upon the Altar of the Nation: A Moral History of the Civil War*. New York: Viking, 2006.

Sutherland, Daniel E., ed. *Guerrillas, Unionists, and Violence on the Confederate Homefront*. Fayetteville: University of Arkansas Press, 1999.

———. *A Savage Conflict: The Decisive Role of Guerrillas in the American Civil War*. Chapel Hill: University of North Carolina Press, 2010.

Tap, Bruce. *Over Lincoln's Shoulder: The Committee on the Conduct of the War*. Lawrence: University Press of Kansas, 1998.

Urwin, Gregory J. W., ed. *Black Flag over Dixie: Racial Atrocities and Reprisals in the Civil War*. Carbondale: Southern Illinois University Press, 2004.

Walters, John Bennett. *Merchant of Terror: General Sherman and Total War*. Indianapolis, Ind.: Bobbs-Merrill, 1973.

Waugh, Joan and Gary W. Gallagher, eds. *Wars Within a War: Controversy and Conflict over the American Civil War*. Chapel Hill: The University of North Carolina Press, 2009.

Weber, Jennifer L. *Copperheads: The Rise and Fall of Lincoln's Opponents in the North*. New York: Oxford University Press, 2006.

Weigley, Russell F. *The American Way of War*. New York: Macmillan, 1973.

———. *A Great Civil War*. Indianapolis: Indiana University Press, 2000.

Werlich, Robert. *"Beast" Butler: The Incredible Career of Major General Benjamin Franklin Butler*. Washington, D.C.: Quaker Press, 1962.

Wert, Jeffry D. *From Winchester to Cedar Creek: The Shenandoah Campaign of 1864*. Mechanicsburg, Pa.: Stackpole Books, 1987.

———. *Mosby's Rangers*. New York: Simon and Schuster, 1990.

Williams, T. Harry. *McClellan, Sherman, and Grant*. New Brunswick, N.J.: Rutgers University Press, 1962.

Winters, John D. *Louisiana in the Confederacy*. Baton Rouge: Louisiana State University Press, 1963.

Witt, John Fabian. *Lincoln's Code: The Laws of War in American History*. New York: Free Press, 2012.

ARTICLES

Baxter, R. R. "The First Modern Codification of the Law of War: Francis Lieber and General Order No. 100." *International Review of the Red Cross* 25 (April 1963): 171–89.

Boyle, William E. "Under the Black Flag: Execution and Retaliation in Mosby's Confederacy." *Military Law Review* 144 (Spring 1994): 148–68.

Browning, Judkin. "'I Am Not So Patriotic as I Was Once': The Effects of Military Occupation on the Occupying Union Soldiers during the Civil War," *Civil War History* 55, no. 2 (June 2009): 217–43.

Campbell, Jacqueline G. "'The Unmeaning Twaddle about Order 28': Benjamin F. Butler and Confederate Women in Occupied New Orleans, 1862." *The Journal of the Civil War Era* 2, no. 1 (March 2012): 11–30.

Carnahan, Burrus M. "Lincoln, Lieber and the Laws of War: The Origins and Limits of Military Necessity." *American Journal of International Law* 92 (1998): 213–31.

Childress, James. "Francis Lieber's Interpretation of the Law of War: General Orders No. 100 in the Context of his Life and Thought." *American Journal of Jurisprudence* 21 (1976): 34–70.

Curti, Merle. "Francis Lieber and Nationalism." *Huntington Library Quarterly* 4 (1941): 263–92.

Dilbeck, D. H. "'The Genesis of this Little Tablet with My Name': Francis Lieber and His Reasons for Drafting General Orders No. 100." *Journal of the Civil War Era* 5. no. 2 (June 2015): 231–53.

Fisher, Noel C. "Prepare Them for My Coming: General William T. Sherman, Total War, and Pacification in West Tennessee," *Tennessee Historical Quarterly* 51, no. 2 (Summer 1992): 75–86.

Freidel, Frank. "Francis Lieber, Charles Sumner, and Slavery," *The Journal of Southern History* 9, no. 1 (February 1943): 75–93.

Hacker, J. David. "A Census-Based Count of the Civil War Dead," *Civil War History* 57, no. 4 (December 2011): 306–47.

Hsieh, Wayne Wei-siang. "Total War and the American Civil War Reconsidered: The End of an Outdated 'Master Narrative,'" *The Journal of the Civil War Era* 1, no. 3 (September 2011): 394–408.

Janda, Lance. "Shutting the Gates of Mercy: The American Origins of Total War, 1860–1880," *The Journal of Military History* 59, no. 1 (January 1959); 7–26.

Keil, Hartmut. "Francis Lieber's Attitudes on Race, Slavery, and Abolition." *Journal of American Ethnic History* 28 (2008): 13–33.

Lash, Jeffrey N. "The Federal Tyrant at Memphis: General Stephen A. Hurlbut and the Union Occupation of West Tennessee, 1862–64," *Tennessee Historical Quarterly* 48, no. 1 (Spring 1989): 15–28.

Lippincott, George E. "Lee-Sawyer Exchange." *Civil War Times Illustrated* 1, no. 3 (June 1962): 39–41.

Mancini, Matthew J. "Francis Lieber, Slavery, and the 'Genesis' of the Laws of War." *Journal of Southern History* 77 (2011): 325–48.

———. "Two Strategies of Victory: William T. Sherman in the Civil War." *Atlanta History* 33 (1990): 5–17.

Merton, Theodor. "Francis Lieber's Code and the Principles of Humanity." *Columbia Journal of Transnational Law* 36 (1997): 269–81.

Neal, Harry E. "Rebels, Ropes, and Reprieves." *Civil War Times Illustrated* 14, no. 10 (February 1976): 30–35.

Neely, Mark. "Was the Civil War a Total War?" *Civil War History* 37, no. 1 (March 1991): 5–28.

Phillips, Christopher. "Lincoln's Grasp of War: Hard War and the Politics of Neutrality and Slavery in the Western Border States, 1861–1862," *The Journal of the Civil War Era* 3, no. 2 (June 2013): 184–210.

Reid, Brian Holden, "Historians and the Joint Committee on the Conduct of the War," *Civil War History* 38 (1992): 319–41.

Smith, W. Wayne. "An Experiment in Counterinsurgency: The Assessment of Confederate Sympathizers in Missouri," *The Journal of Southern History* 35, no. 3 (August 1969): 361–80.

Tap, Bruce. " 'These Devils Are Not Fit to Live on God's Earth': War Crimes and the Committee on the Conduct of the War, 1864–1865." *Civil War History* 42, no. 2 (June 1996): 116–32.

Trefousse, Hans L., "The Joint Committee on the Conduct of the War: A Reappraisal," *Civil War History* 10 (1964): 5–19.

True, Marshall, "A Reluctant Warrior Advises the President; Ethan Allen Hitchcock, Abraham Lincoln and the Union Army, Spring 1862." *Vermont History* 50, no. 3 (Summer 1982): 129–50.

Urwin, Gregory J. W. " 'We Cannot Treat Negroes . . . as Prisoners of War': Racial Atrocities and Reprisals in Civil War Arkansas." *Civil War History* 42, no. 3 (September 1996): 193–210.

DISSERTATIONS

Hooper, Ernest Walter. "Memphis, Tennessee: Federal Occupation and Reconstruction, 1862–1870." PhD diss., University of North Carolina, 1957.

Lang, Andrew F. "The Garrison War: Culture, Race, and the Problem of Military Occupation during the American Civil War Era." PhD diss., Rice University, 2013.

Sude, Barry. "Federal Military Policy and Strategy in Missouri and Arkansas, 1861–1863: A Study in Command Level Conflict. PhD diss., Temple University, 1986.

Index